SUPREME POWER

POWERS &
PRINCIPALITIES

SUPREME POWER

POWERS & PRINCIPALITIES

WRITER: J. Michael Straczynski
ARTIST: Gary Frank
INKER: Jon Sibal

COLORS: Chris Sotomayor
LETTERS: Virtual Calligraphy's Rus Wooton
COVER ART: Gary Frank & Richard Isanove
ASSISTANT EDITOR: John Barber
EDITOR: Nick Lowe
STORY EDITOR: Joe Quesada

COLLECTIONS EDITOR: Jeff Youngquist
ASSISTANT EDITOR: Jennifer Grünwald
BOOK DESIGNER: Patrick McGrath
CREATIVE DIRECTOR: Tom Marvelli

EDITOR IN CHIEF: Joe Quesada
PUBLISHER: Dan Buckley

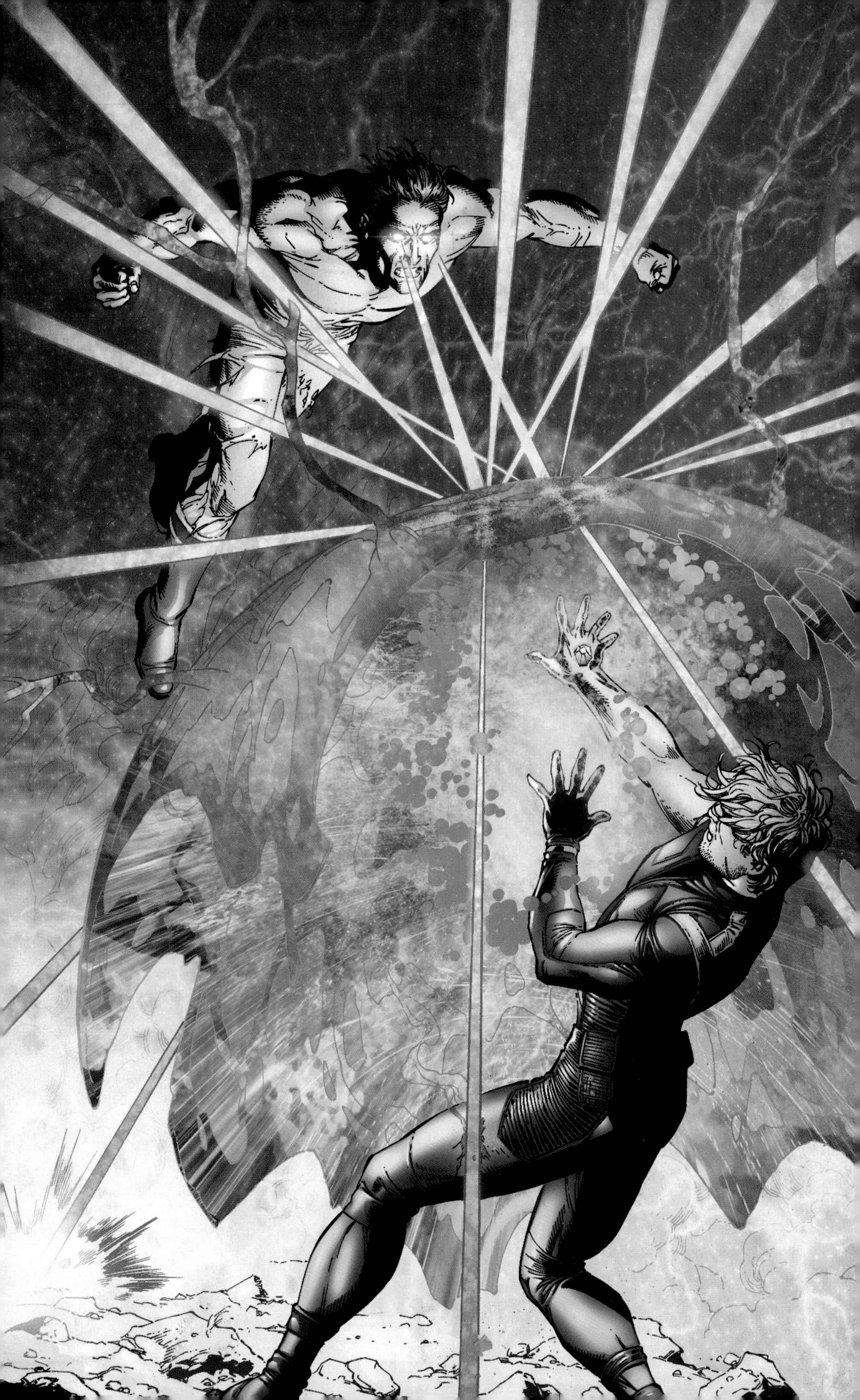

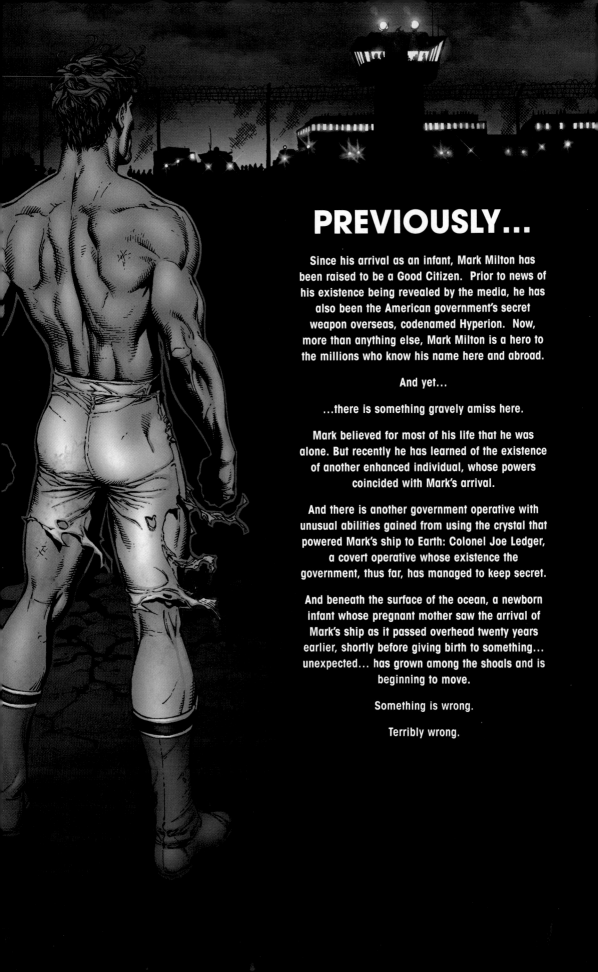

PREVIOUSLY...

Since his arrival as an infant, Mark Milton has been raised to be a Good Citizen. Prior to news of his existence being revealed by the media, he has also been the American government's secret weapon overseas, codenamed Hyperion. Now, more than anything else, Mark Milton is a hero to the millions who know his name here and abroad.

And yet...

...there is something gravely amiss here.

Mark believed for most of his life that he was alone. But recently he has learned of the existence of another enhanced individual, whose powers coincided with Mark's arrival.

And there is another government operative with unusual abilities gained from using the crystal that powered Mark's ship to Earth: Colonel Joe Ledger, a covert operative whose existence the government, thus far, has managed to keep secret.

And beneath the surface of the ocean, a newborn infant whose pregnant mother saw the arrival of Mark's ship as it passed overhead twenty years earlier, shortly before giving birth to something... unexpected... has grown among the shoals and is beginning to move.

Something is wrong.

Terribly wrong.

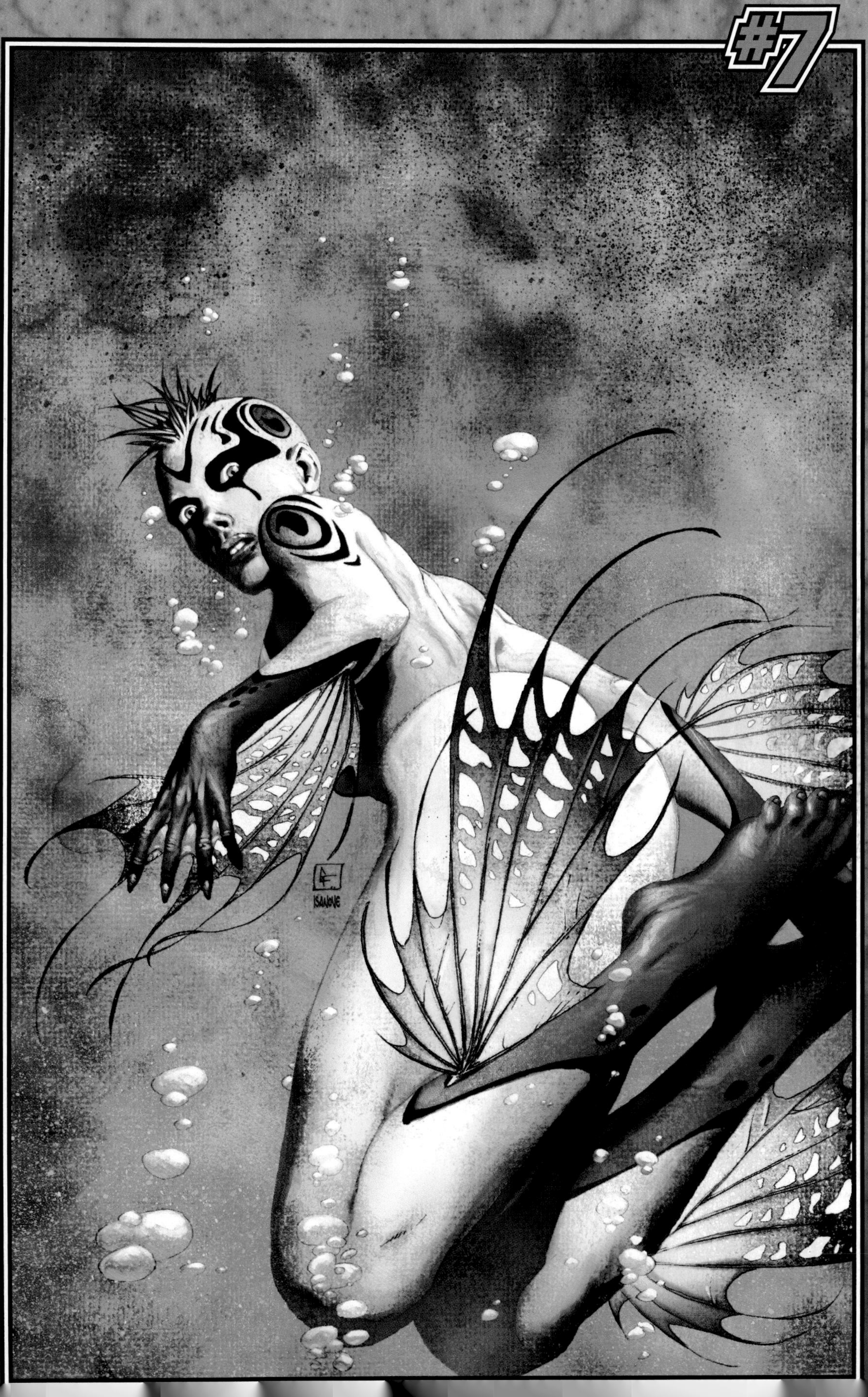
#7
ISANOVE

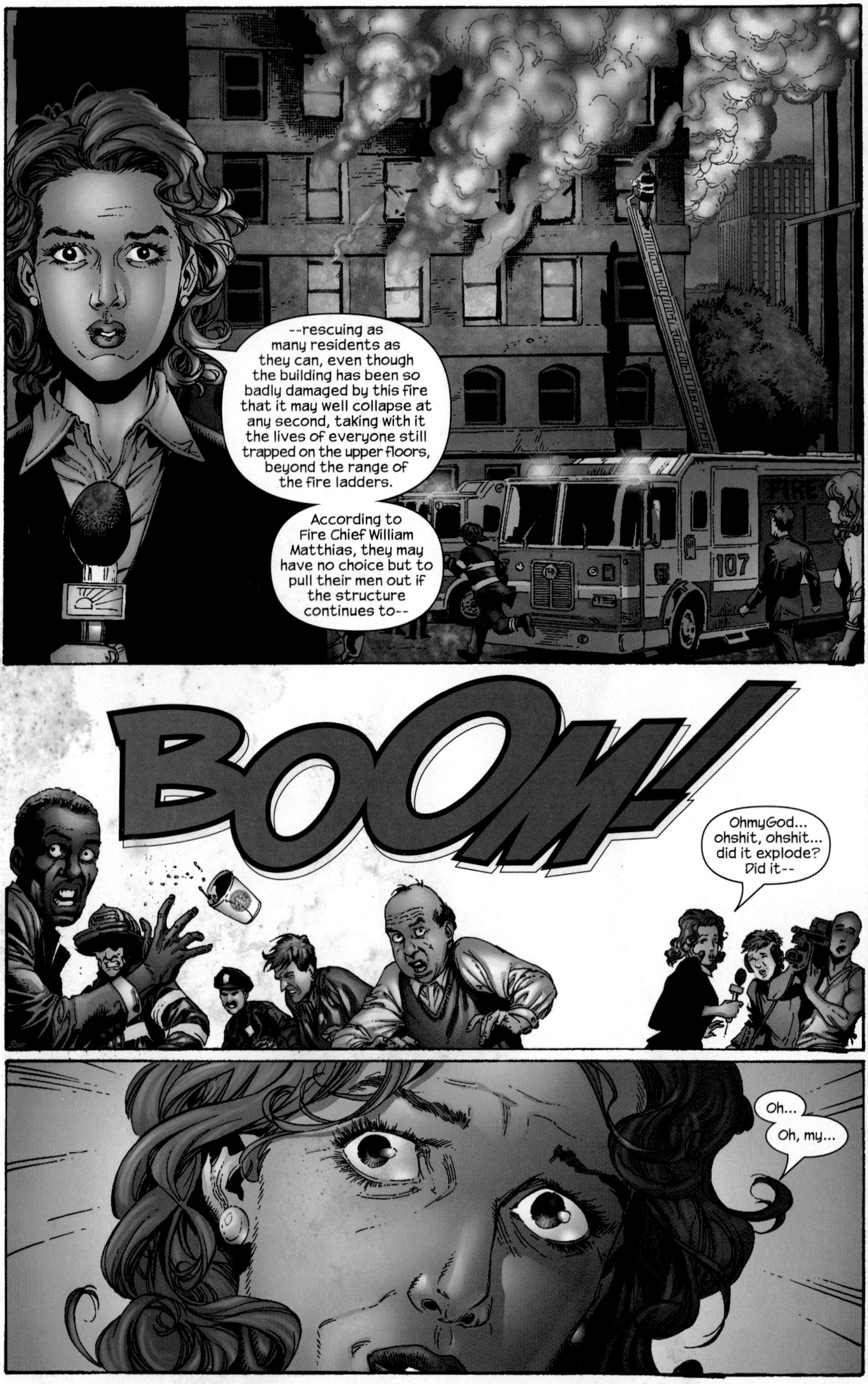
--rescuing as many residents as they can, even though the building has been so badly damaged by this fire that it may well collapse at any second, taking with it the lives of everyone still trapped on the upper floors, beyond the range of the fire ladders.
According to Fire Chief William Matthias, they may have no choice but to pull their men out if the structure continues to--
FIRE
107
BOOM!
OhmyGod... ohshit, ohshit... did it explode? Did it--
Oh...
Oh, my...

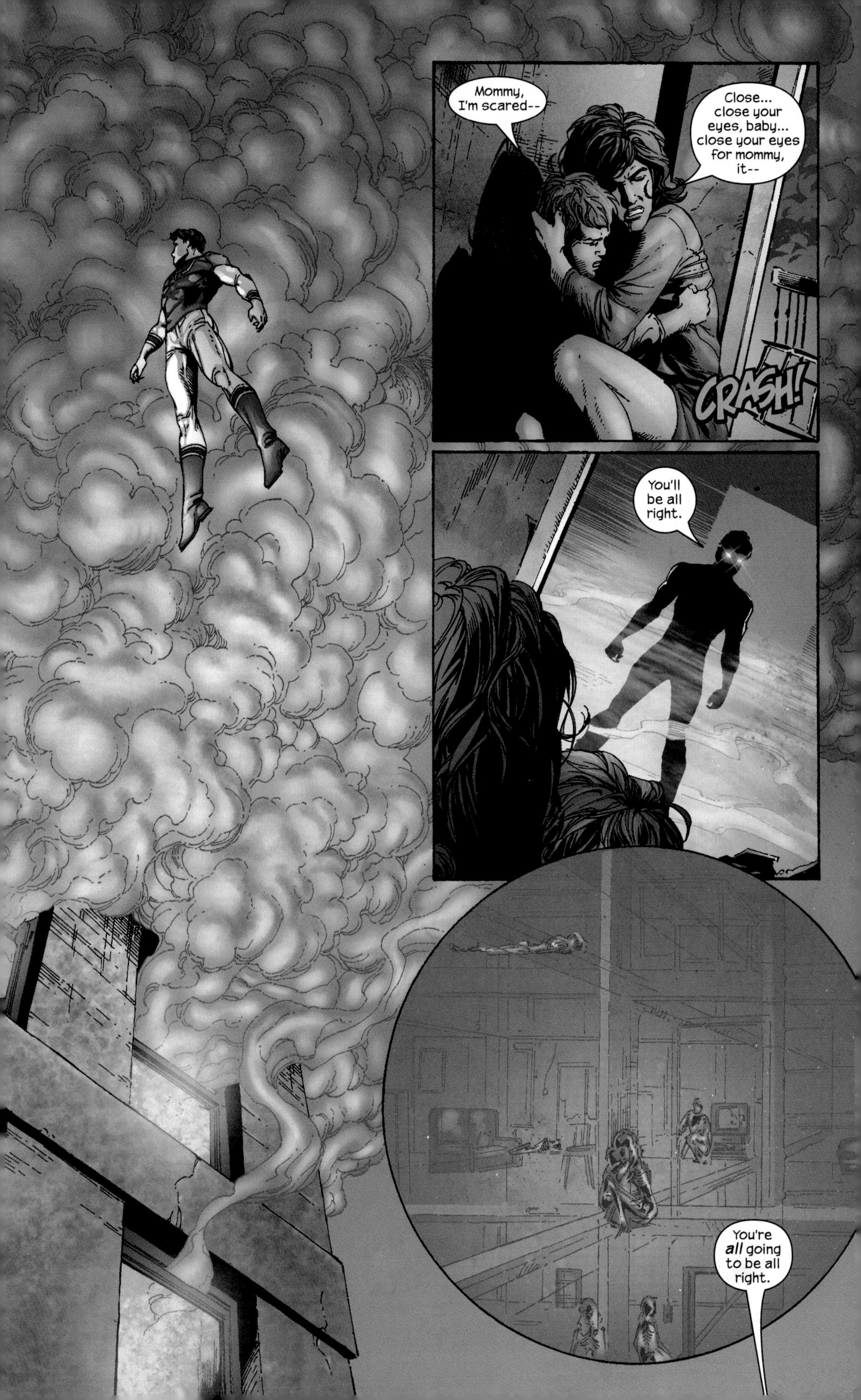

Mommy, I'm scared--
Close... close your eyes, baby... close your eyes for mommy, it--
CRASH!
You'll be all right.
You're *all* going to be all right.

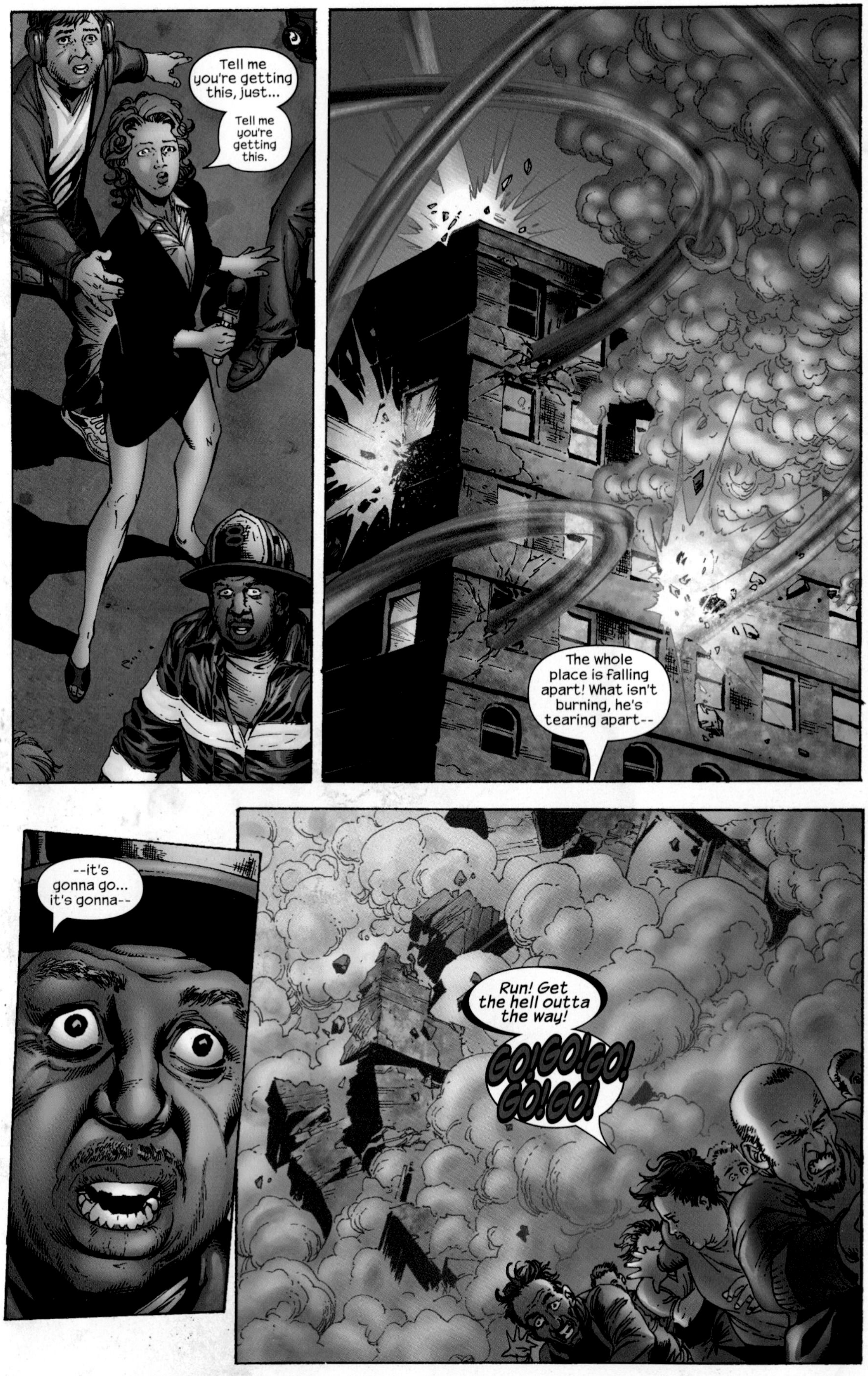
Tell me you're getting this, just...
Tell me you're getting this.
The whole place is falling apart! What isn't burning, he's tearing apart--
--it's gonna go... it's gonna--
Run! Get the hell outta the way!
GO!GO!GO! GO!GO!

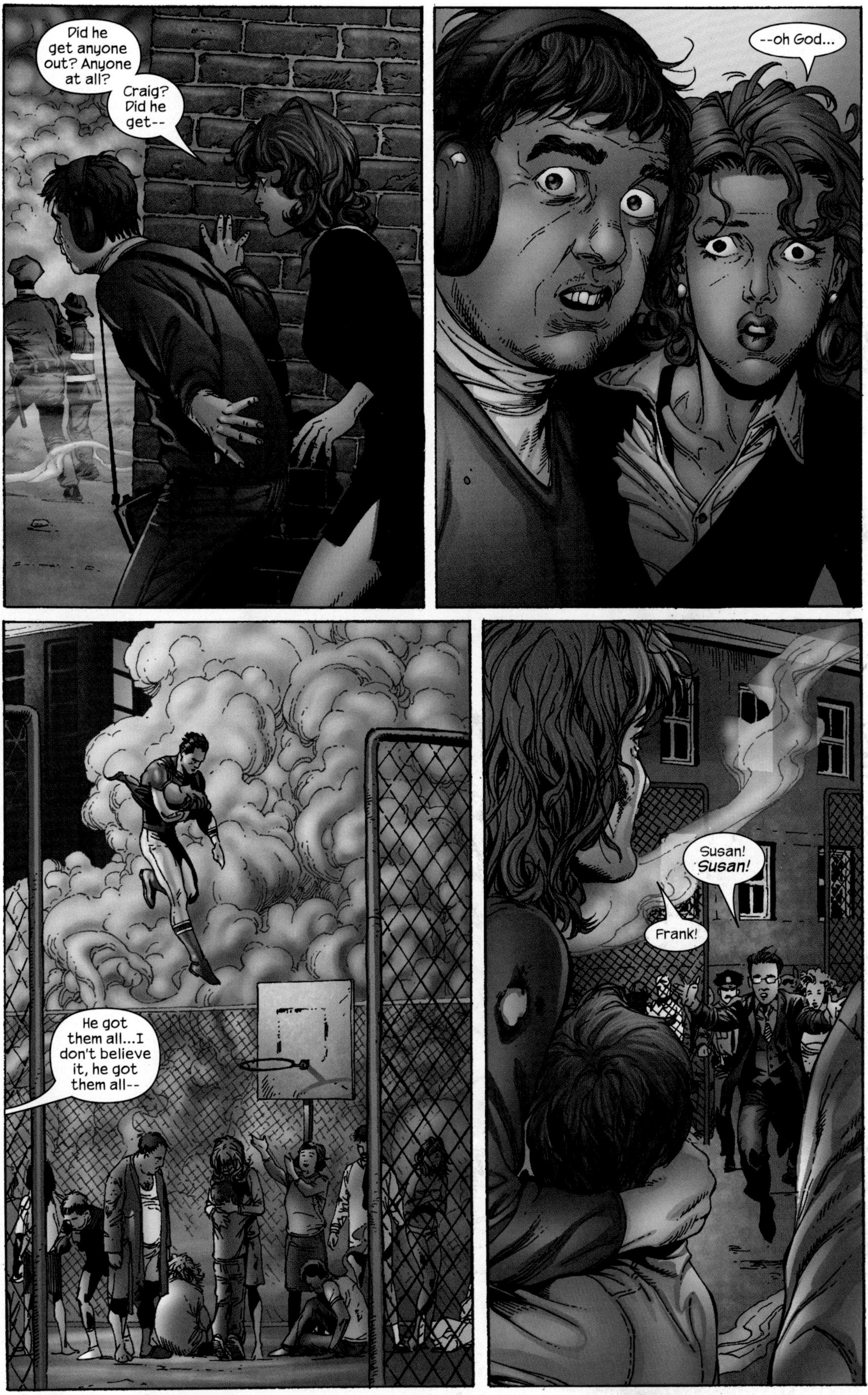
Did he get anyone out? Anyone at all?
Craig? Did he get--
--oh God...
He got them all...I don't believe it, he got them all--
Susan! Susan!
Frank!

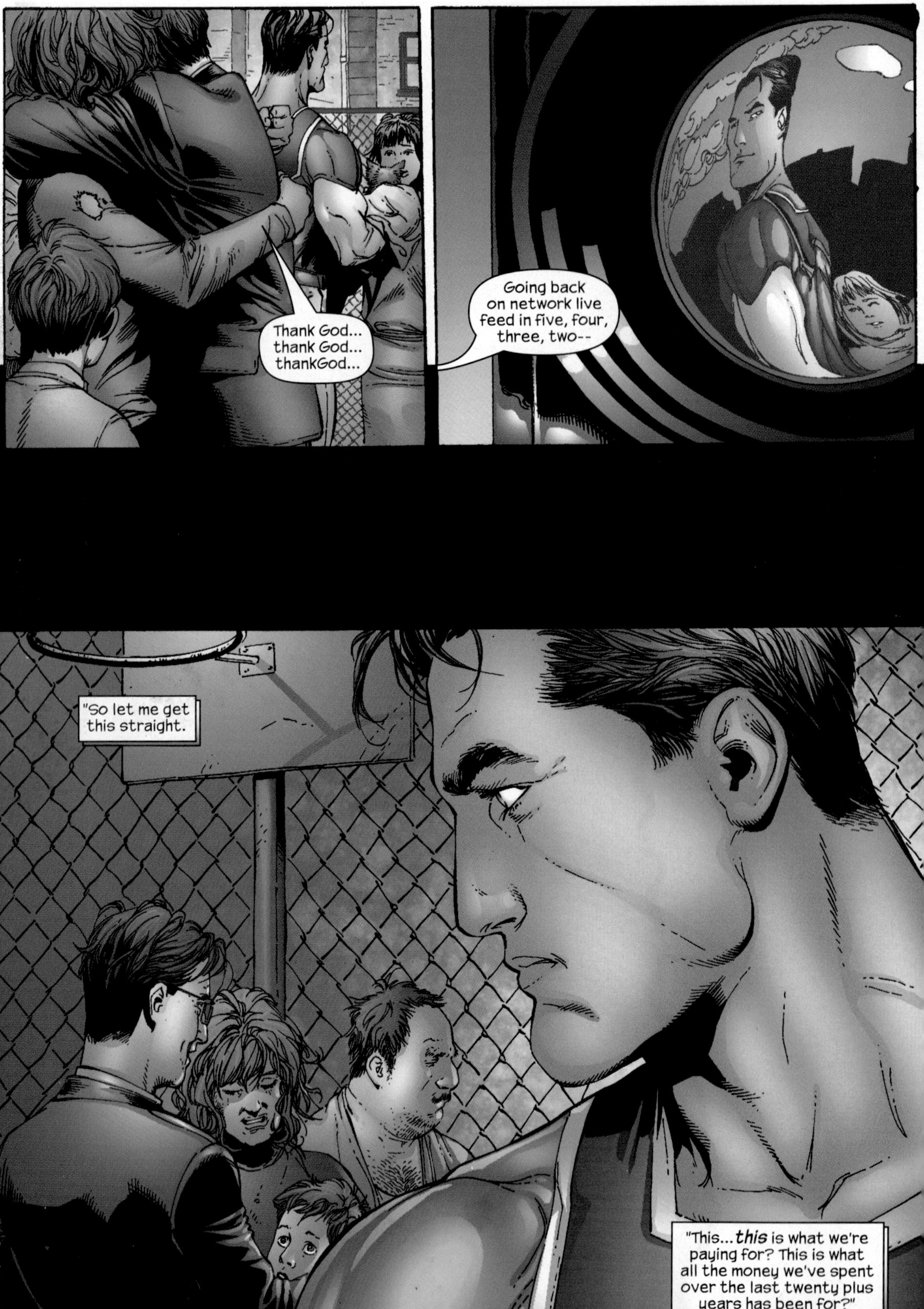
Thank God...
thank God...
thankGod...
Going back on network live feed in five, four, three, two--
"So let me get this straight.
"This...*this* is what we're paying for? This is what all the money we've spent over the last twenty plus years has been for?"

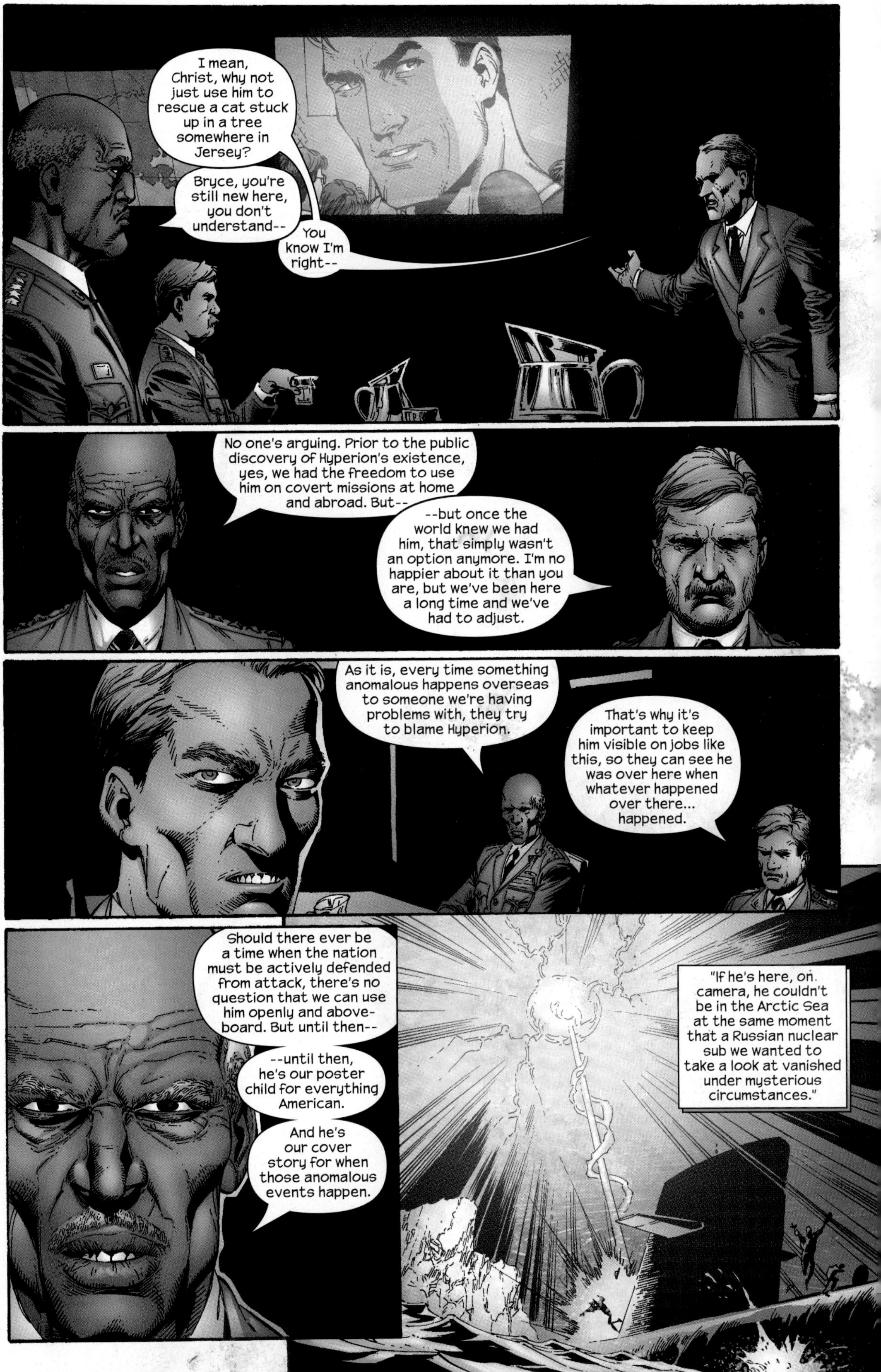
I mean, Christ, why not just use him to rescue a cat stuck up in a tree somewhere in Jersey?
Bryce, you're still new here, you don't understand--
You know I'm right--
No one's arguing. Prior to the public discovery of Hyperion's existence, yes, we had the freedom to use him on covert missions at home and abroad. But--
--but once the world knew we had him, that simply wasn't an option anymore. I'm no happier about it than you are, but we've been here a long time and we've had to adjust.
As it is, every time something anomalous happens overseas to someone we're having problems with, they try to blame Hyperion.
That's why it's important to keep him visible on jobs like this, so they can see he was over here when whatever happened over there... happened.
Should there ever be a time when the nation must be actively defended from attack, there's no question that we can use him openly and above-board. But until then--
--until then, he's our poster child for everything American.
And he's our cover story for when those anomalous events happen.
"If he's here, on camera, he couldn't be in the Arctic Sea at the same moment that a Russian nuclear sub we wanted to take a look at vanished under mysterious circumstances."

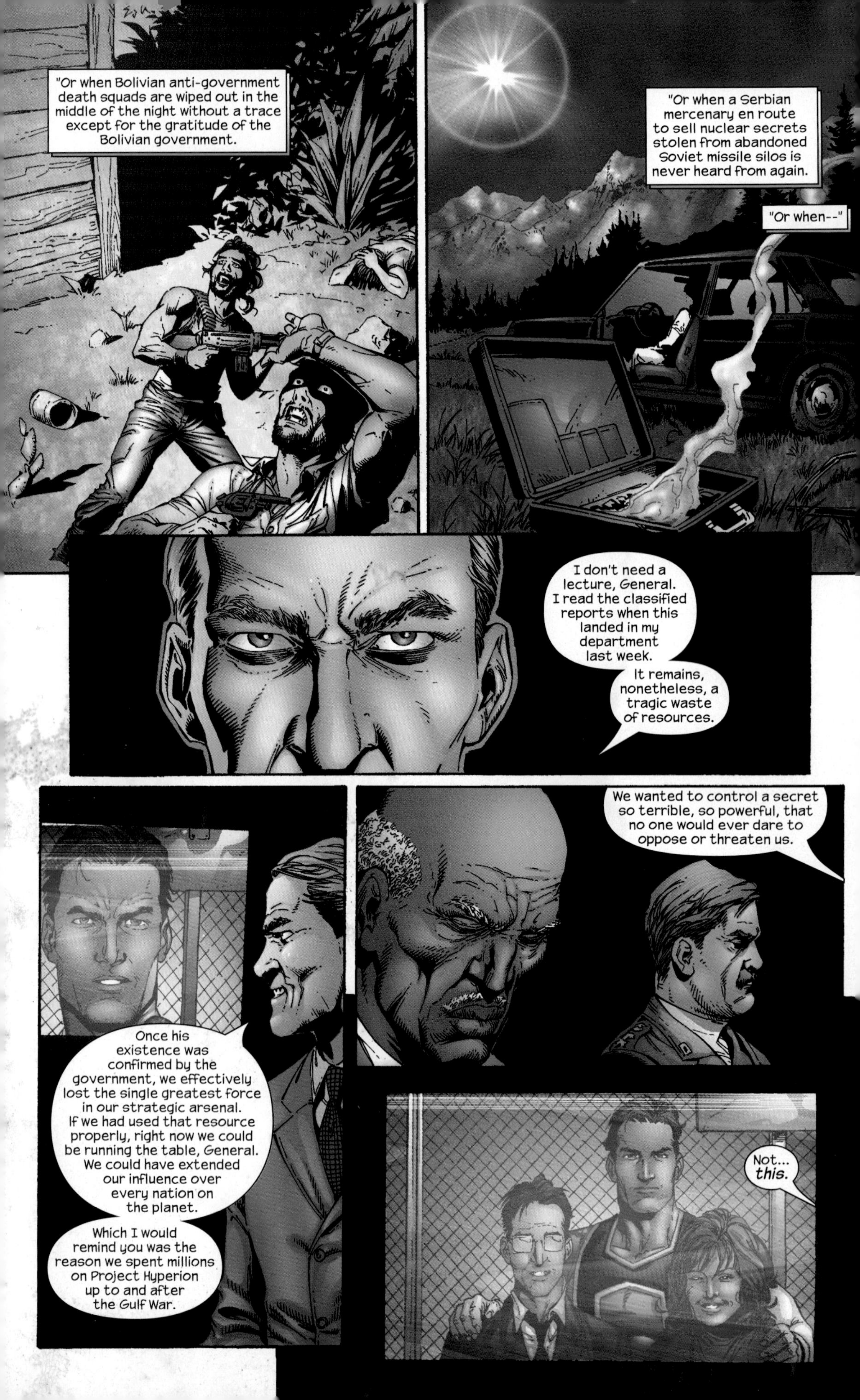
"Or when Bolivian anti-government death squads are wiped out in the middle of the night without a trace except for the gratitude of the Bolivian government.
"Or when a Serbian mercenary en route to sell nuclear secrets stolen from abandoned Soviet missile silos is never heard from again.
"Or when--"
I don't need a lecture, General. I read the classified reports when this landed in my department last week.
It remains, nonetheless, a tragic waste of resources.
Once his existence was confirmed by the government, we effectively lost the single greatest force in our strategic arsenal. If we had used that resource properly, right now we could be running the table, General. We could have extended our influence over every nation on the planet.
Which I would remind you was the reason we spent millions on Project Hyperion up to and after the Gulf War.
We wanted to control a secret so terrible, so powerful, that no one would ever dare to oppose or threaten us.
Not... *this.*

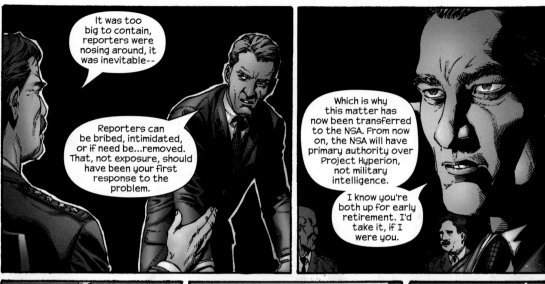

It was too big to contain, reporters were nosing around, it was inevitable--

Reporters can be bribed, intimidated, or if need be...removed. That, not exposure, should have been your first response to the problem.

Which is why this matter has now been transferred to the NSA. From now on, the NSA will have primary authority over Project Hyperion, not military intelligence.

I know you're both up for early retirement. I'd take it, if I were you.

"Because there are going to be some changes made. Starting now."

Excuse me--

Before you go, I wanted to thank you for all your good works.

I appreciate that, but there's really no--

Good luck to you.

May you find what you are looking for.

"Or, perhaps, what is looking for you."

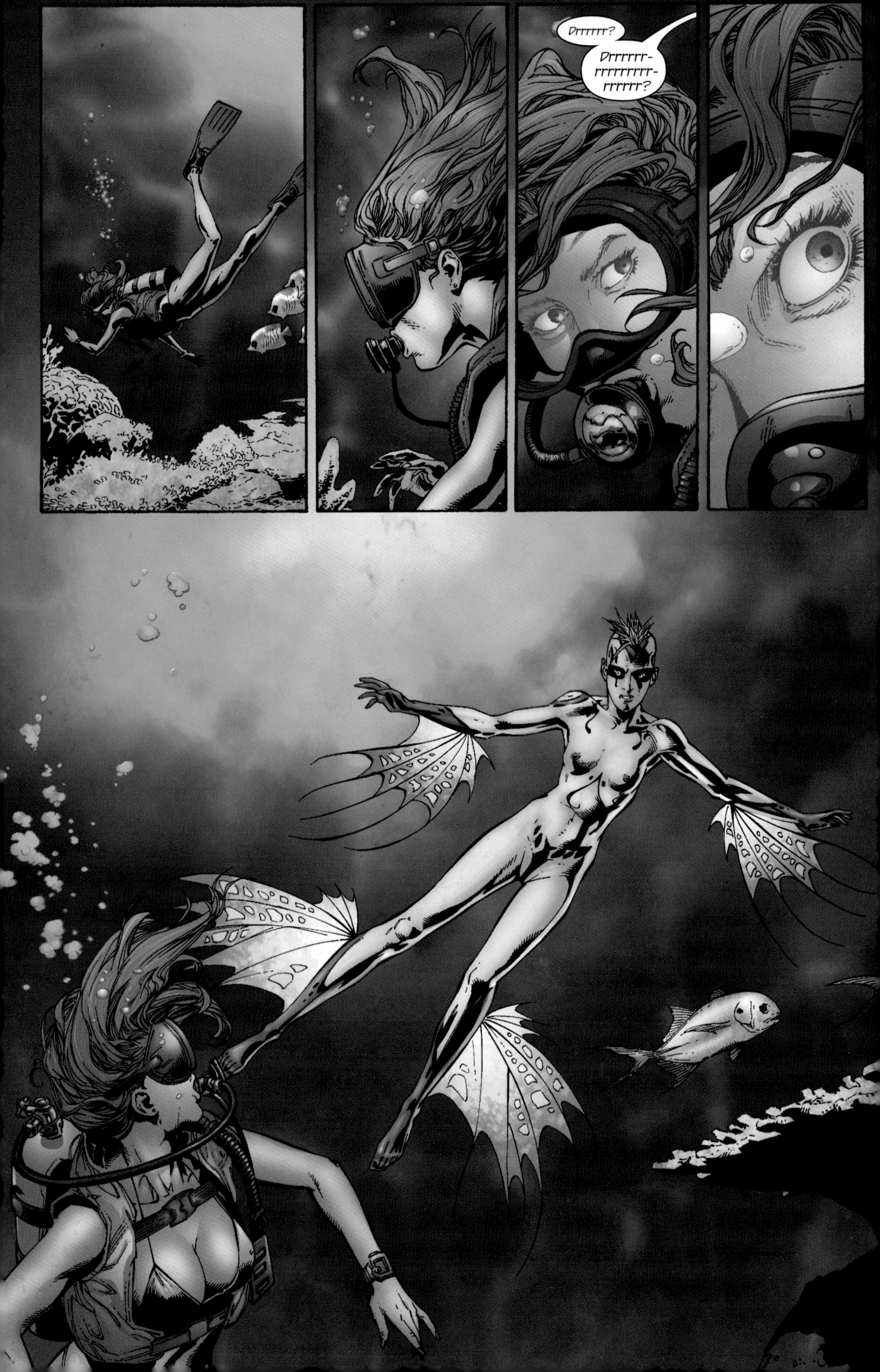
Drrrrrr?
Drrrrrr-rrrrrrrrr-rrrrrr?

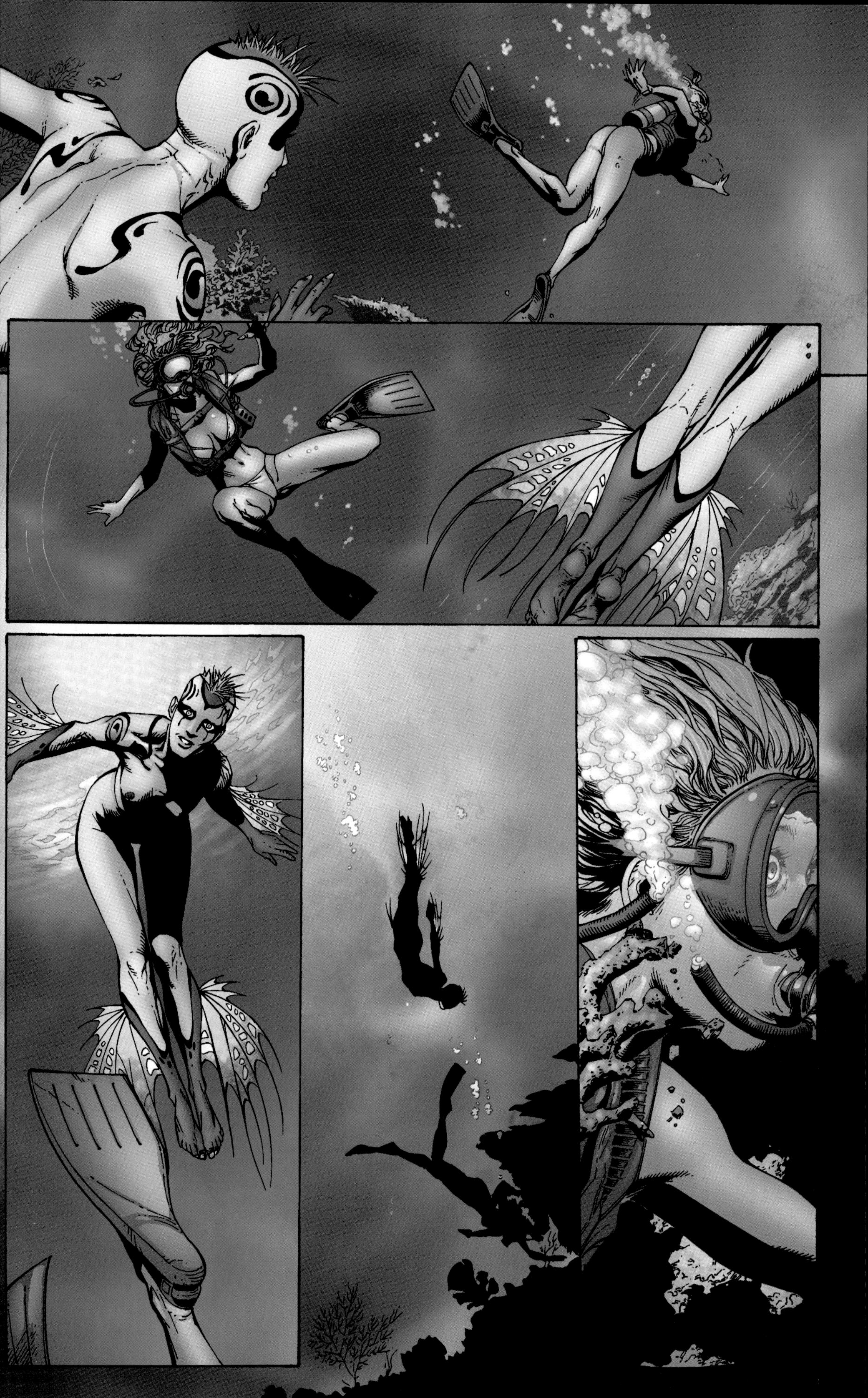

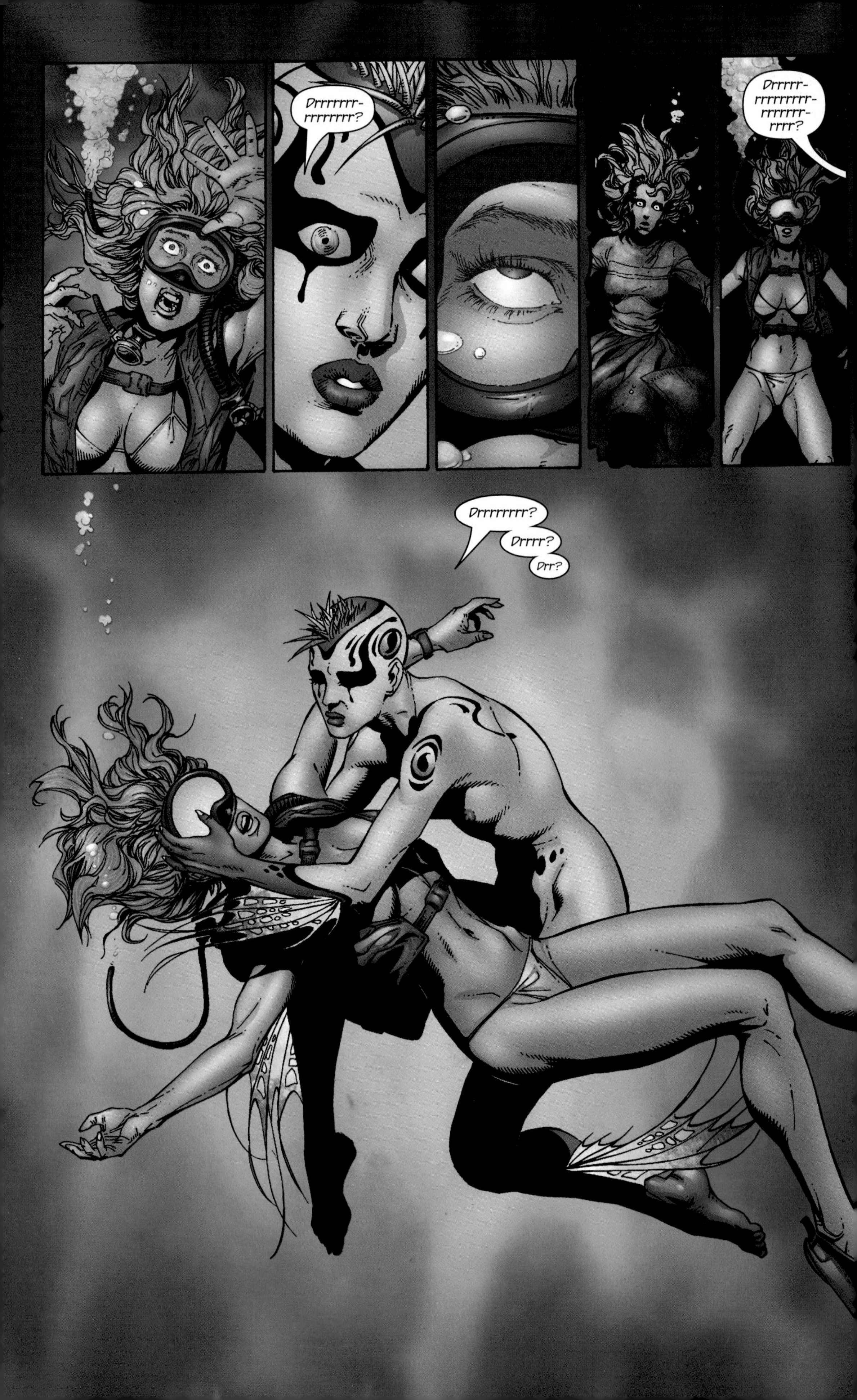
Drrrrrrr-
rrrrrrrr?
Drrrrr-
rrrrrrrrrr-
rrrrrrr-
rrrr?
Drrrrrrrr?
Drrrr?
Drr?

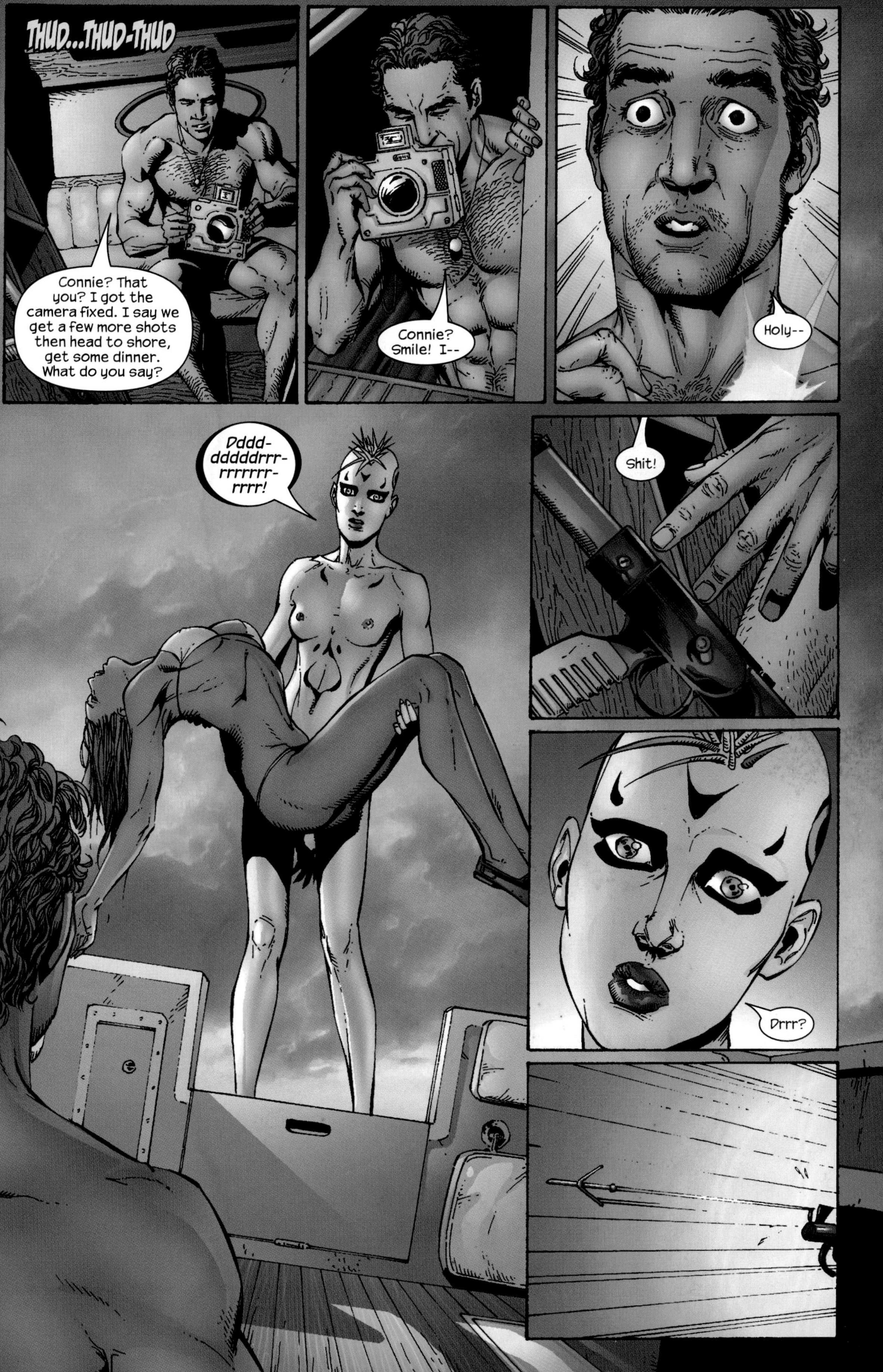
THUD...THUD-THUD
Connie? That you? I got the camera fixed. I say we get a few more shots then head to shore, get some dinner. What do you say?
Connie? Smile! I--
Holy--
Dddd-dddddrrr-rrrrrrr-rrrr!
Shit!
Drrr?

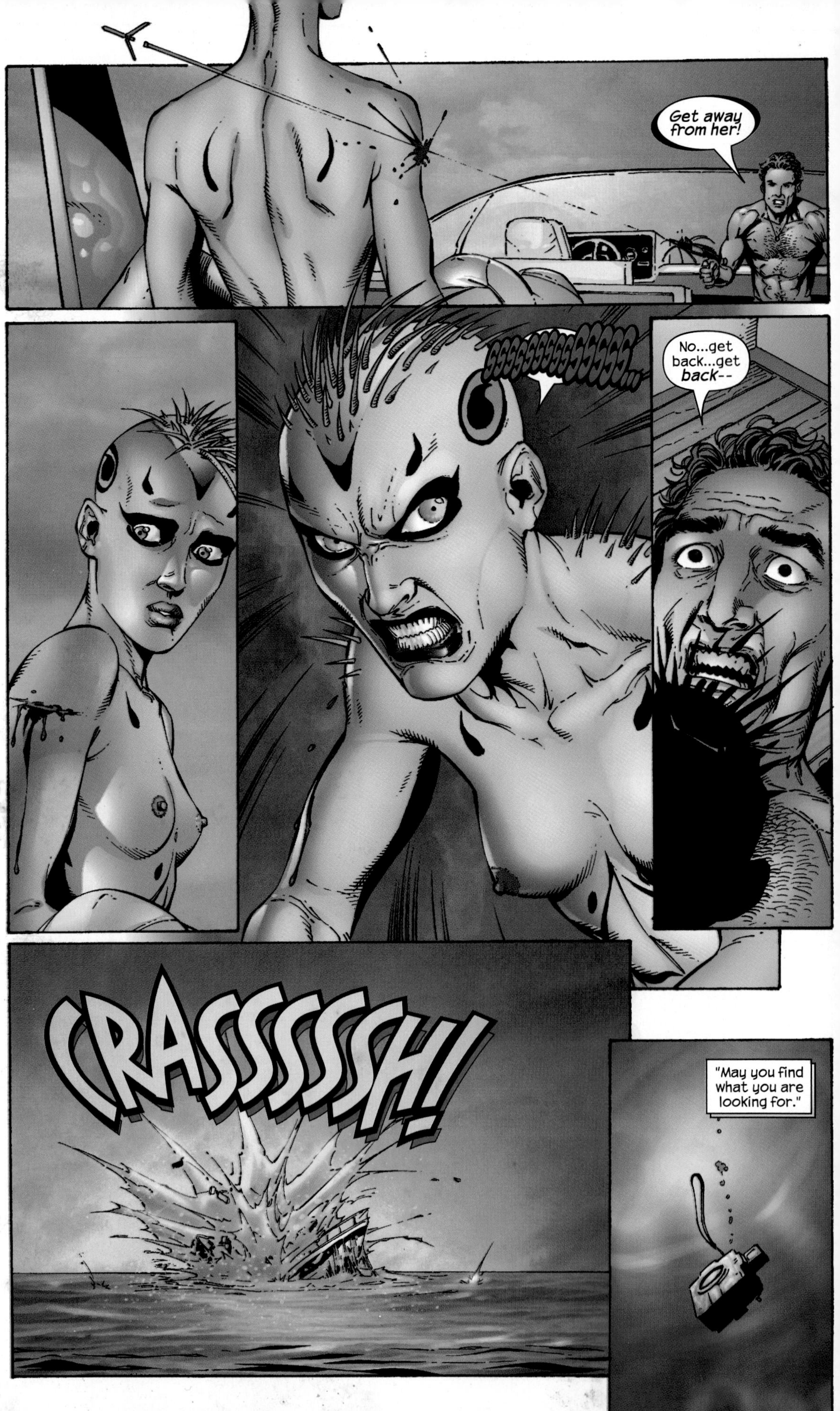
Get away from her!
No...get back...get back--
SSSSSSSSSSSSSSS...
CRASSSSSH!
"May you find what you are looking for."

"Or, perhaps, what is looking for you."

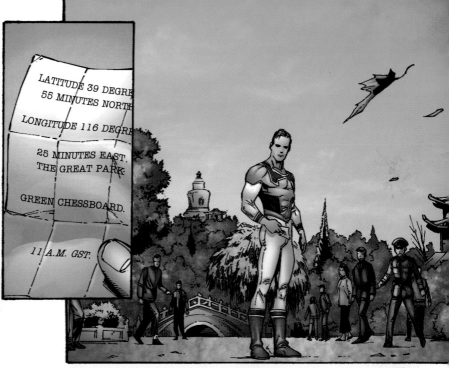

LATITUDE 39 DEGRE[ ]
55 MINUTES NORTH[ ]

LONGITUDE 116 DEGRE[ ]

25 MINUTES EAST.
THE GREAT PARK:

GREEN CHESSBOARD.

11 A.M. GST.

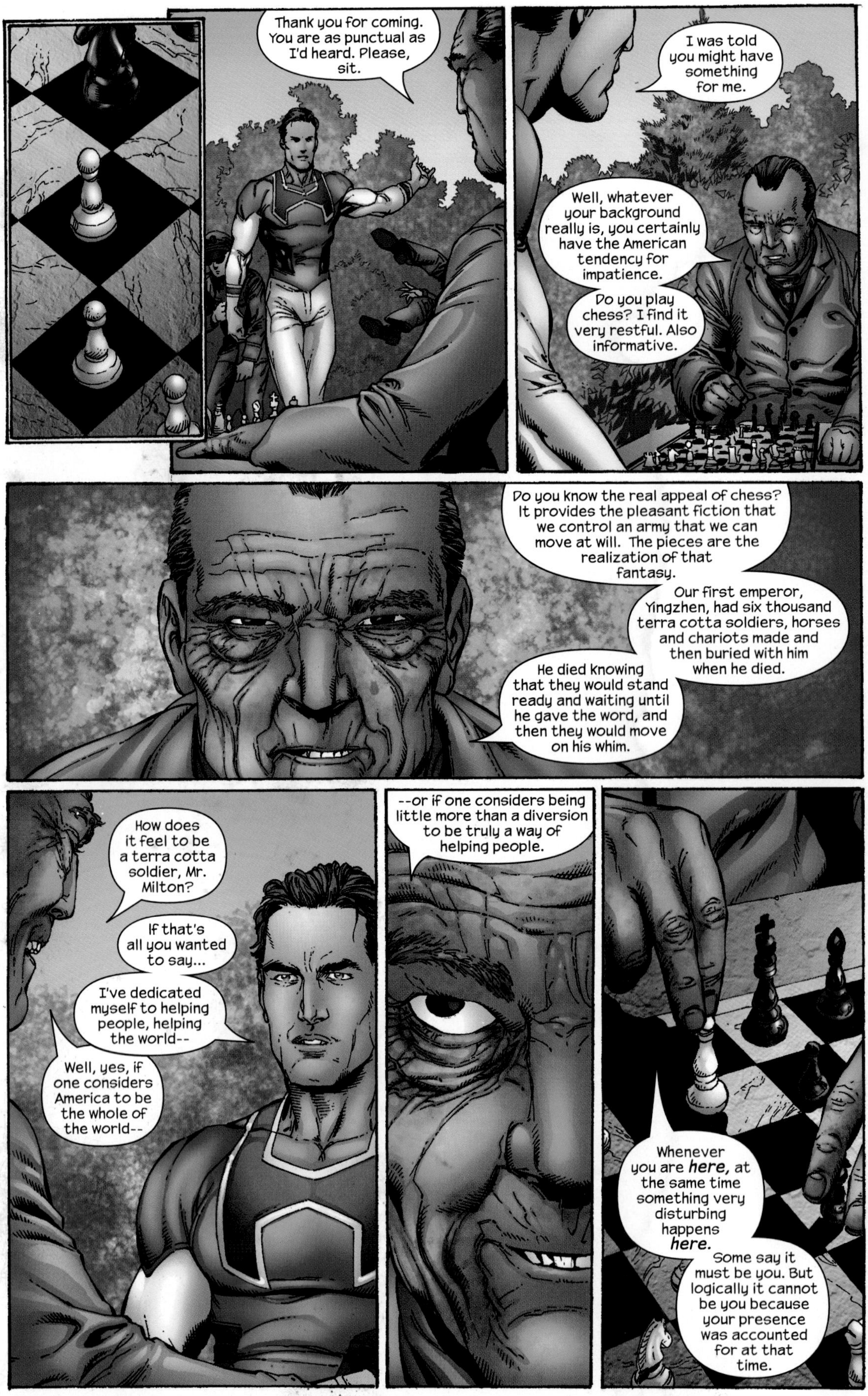
Thank you for coming. You are as punctual as I'd heard. Please, sit.
I was told you might have something for me.
Well, whatever your background really is, you certainly have the American tendency for impatience.
Do you play chess? I find it very restful. Also informative.
Do you know the real appeal of chess? It provides the pleasant fiction that we control an army that we can move at will. The pieces are the realization of that fantasy.
Our first emperor, Yingzhen, had six thousand terra cotta soldiers, horses and chariots made and then buried with him when he died.
He died knowing that they would stand ready and waiting until he gave the word, and then they would move on his whim.
How does it feel to be a terra cotta soldier, Mr. Milton?
If that's all you wanted to say...
I've dedicated myself to helping people, helping the world--
Well, yes, if one considers America to be the whole of the world--
--or if one considers being little more than a diversion to be truly a way of helping people.
Whenever you are *here,* at the same time something very disturbing happens *here.*
Some say it must be you. But logically it cannot be you because your presence was accounted for at that time.

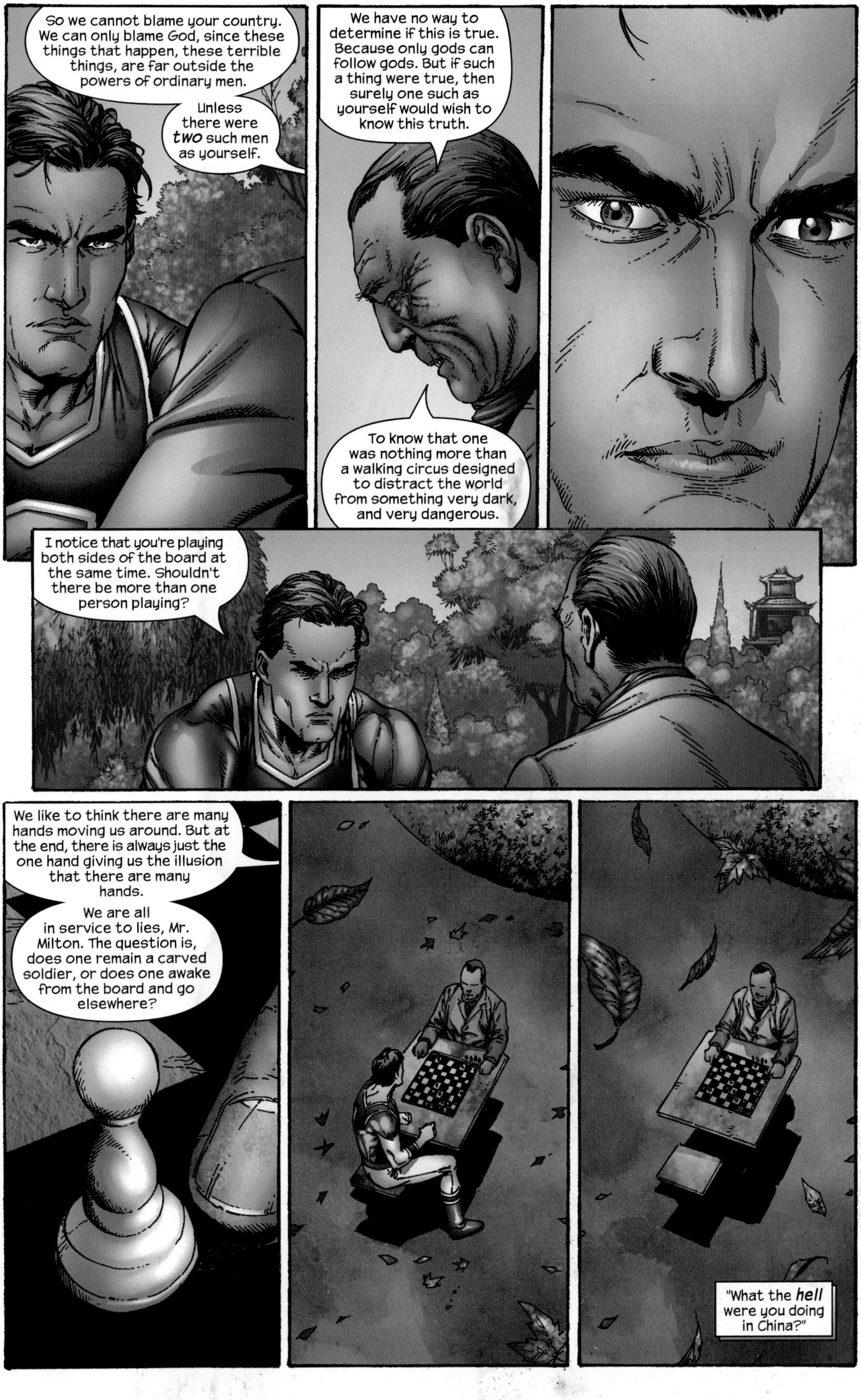
So we cannot blame your country. We can only blame God, since these things that happen, these terrible things, are far outside the powers of ordinary men.
Unless there were *two* such men as yourself.
We have no way to determine if this is true. Because only gods can follow gods. But if such a thing were true, then surely one such as yourself would wish to know this truth.
To know that one was nothing more than a walking circus designed to distract the world from something very dark, and very dangerous.
I notice that you're playing both sides of the board at the same time. Shouldn't there be more than one person playing?
We like to think there are many hands moving us around. But at the end, there is always just the one hand giving us the illusion that there are many hands.
We are all in service to lies, Mr. Milton. The question is, does one remain a carved soldier, or does one awake from the board and go elsewhere?
"What the *hell* were you doing in China?"

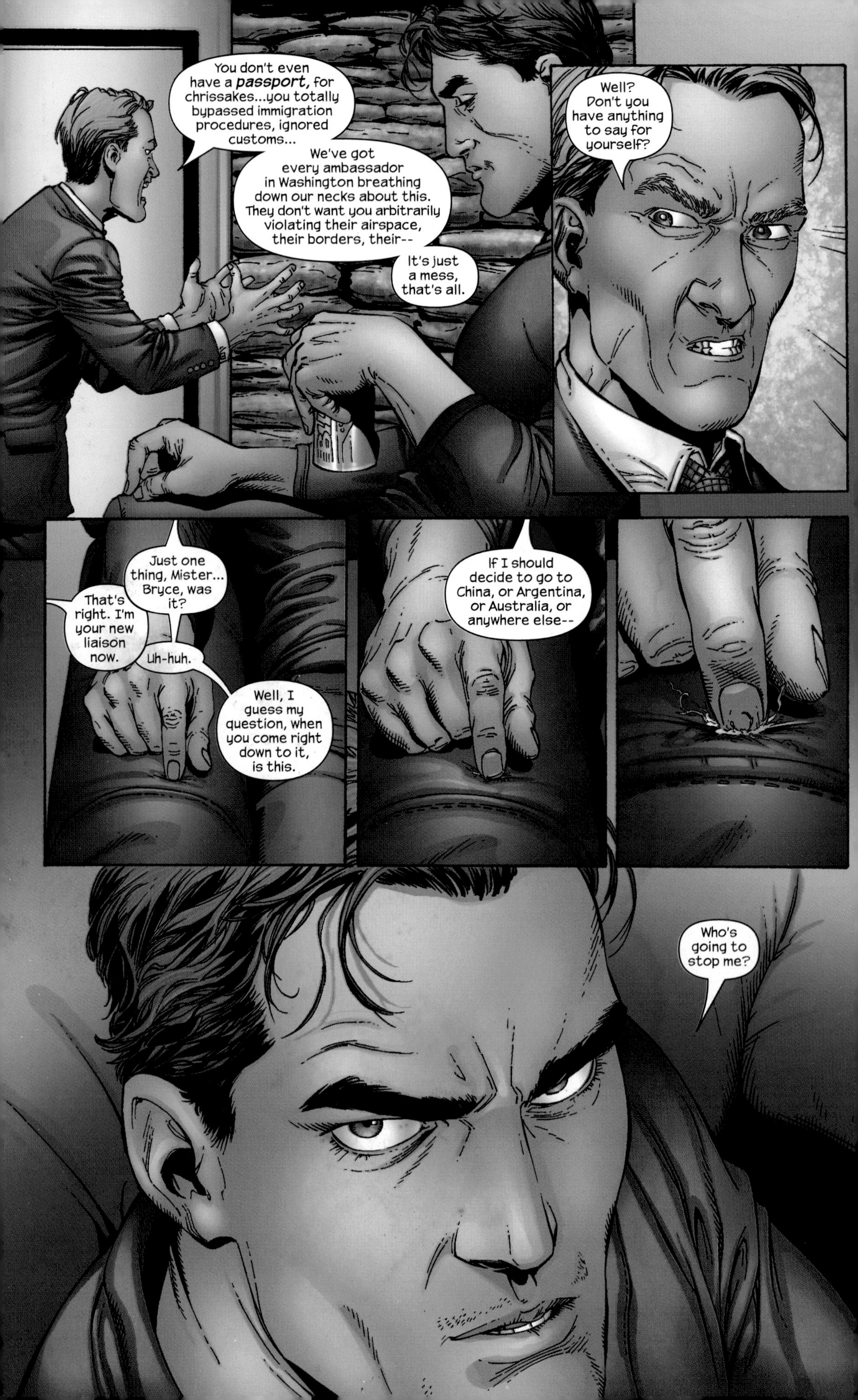
You don't even have a *passport,* for chrissakes...you totally bypassed immigration procedures, ignored customs...
We've got every ambassador in Washington breathing down our necks about this. They don't want you arbitrarily violating their airspace, their borders, their--
It's just a mess, that's all.
Well? Don't you have anything to say for yourself?
Just one thing, Mister... Bryce, was it?
That's right. I'm your new liaison now.
Uh-huh.
Well, I guess my question, when you come right down to it, is this.
If I should decide to go to China, or Argentina, or Australia, or anywhere else--
Who's going to stop me?

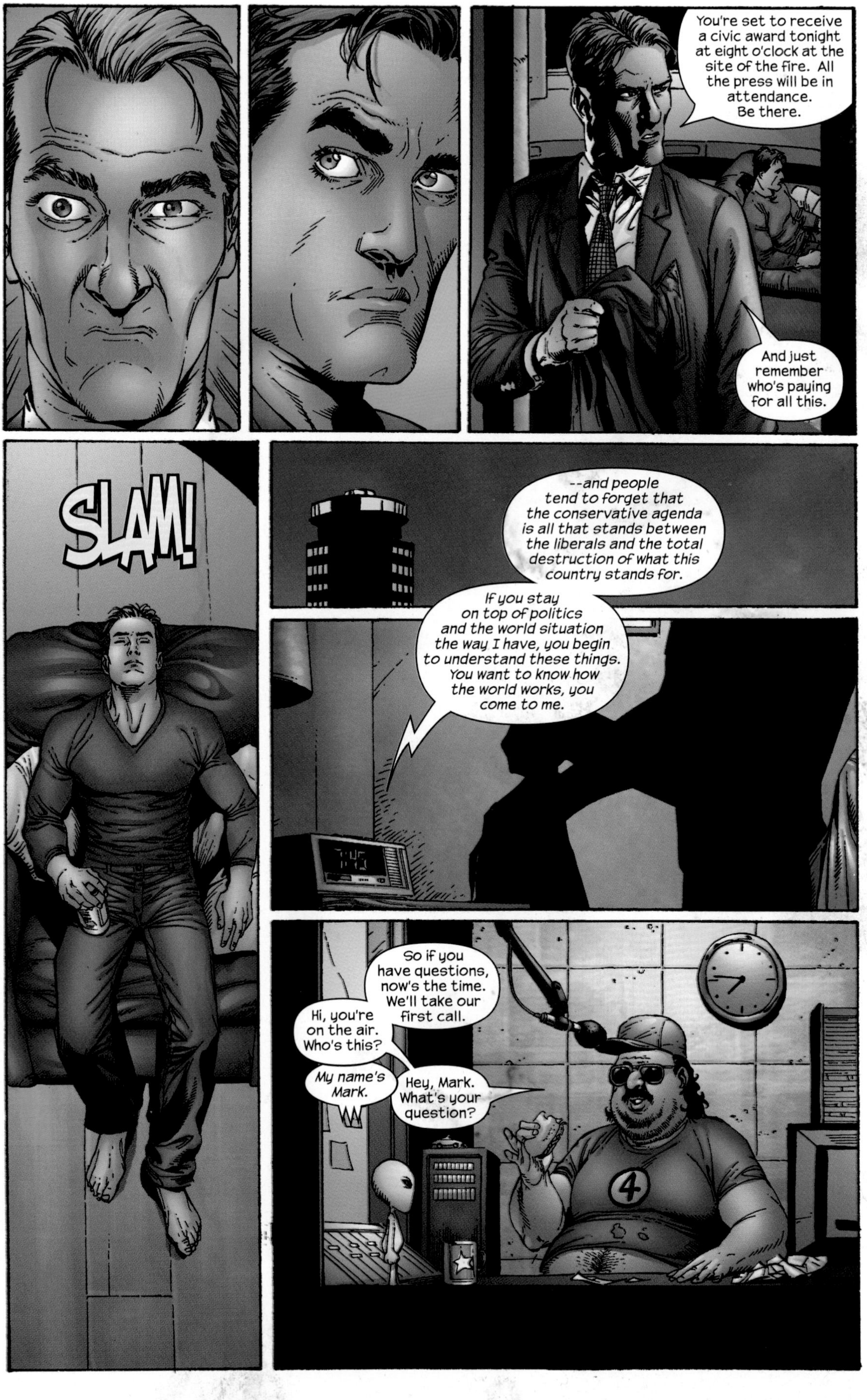
You're set to receive a civic award tonight at eight o'clock at the site of the fire. All the press will be in attendance. Be there.
And just remember who's paying for all this.
SLAM!
--and people tend to forget that the conservative agenda is all that stands between the liberals and the total destruction of what this country stands for.
If you stay on top of politics and the world situation the way I have, you begin to understand these things. You want to know how the world works, you come to me.
So if you have questions, now's the time. We'll take our first call.
Hi, you're on the air. Who's this?
My name's Mark.
Hey, Mark. What's your question?

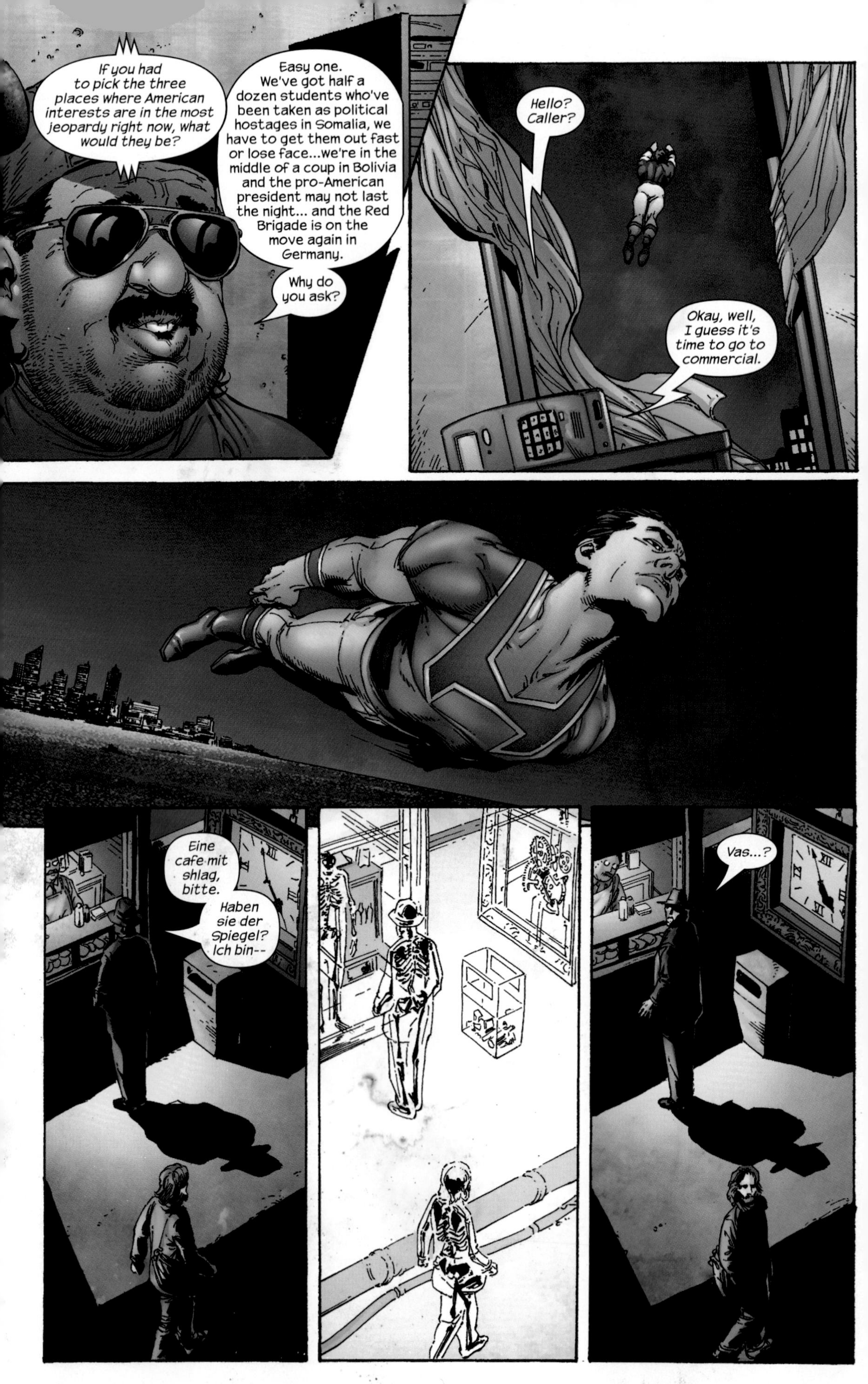
If you had to pick the three places where American interests are in the most jeopardy right now, what would they be?
Easy one. We've got half a dozen students who've been taken as political hostages in Somalia, we have to get them out fast or lose face...we're in the middle of a coup in Bolivia and the pro-American president may not last the night... and the Red Brigade is on the move again in Germany.
Why do you ask?
Hello? Caller?
Okay, well, I guess it's time to go to commercial.
Eine cafe mit shlag, bitte.
Haben sie der Spiegel? Ich bin--
Vas...?

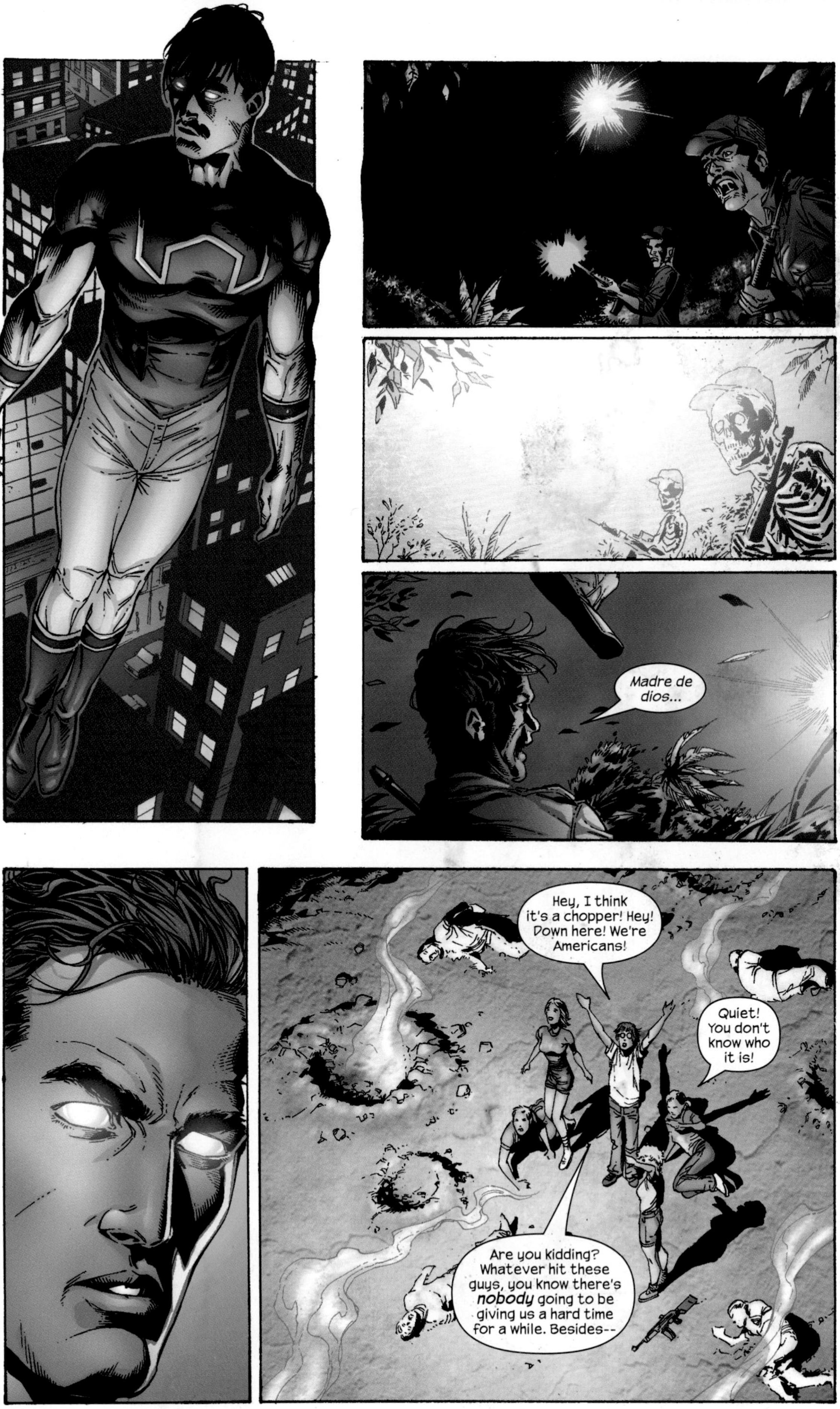
Madre de dios...
Hey, I think it's a chopper! Hey! Down here! We're Americans!
Quiet! You don't know who it is!
Are you kidding? Whatever hit these guys, you know there's *nobody* going to be giving us a hard time for a while. Besides--

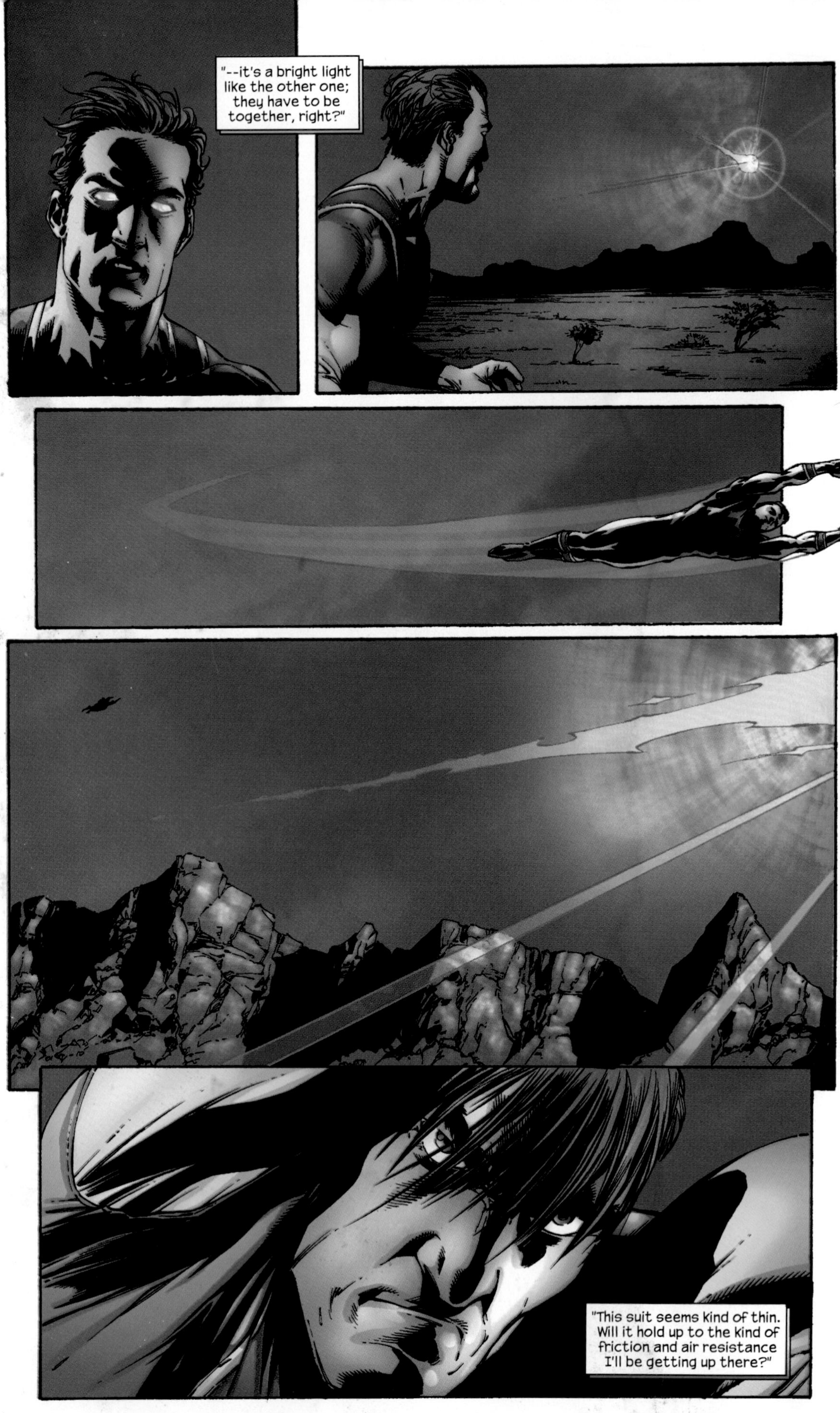
"--it's a bright light like the other one; they have to be together, right?"
"This suit seems kind of thin. Will it hold up to the kind of friction and air resistance I'll be getting up there?"

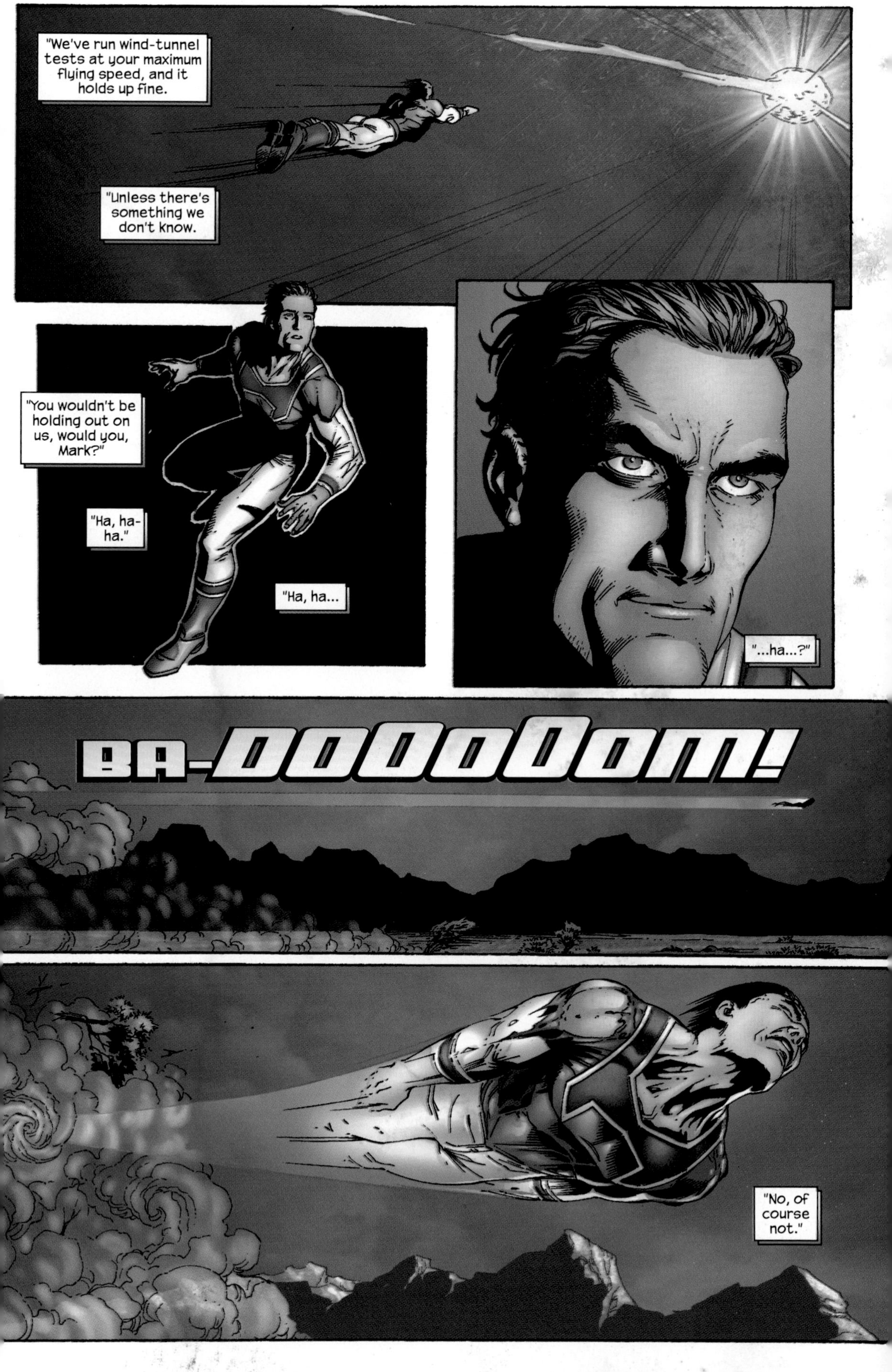
"We've run wind-tunnel tests at your maximum flying speed, and it holds up fine.
"Unless there's something we don't know.
"You wouldn't be holding out on us, would you, Mark?"
"Ha, ha-ha."
"Ha, ha...
"...ha...?"
BA-DOOOOOM!
"No, of course not."

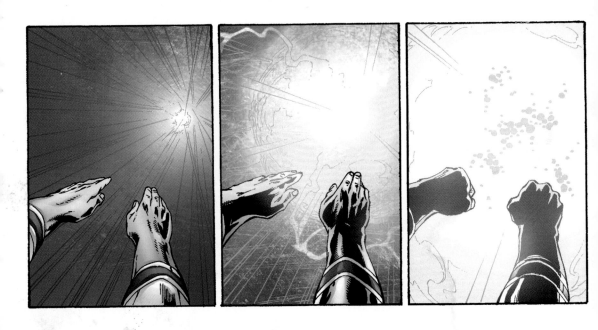

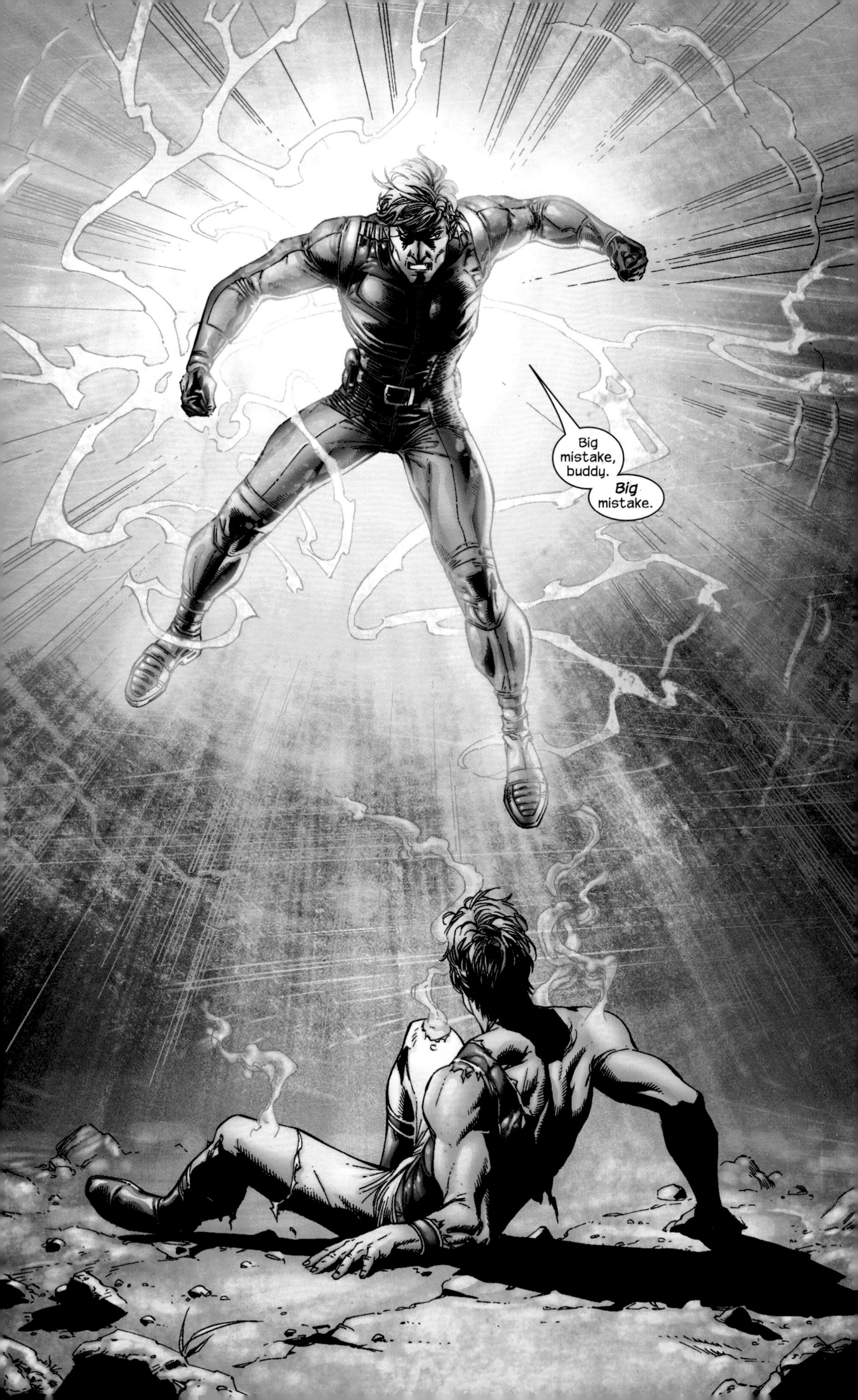
Big mistake, buddy.
Big mistake.

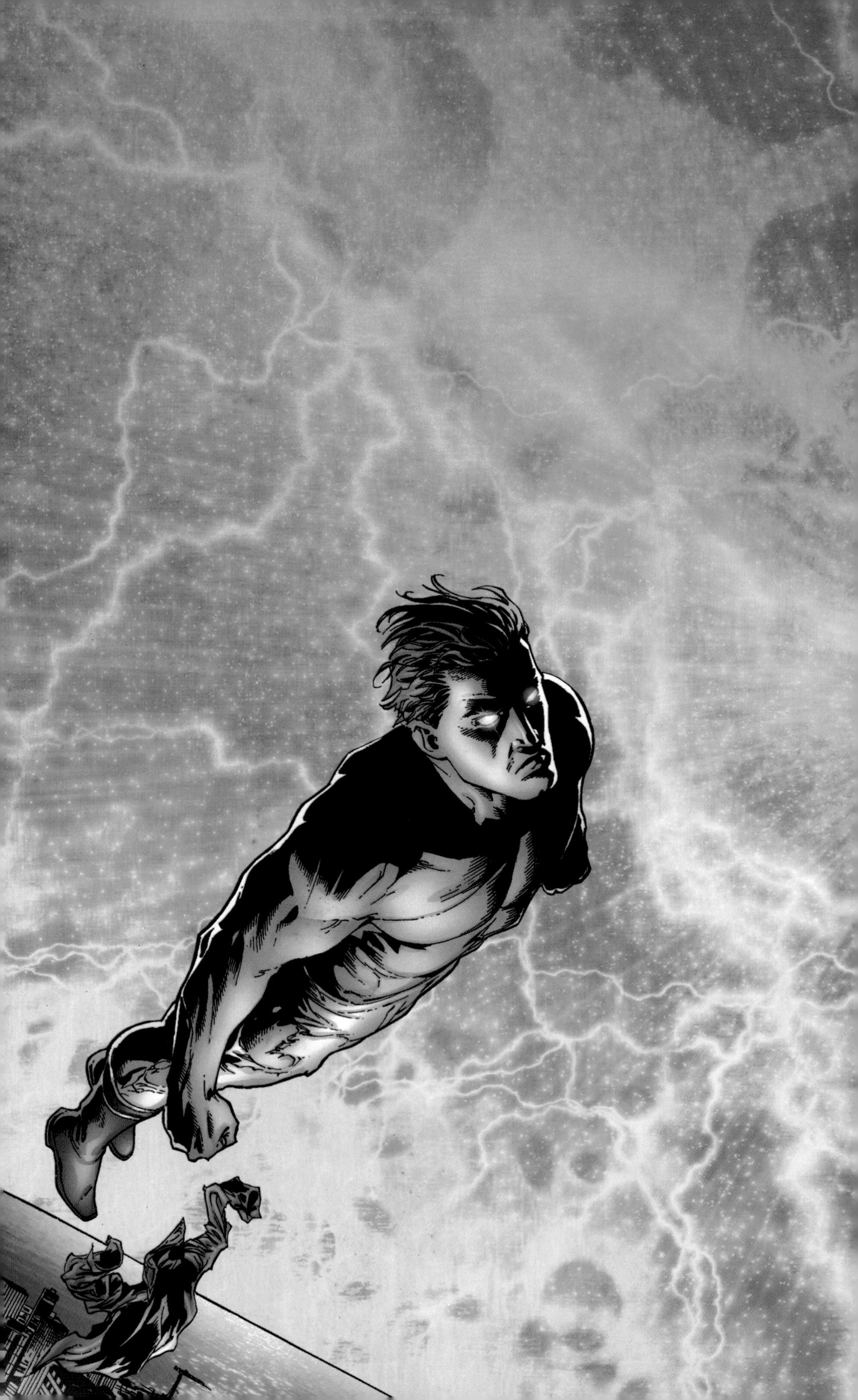

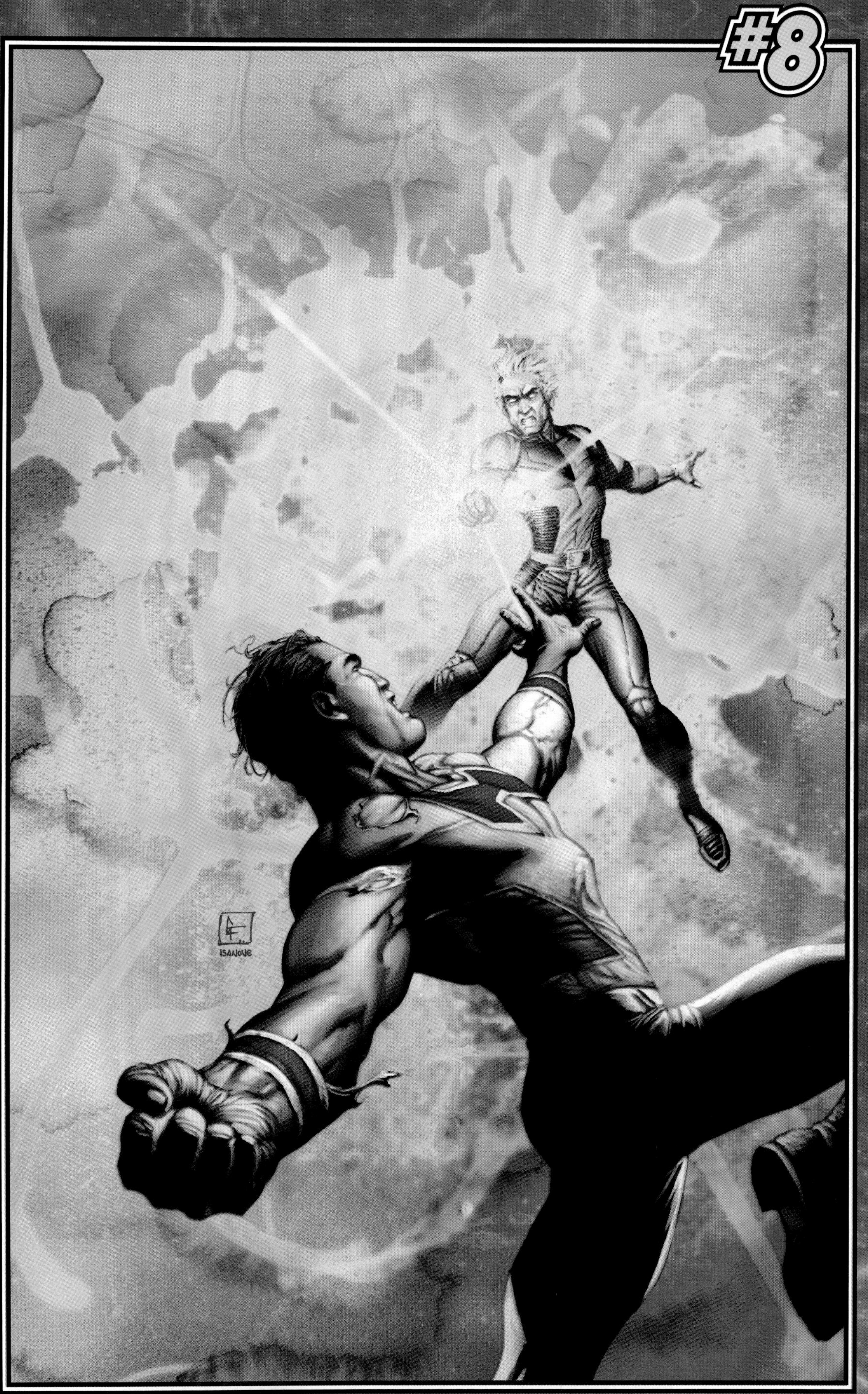
#8

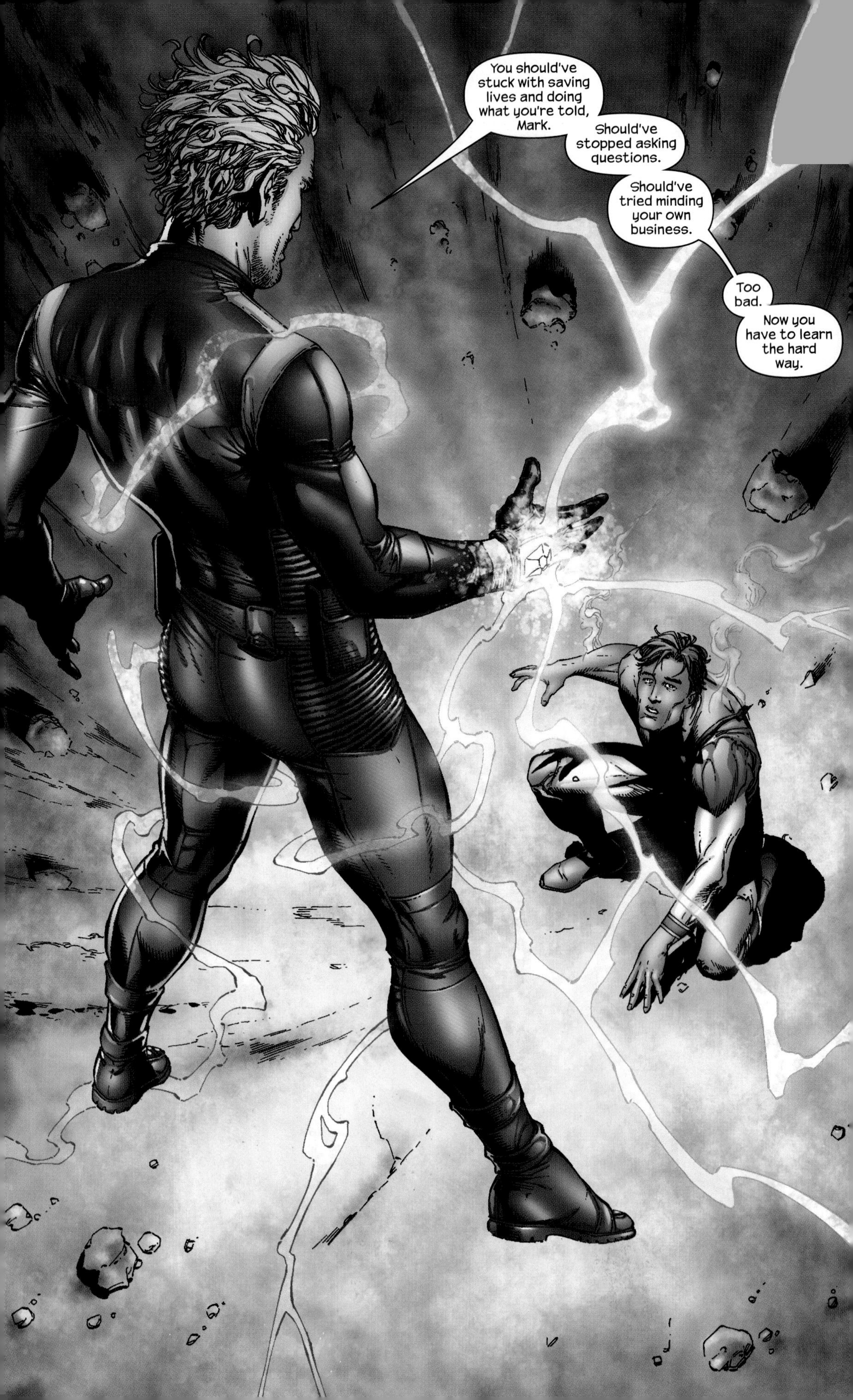
You should've stuck with saving lives and doing what you're told, Mark.
Should've stopped asking questions.
Should've tried minding your own business.
Too bad.
Now you have to learn the hard way.

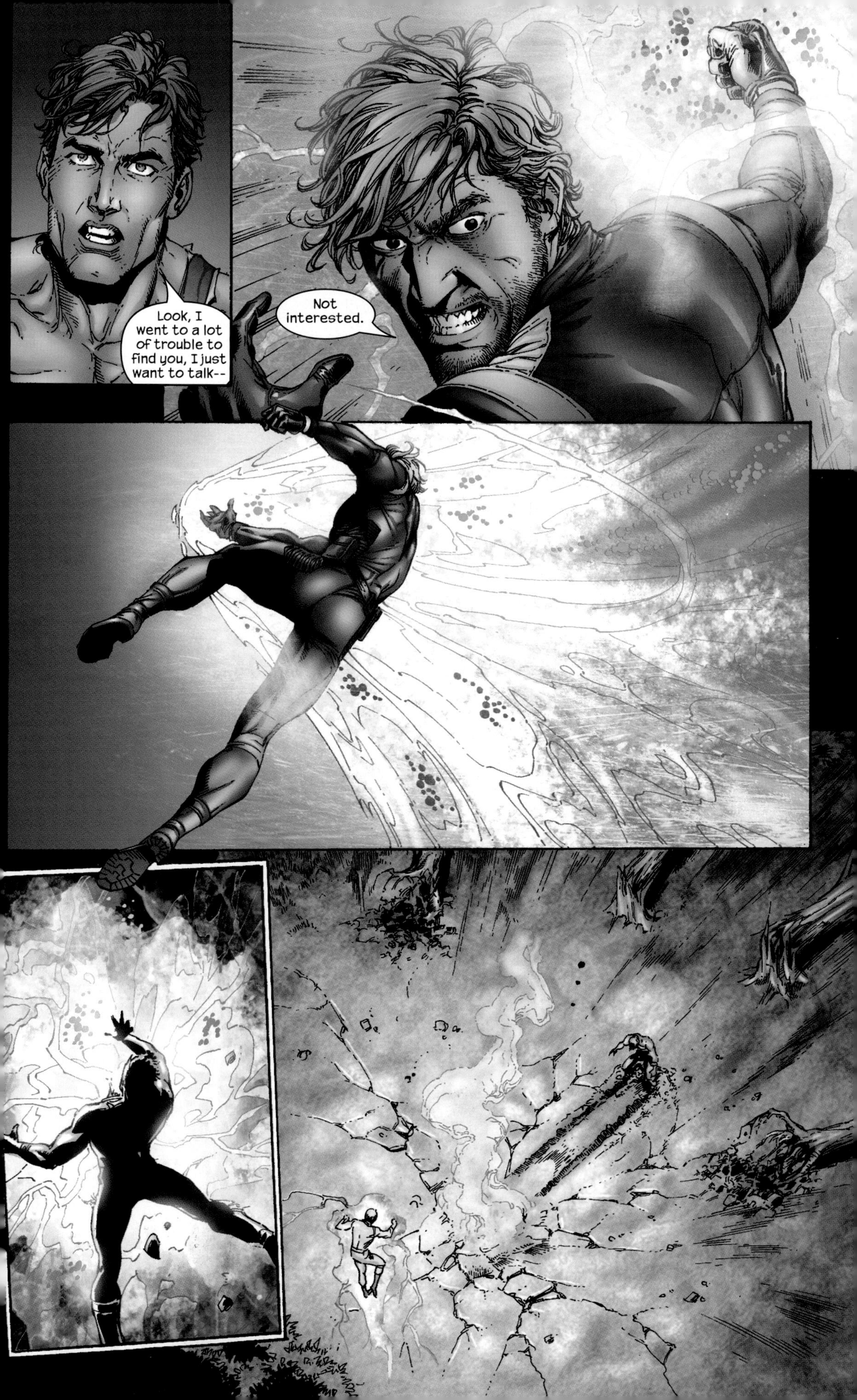
Look, I went to a lot of trouble to find you, I just want to talk--
Not interested.

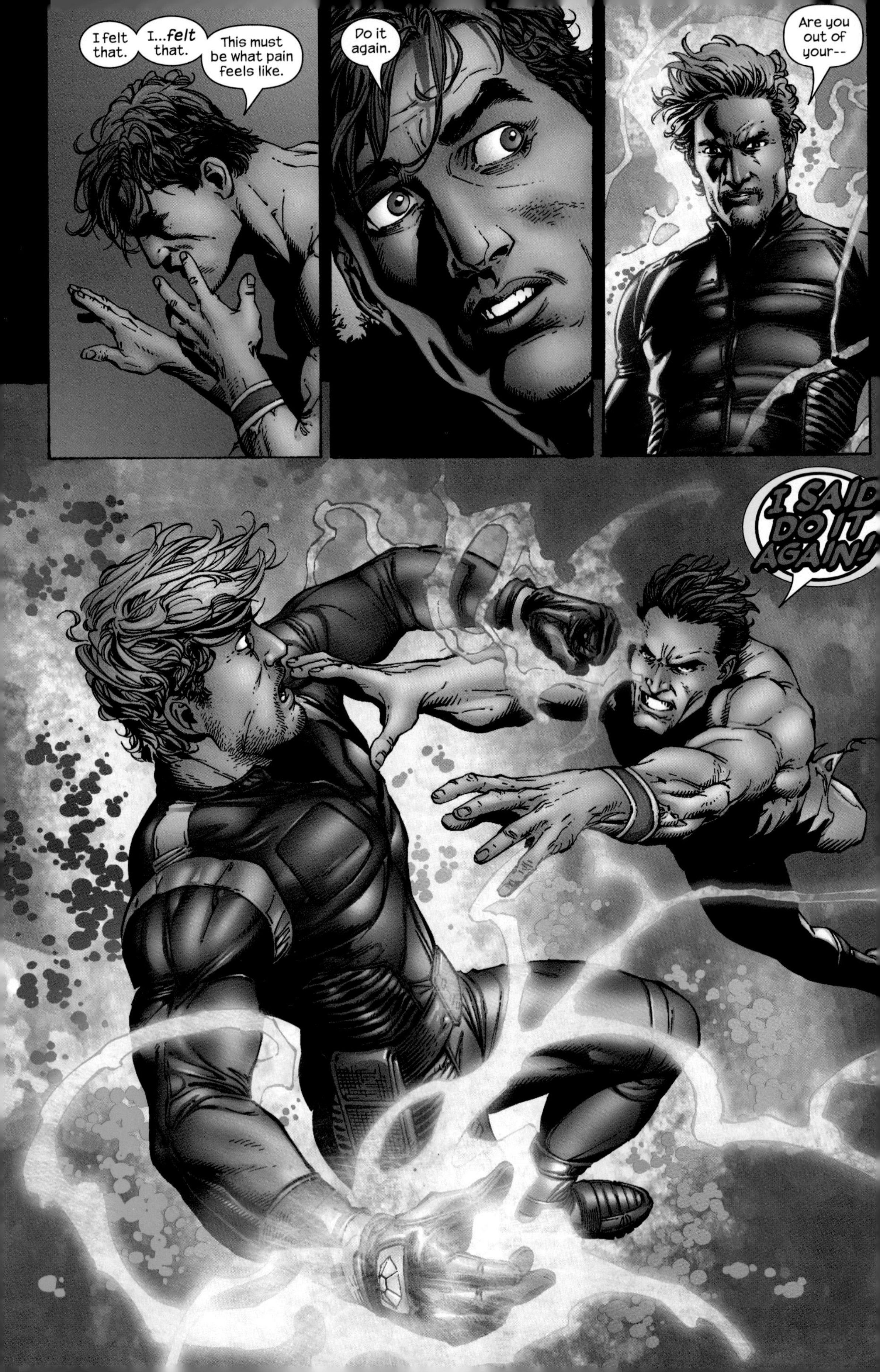
I felt that.
I...*felt* that.
This must be what pain feels like.
Do it again.
Are you out of your--
I SAID DO IT AGAIN!

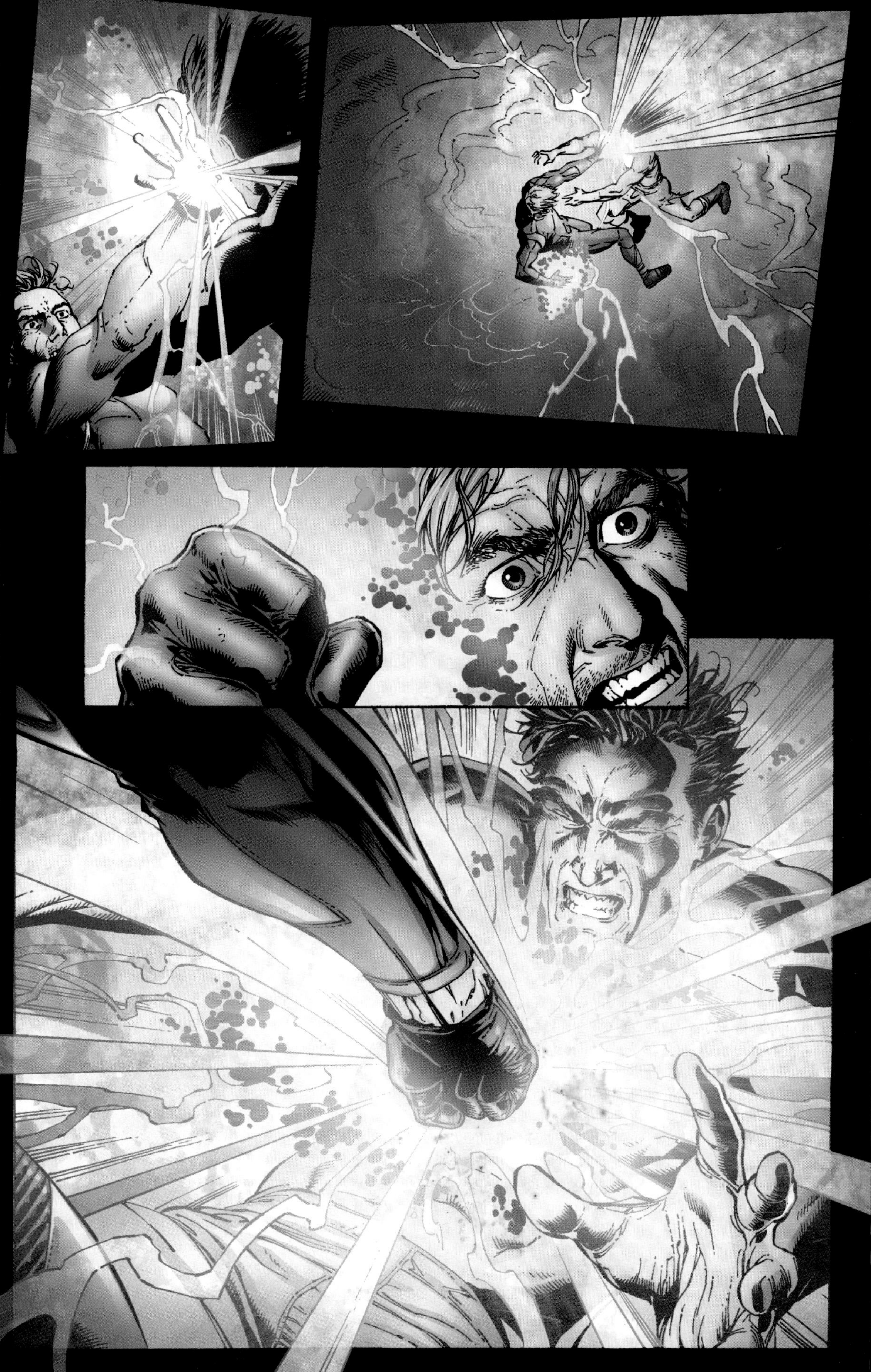

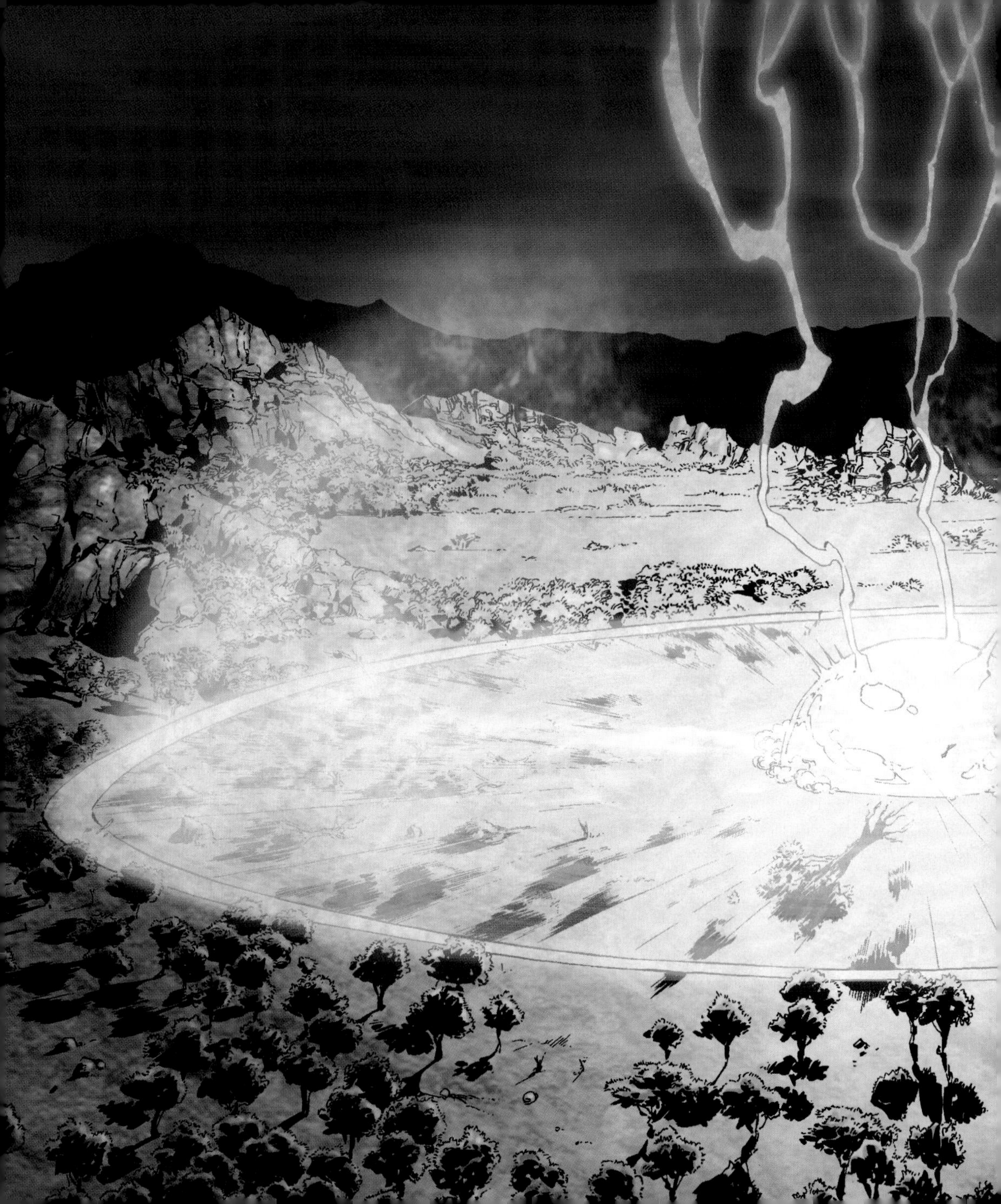

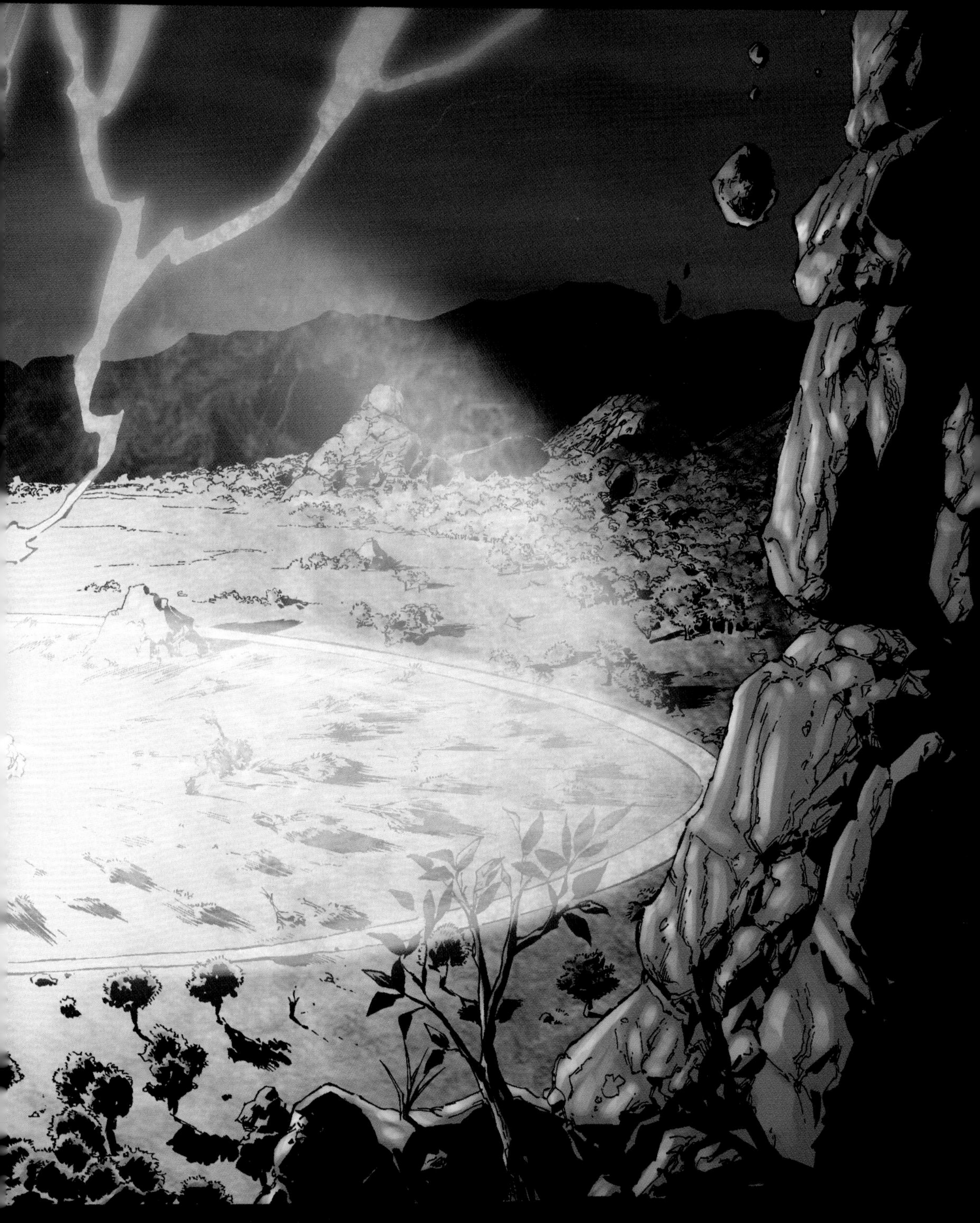

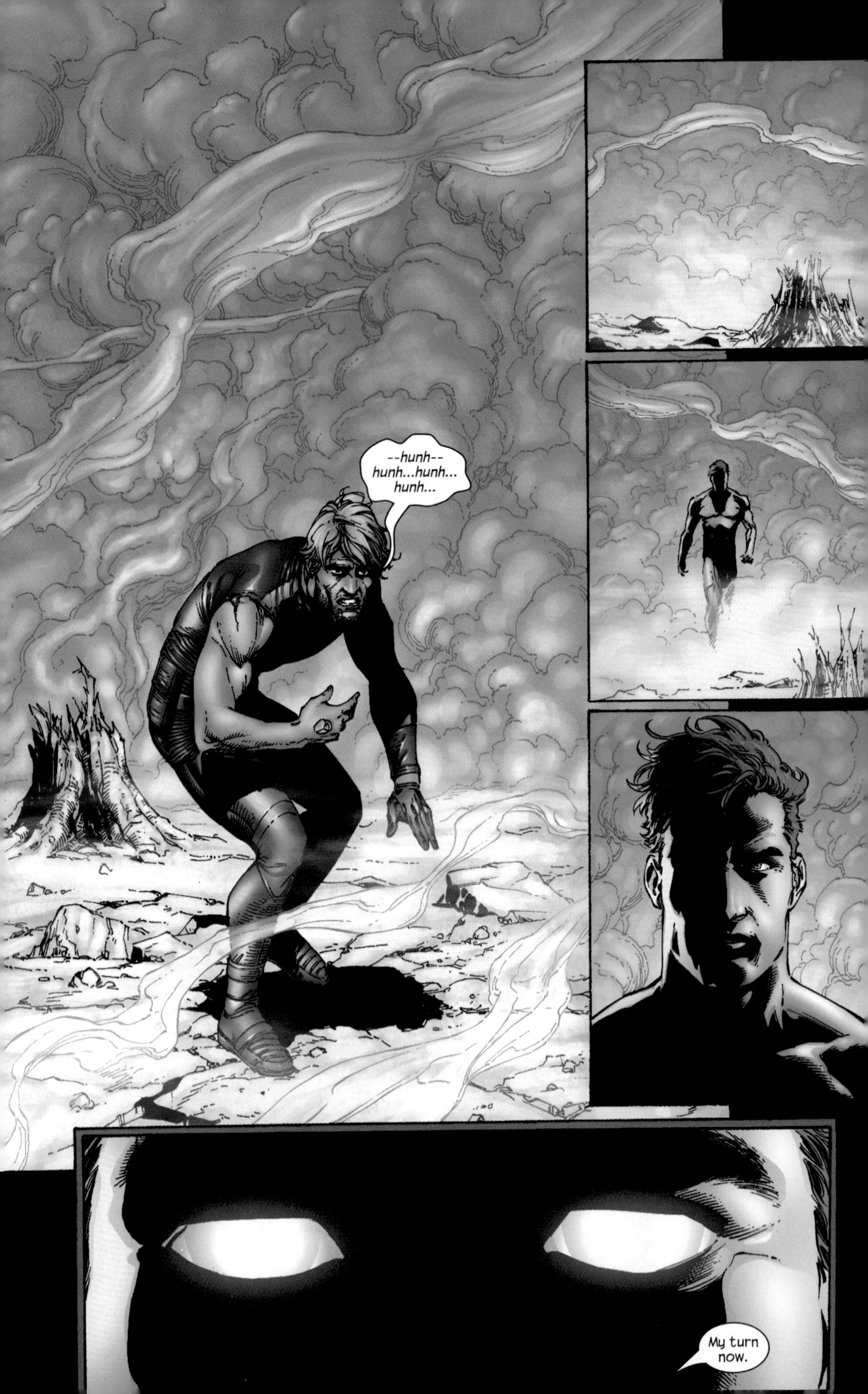
--hunh--
hunh...hunh...
hunh...
My turn now.

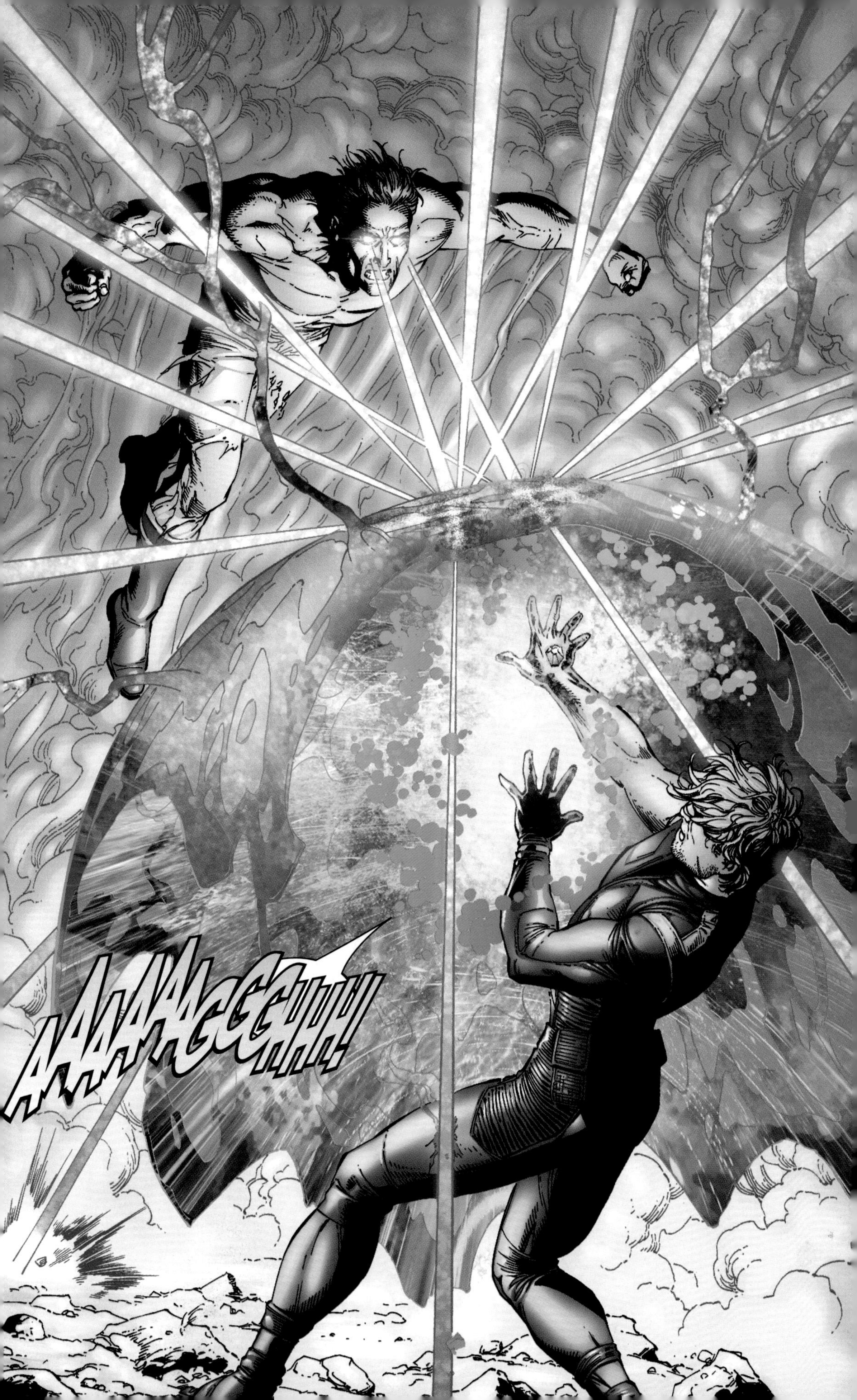
AAAAAGGGHHH!

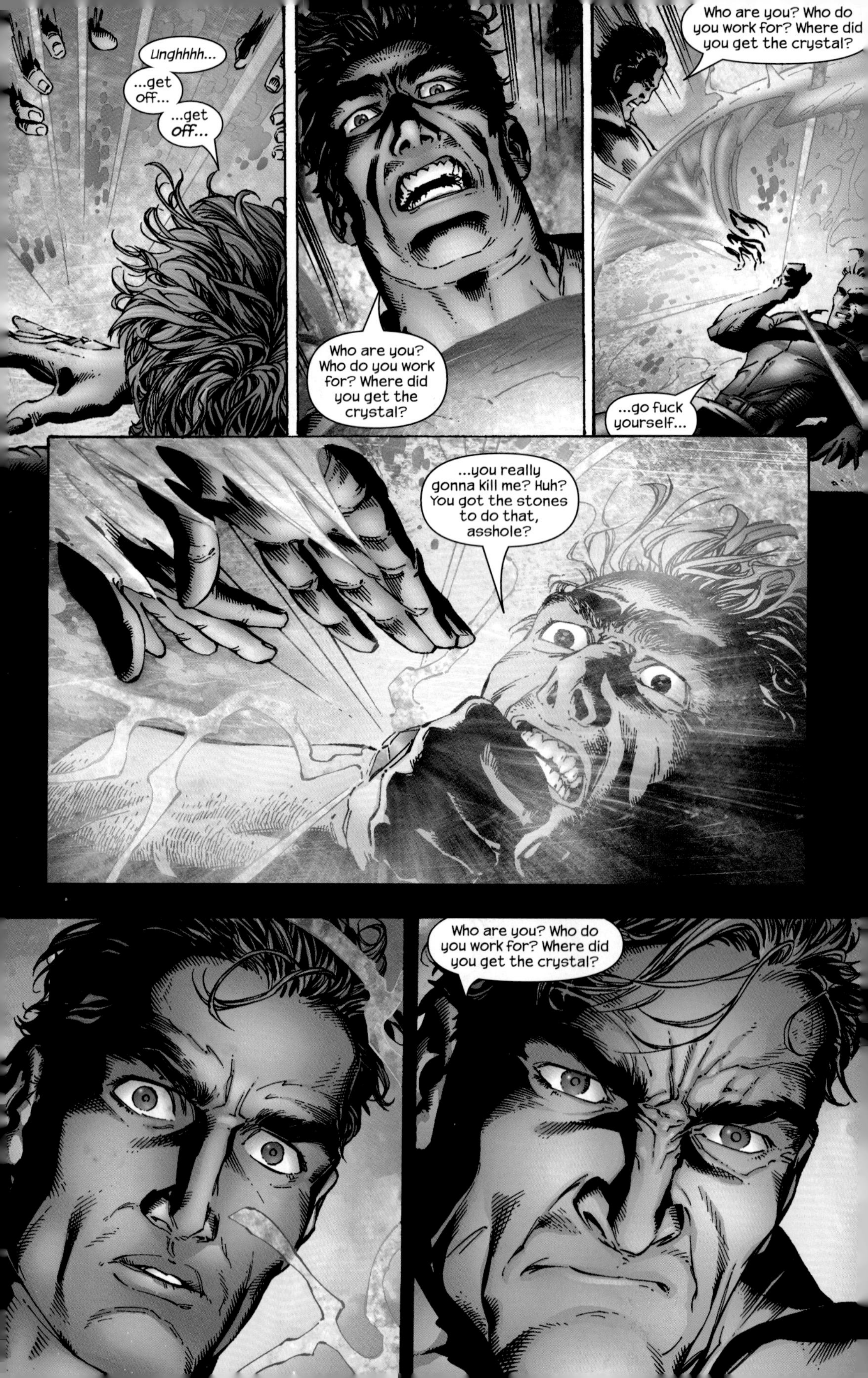
Unghhhh...
...get off...
...get off...
Who are you? Who do you work for? Where did you get the crystal?
Who are you? Who do you work for? Where did you get the crystal?
...go fuck yourself...
...you really gonna kill me? Huh? You got the stones to do that, asshole?
Who are you? Who do you work for? Where did you get the crystal?

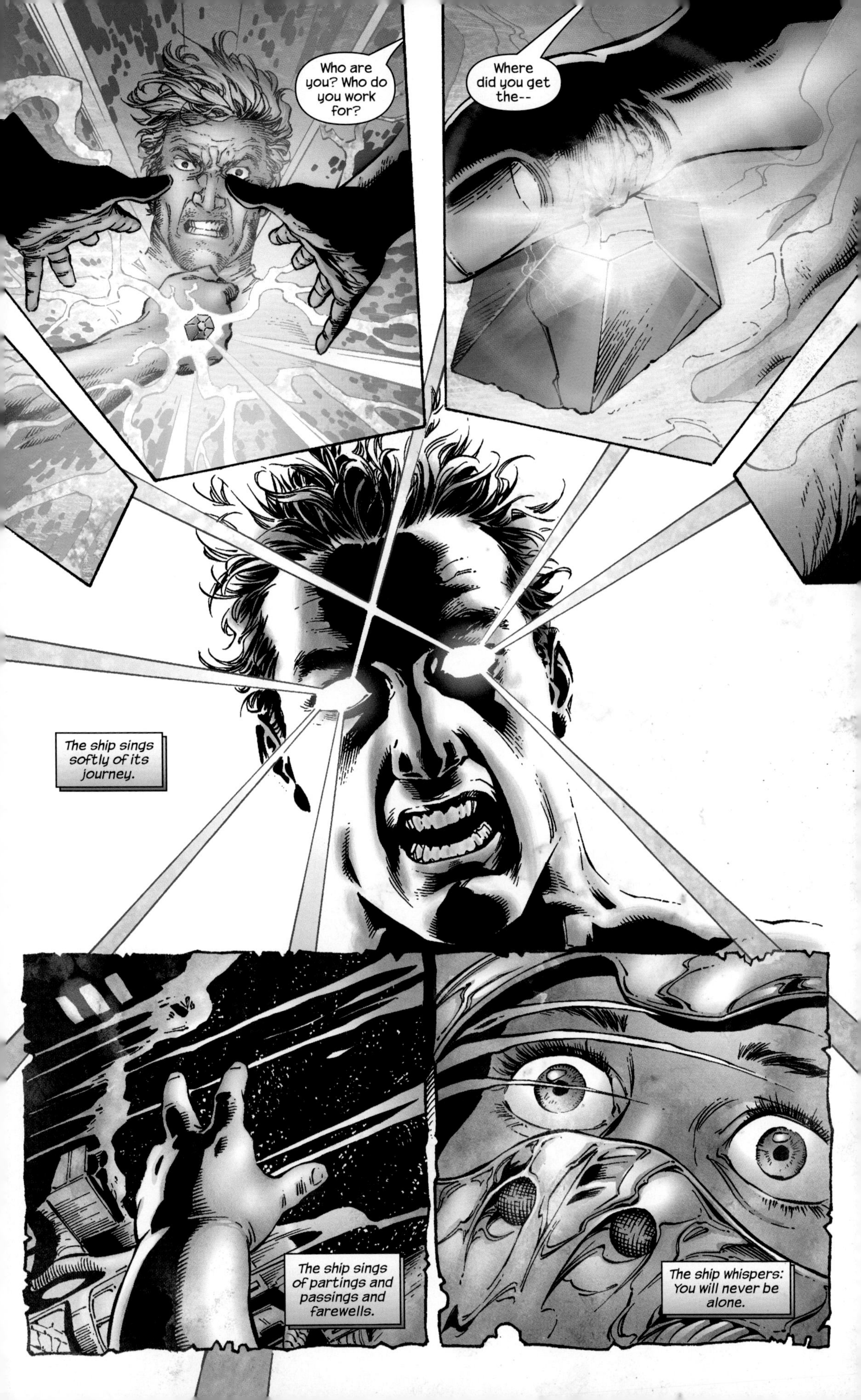
Who are you? Who do you work for?
Where did you get the--
The ship sings softly of its journey.
The ship sings of partings and passings and farewells.
The ship whispers: You will never be alone.

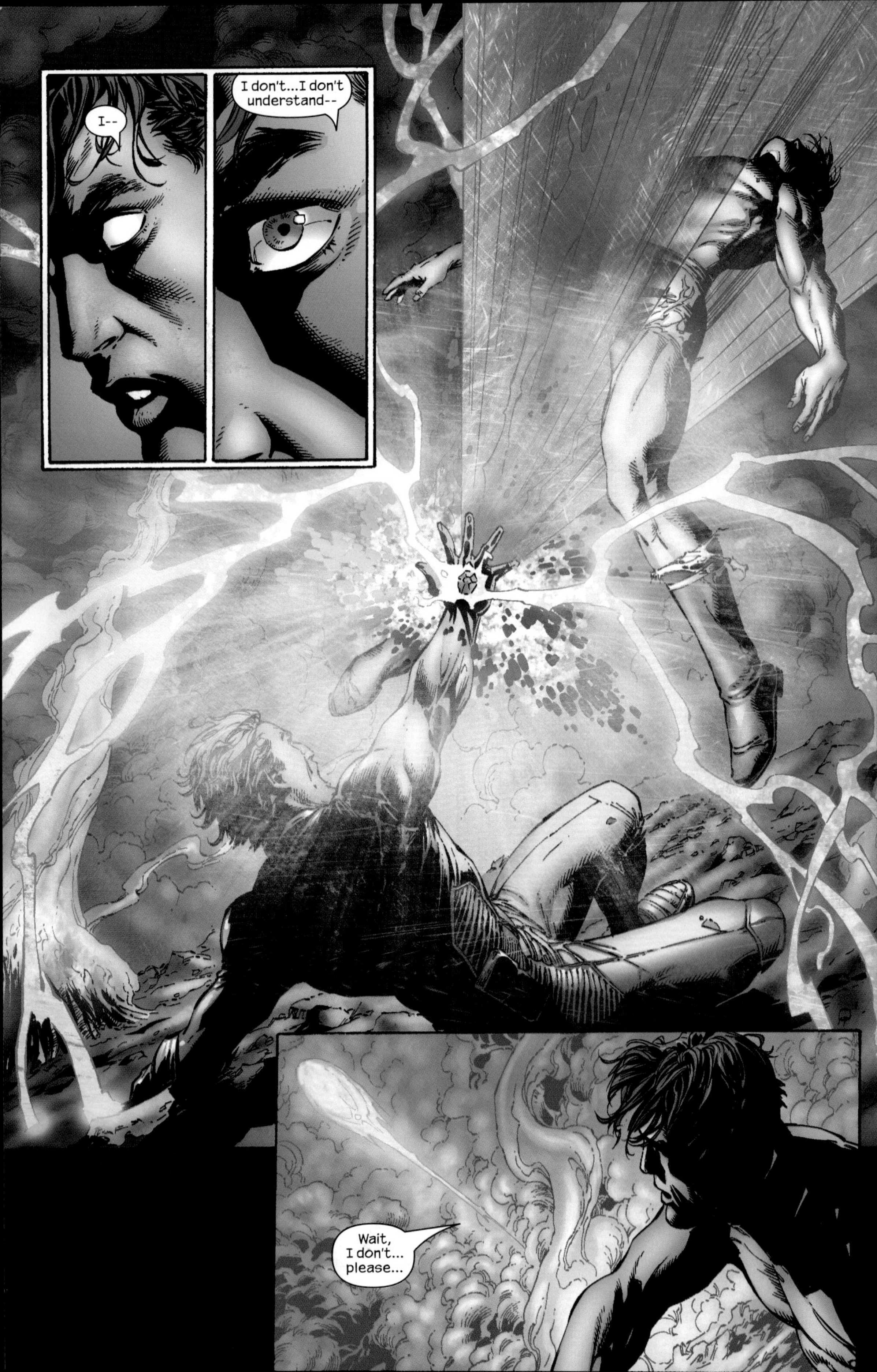
I--
I don't...I don't understand--
Wait, I don't... please...

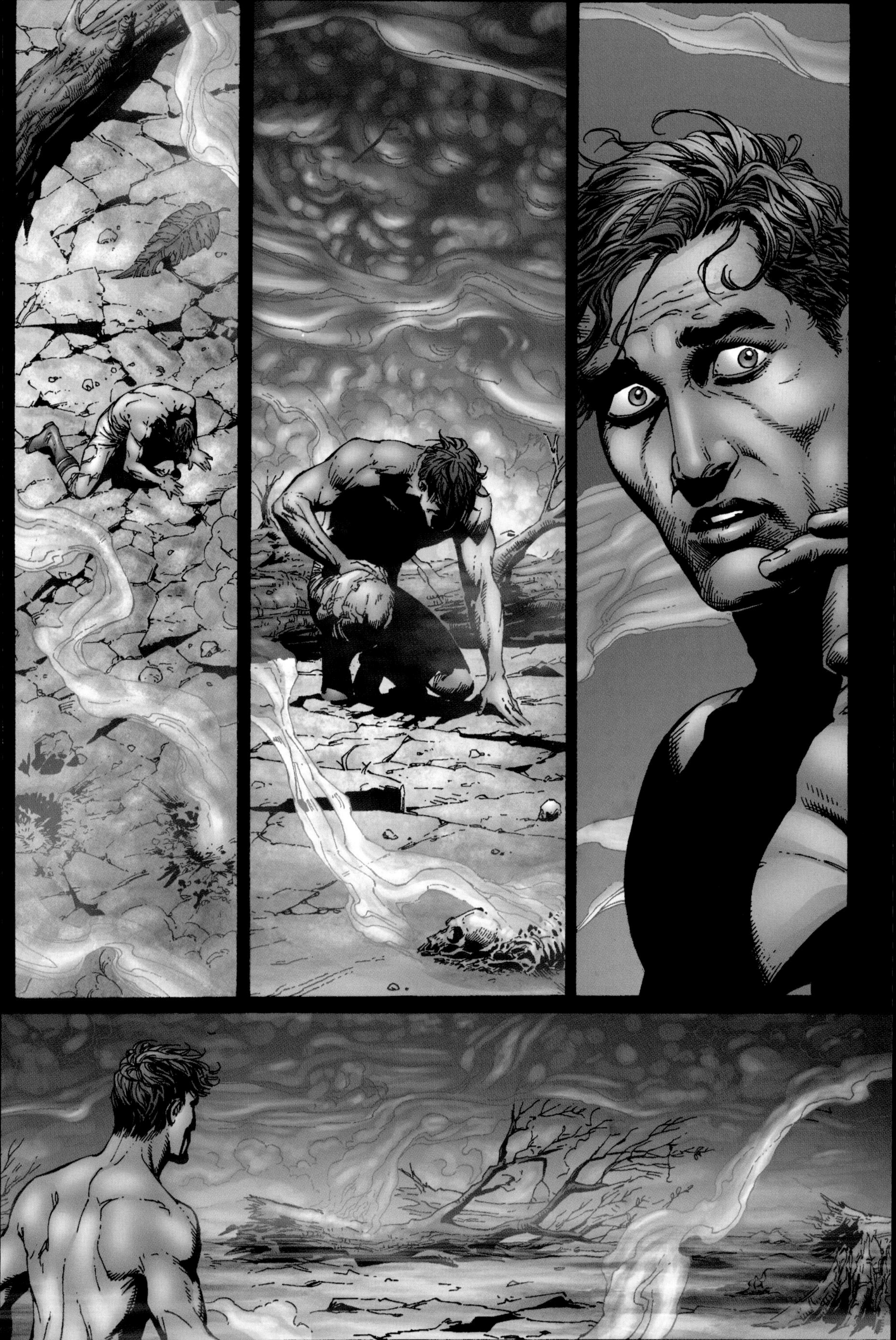

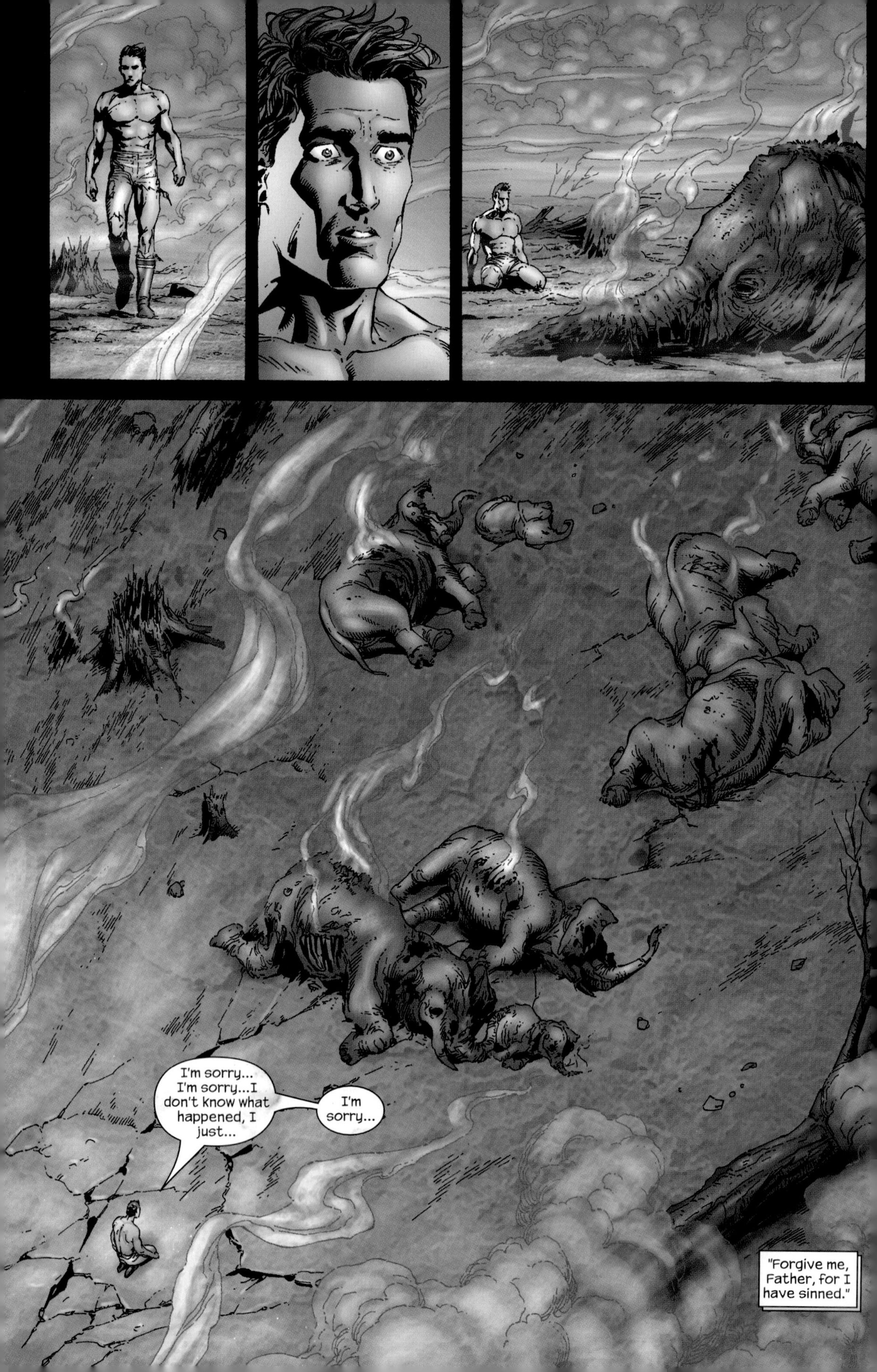
I'm sorry...
I'm sorry...I don't know what happened, I just...
I'm sorry...
"Forgive me, Father, for I have sinned."

It has been two weeks since my last confession.
Go on, my son.
My wife has been visiting her parents, and in her absence I have had impure thoughts. Before she left, my sister-in-law stayed with us a few days, and I peeked at her in the shower.
Go on.
That's... pretty much it, Father. It's--
--heh--
--I guess it's been a slow couple of weeks for sin. She's coming back next week, though. Anyway, that's it.
For these and all my sins I am truly sorry.
You will perform twelve Hail Marys and put a lock on the bathroom door.
Yes, Father.
A thumb-lock, that only opens from the inside.
Yes, Father.
O my God, I am heartily sorry for having offended Thee, and I detest all my sins because I dread the loss of heaven and the pains of hell. But most of all, because they offend Thee, my God, Who art all good and deserving of all my love.
I firmly resolve, with the help of Thy grace, to confess my sins, to do penance, and to amend my life. Amen.
God the Father of Mercies, through the death and resurrection of his Son has reconciled the world to himself and sent the Holy Spirit among us for the forgiveness of sins; through the ministry of the Church may God give you pardon and peace...
...and I absolve you from your sins in the name of the Father, and of the Son, and of the Holy Spirit.
Give thanks to the Lord, for He is good.
His mercy endures forever.
Go in peace.
Bob's Hardware on 14th is open late. I suggest that when you go in peace, you go there.
Yes, Father.
CLICK!

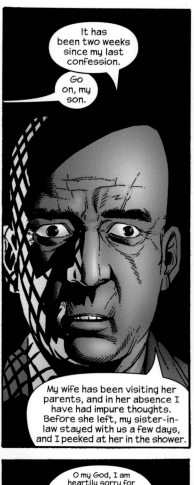

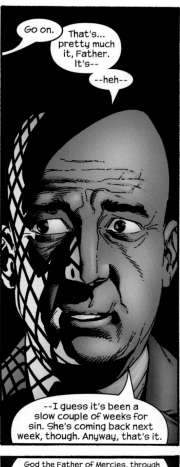

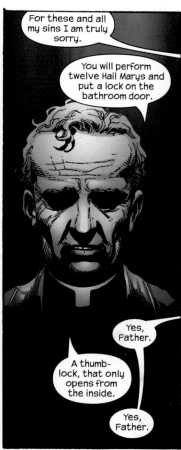

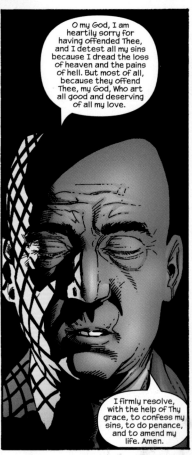

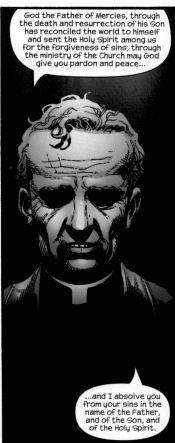

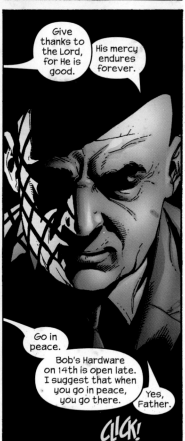

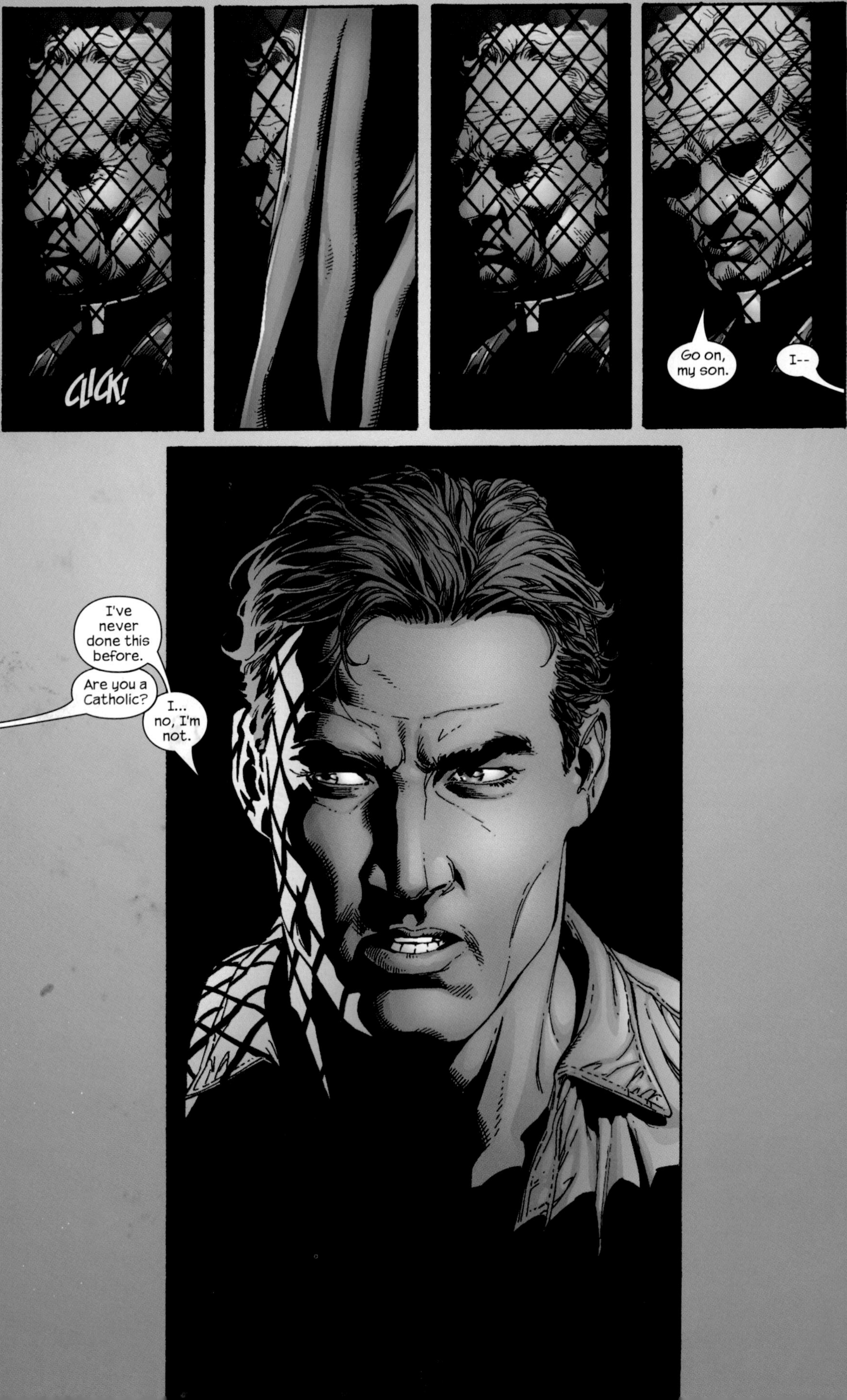
CLICK!
Go on, my son.
I--
I've never done this before.
Are you a Catholic?
I... no, I'm not.

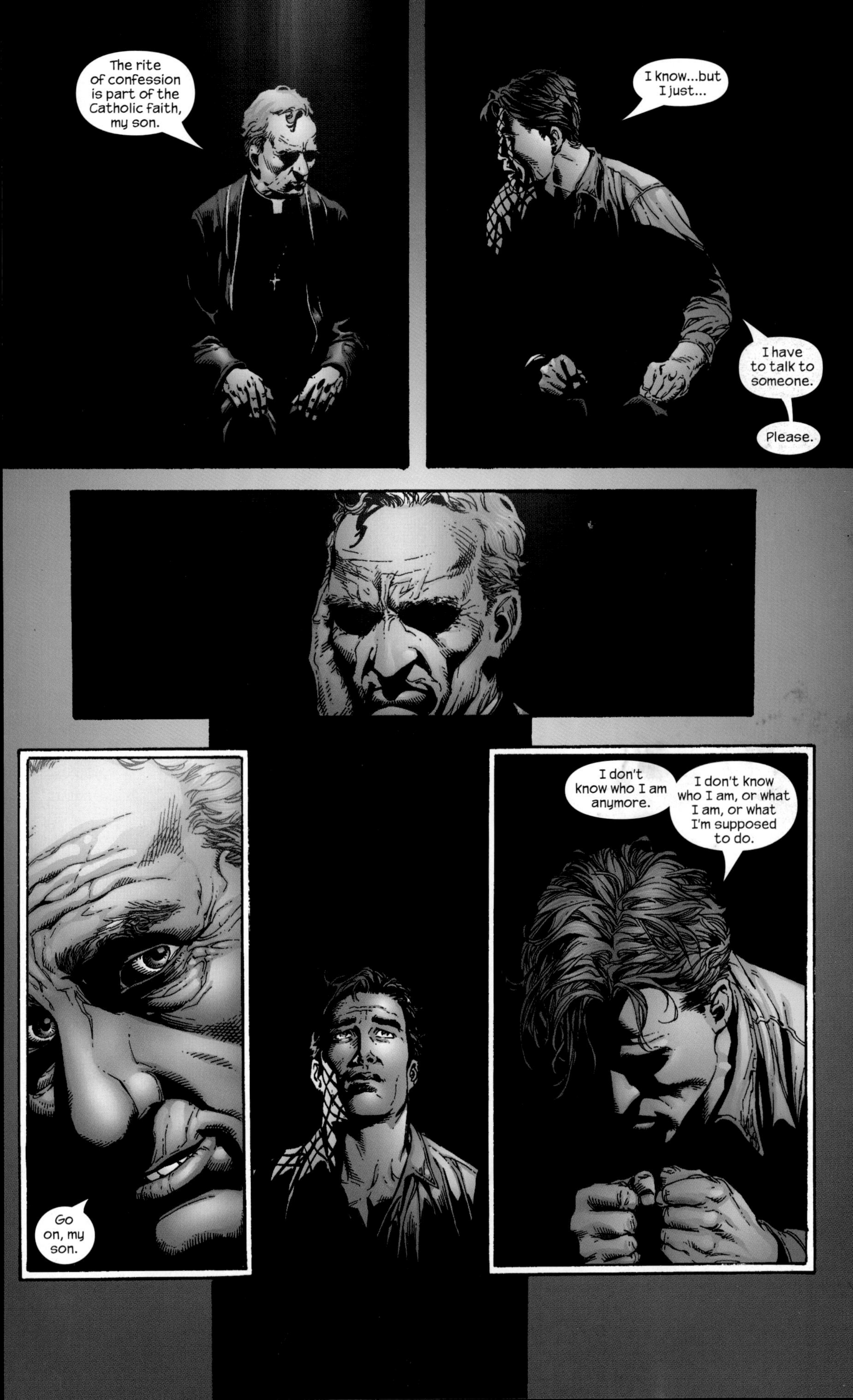
The rite of confession is part of the Catholic faith, my son.
I know...but I just...
I have to talk to someone.
Please.
Go on, my son.
I don't know who I am anymore.
I don't know who I am, or what I am, or what I'm supposed to do.

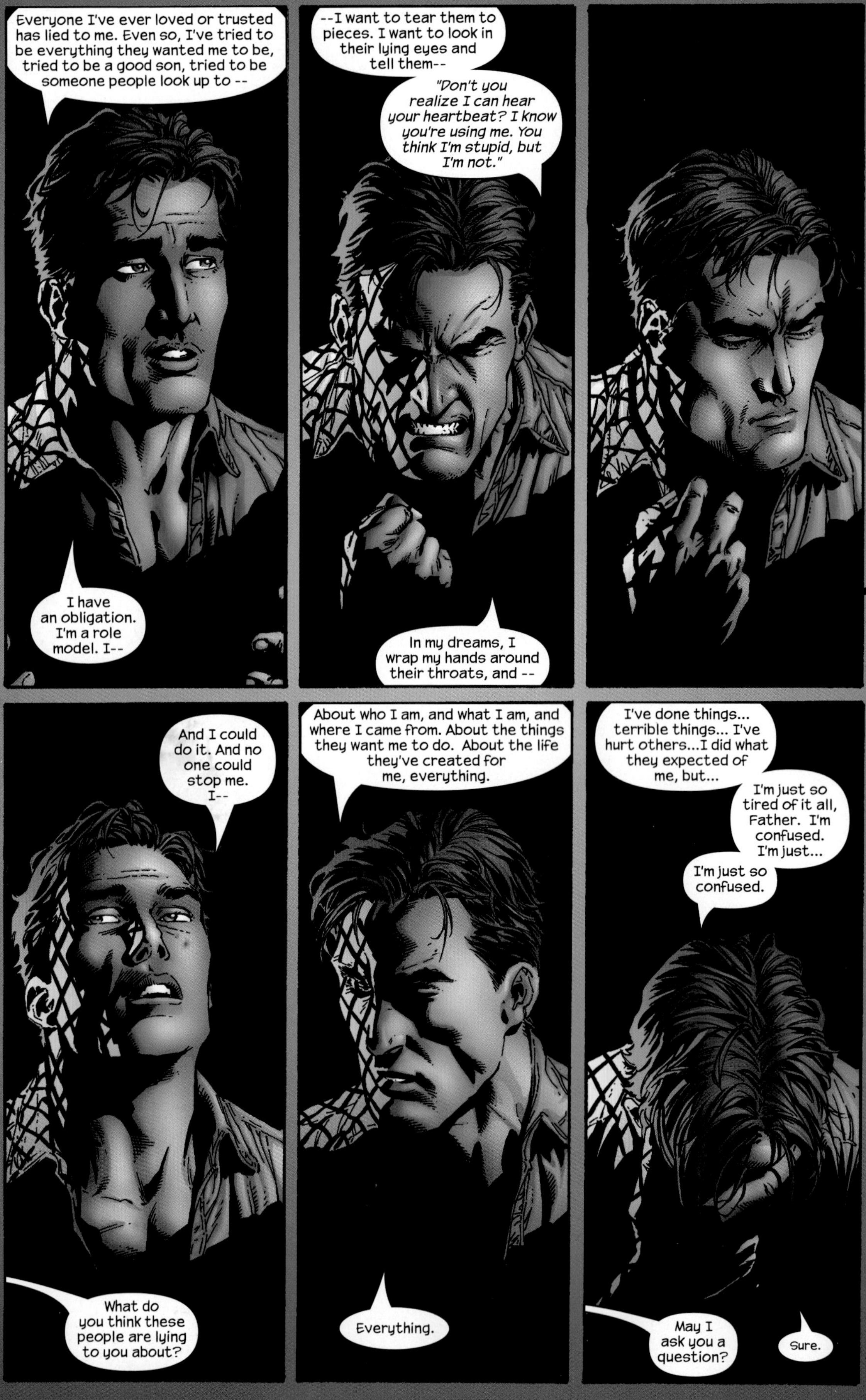
Everyone I've ever loved or trusted has lied to me. Even so, I've tried to be everything they wanted me to be, tried to be a good son, tried to be someone people look up to --
I have an obligation. I'm a role model. I--
--I want to tear them to pieces. I want to look in their lying eyes and tell them--
"Don't you realize I can hear your heartbeat? I know you're using me. You think I'm stupid, but I'm not."
In my dreams, I wrap my hands around their throats, and --
And I could do it. And no one could stop me. I--
What do you think these people are lying to you about?
About who I am, and what I am, and where I came from. About the things they want me to do. About the life they've created for me, everything.
Everything.
I've done things... terrible things... I've hurt others...I did what they expected of me, but...
I'm just so tired of it all, Father. I'm confused. I'm just...
I'm just so confused.
May I ask you a question?
Sure.

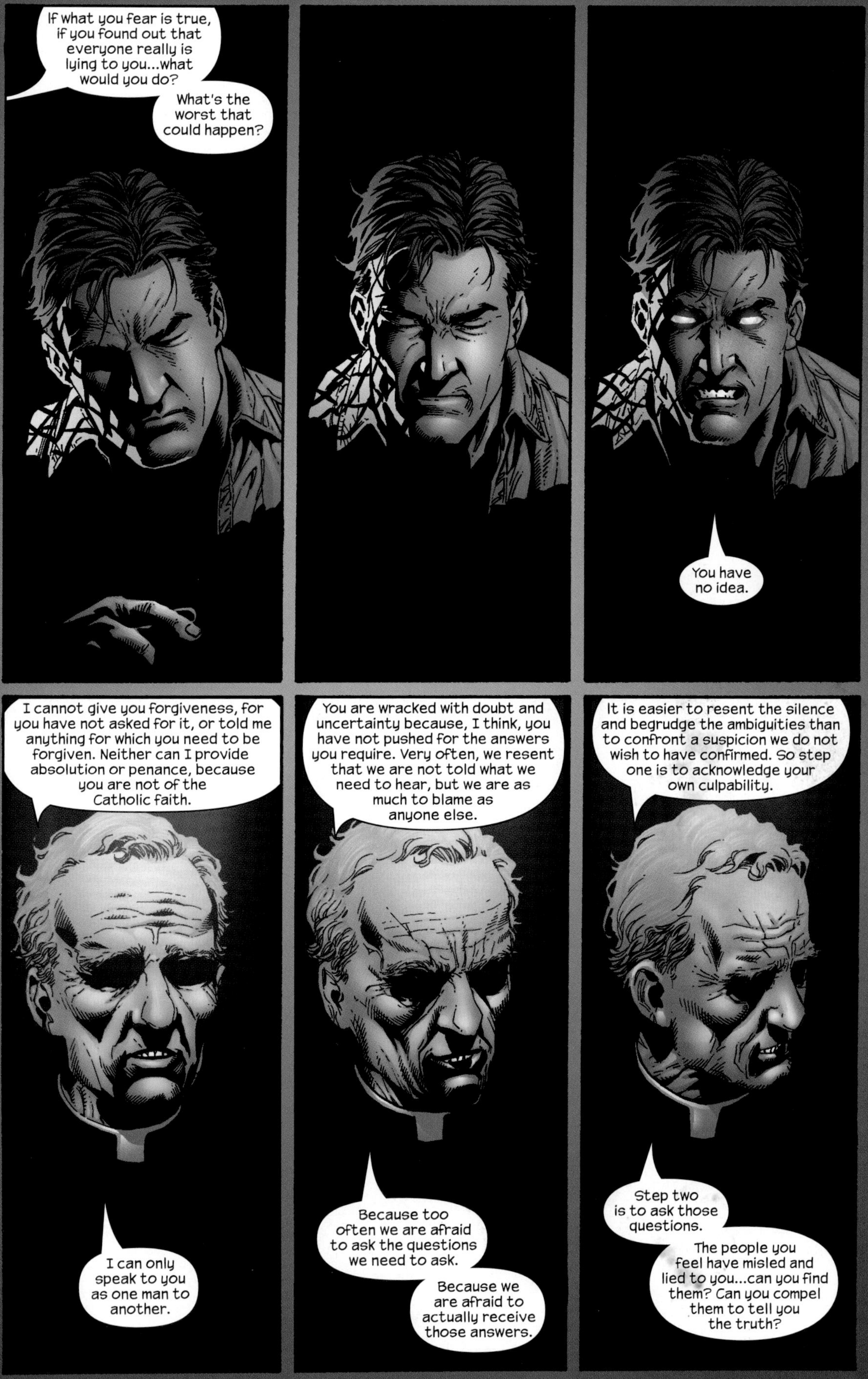

If what you fear is true, if you found out that everyone really is lying to you...what would you do?
What's the worst that could happen?
You have no idea.
I cannot give you forgiveness, for you have not asked for it, or told me anything for which you need to be forgiven. Neither can I provide absolution or penance, because you are not of the Catholic faith.
I can only speak to you as one man to another.
You are wracked with doubt and uncertainty because, I think, you have not pushed for the answers you require. Very often, we resent that we are not told what we need to hear, but we are as much to blame as anyone else.
Because too often we are afraid to ask the questions we need to ask.
Because we are afraid to actually receive those answers.
It is easier to resent the silence and begrudge the ambiguities than to confront a suspicion we do not wish to have confirmed. So step one is to acknowledge your own culpability.
Step two is to ask those questions.
The people you feel have misled and lied to you...can you find them? Can you compel them to tell you the truth?

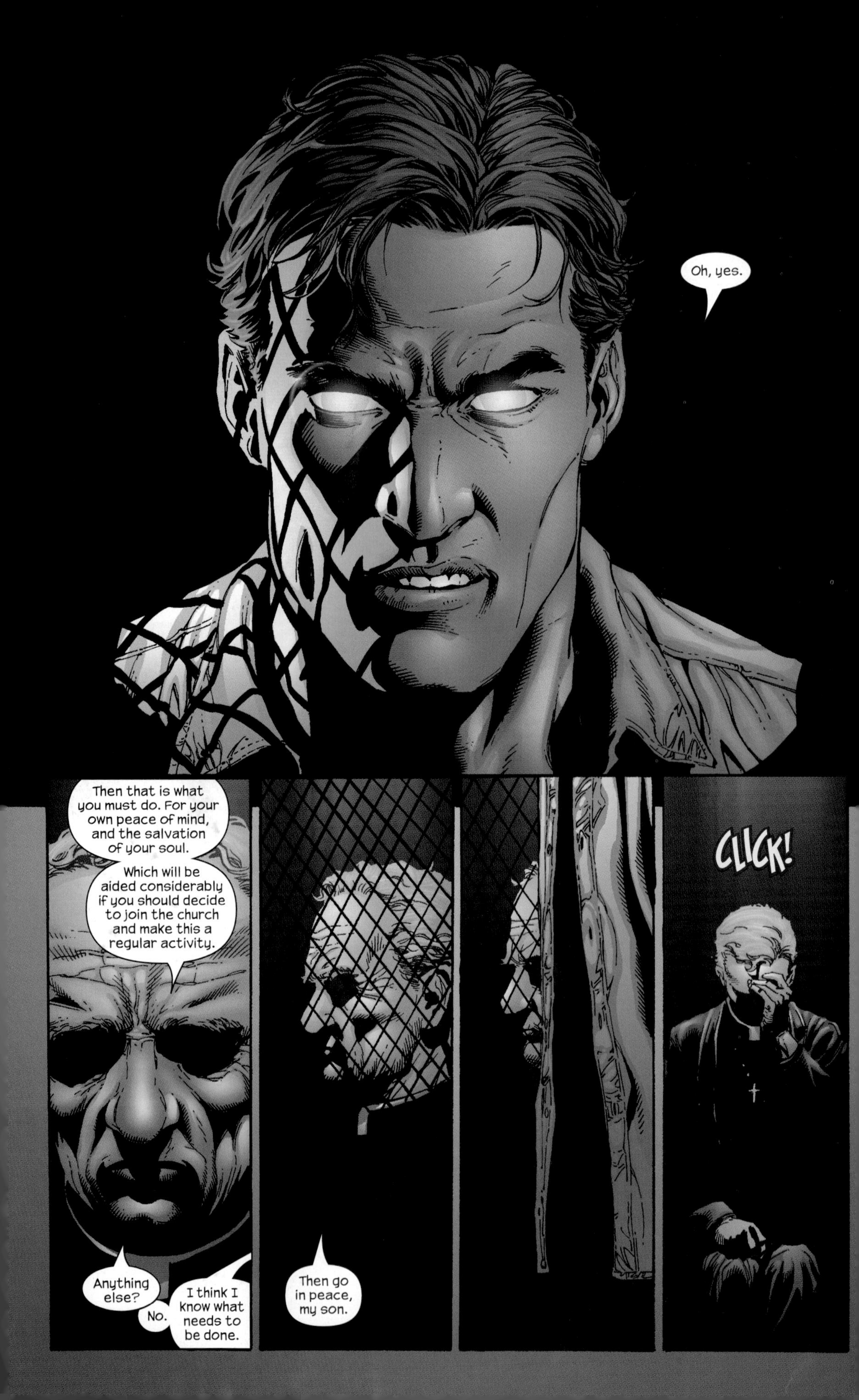
Oh, yes.
Then that is what you must do. For your own peace of mind, and the salvation of your soul.
Which will be aided considerably if you should decide to join the church and make this a regular activity.
Anything else?
No.
I think I know what needs to be done.
Then go in peace, my son.
CLICK!

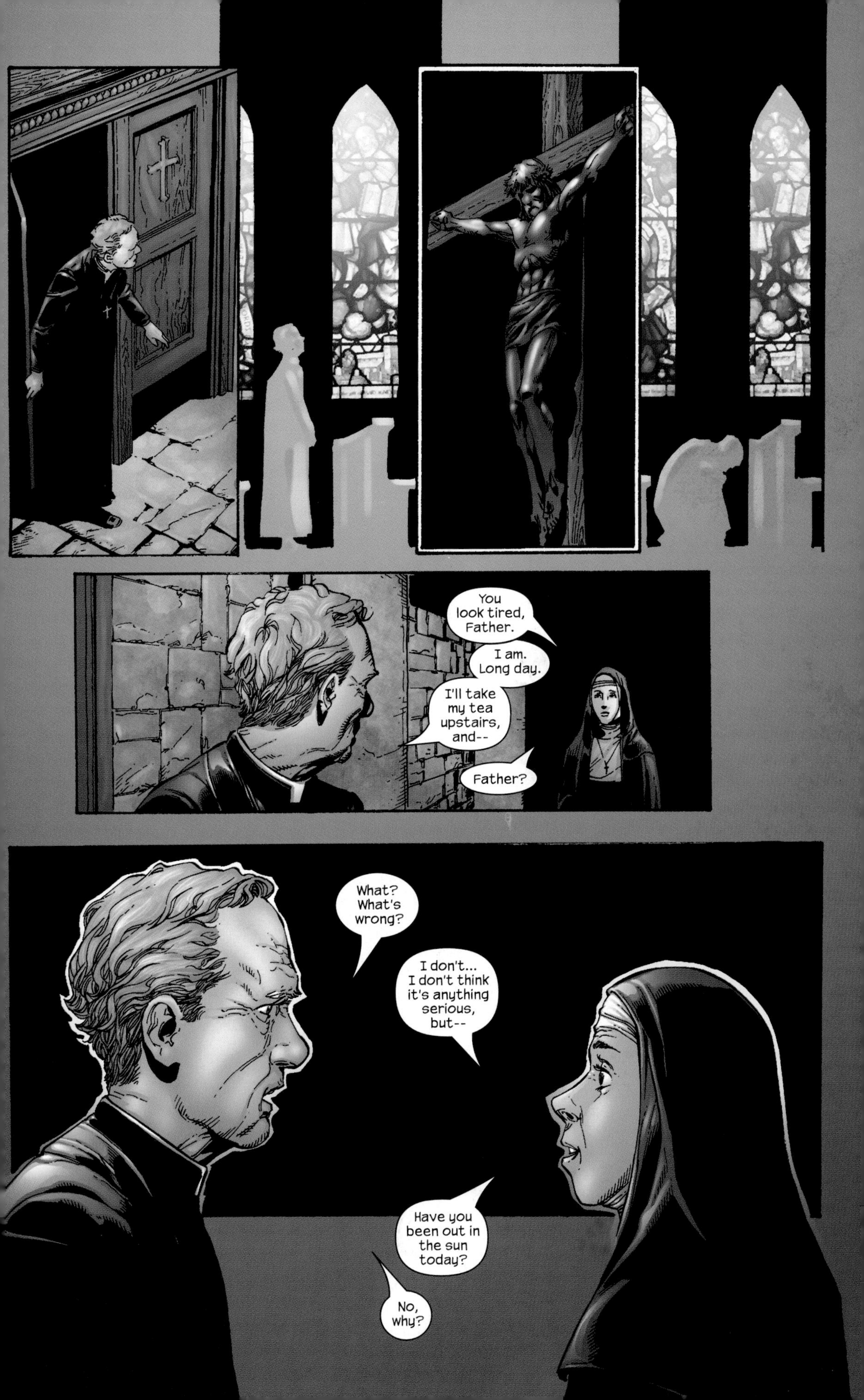
You look tired, Father.
I am. Long day.
I'll take my tea upstairs, and--
Father?
What? What's wrong?
I don't... I don't think it's anything serious, but--
Have you been out in the sun today?
No, why?

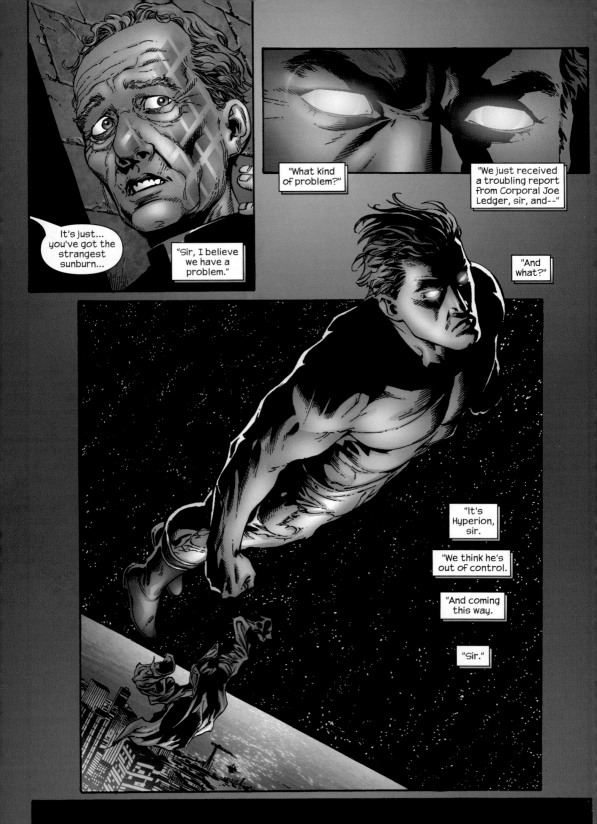

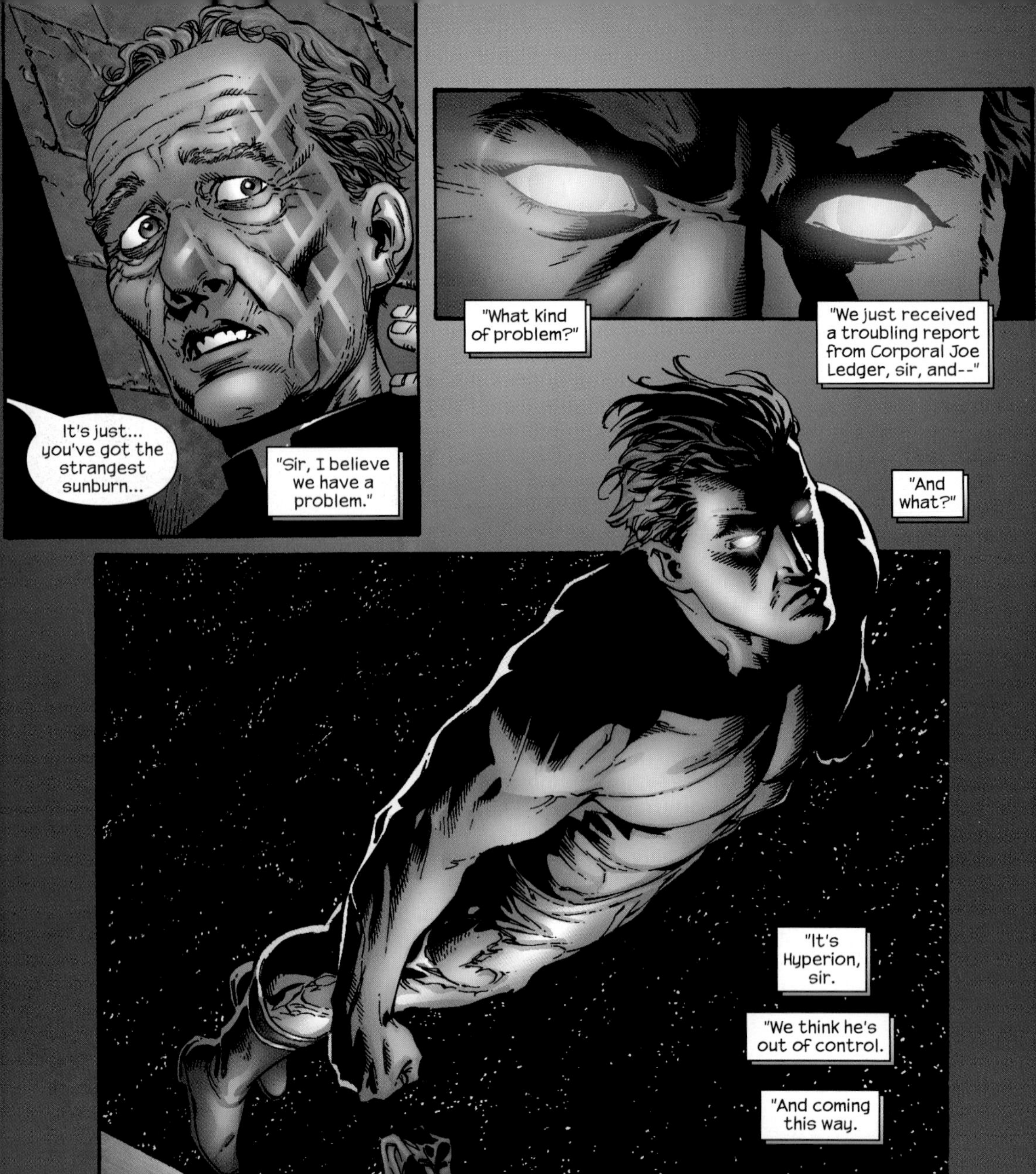
It's just... you've got the strangest sunburn...
"Sir, I believe we have a problem."
"What kind of problem?"
"We just received a troubling report from Corporal Joe Ledger, sir, and--"
"And what?"
"It's Hyperion, sir.
"We think he's out of control.
"And coming this way.
"Sir."

UBI DUBIUM, IBI LIBERTAS

WHERE THERE IS DOUBT, THERE IS FREEDOM

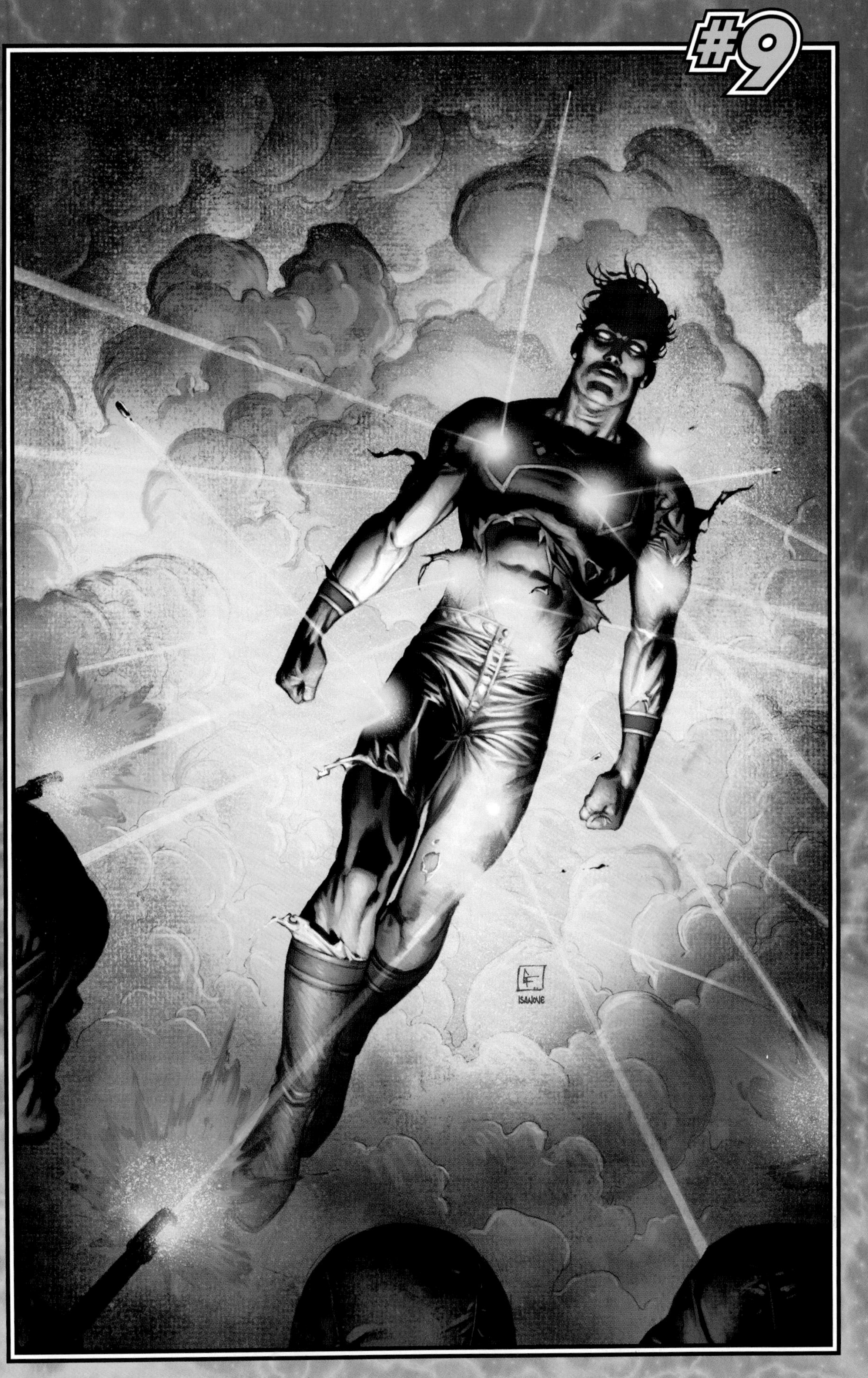
#9
ISANOVE

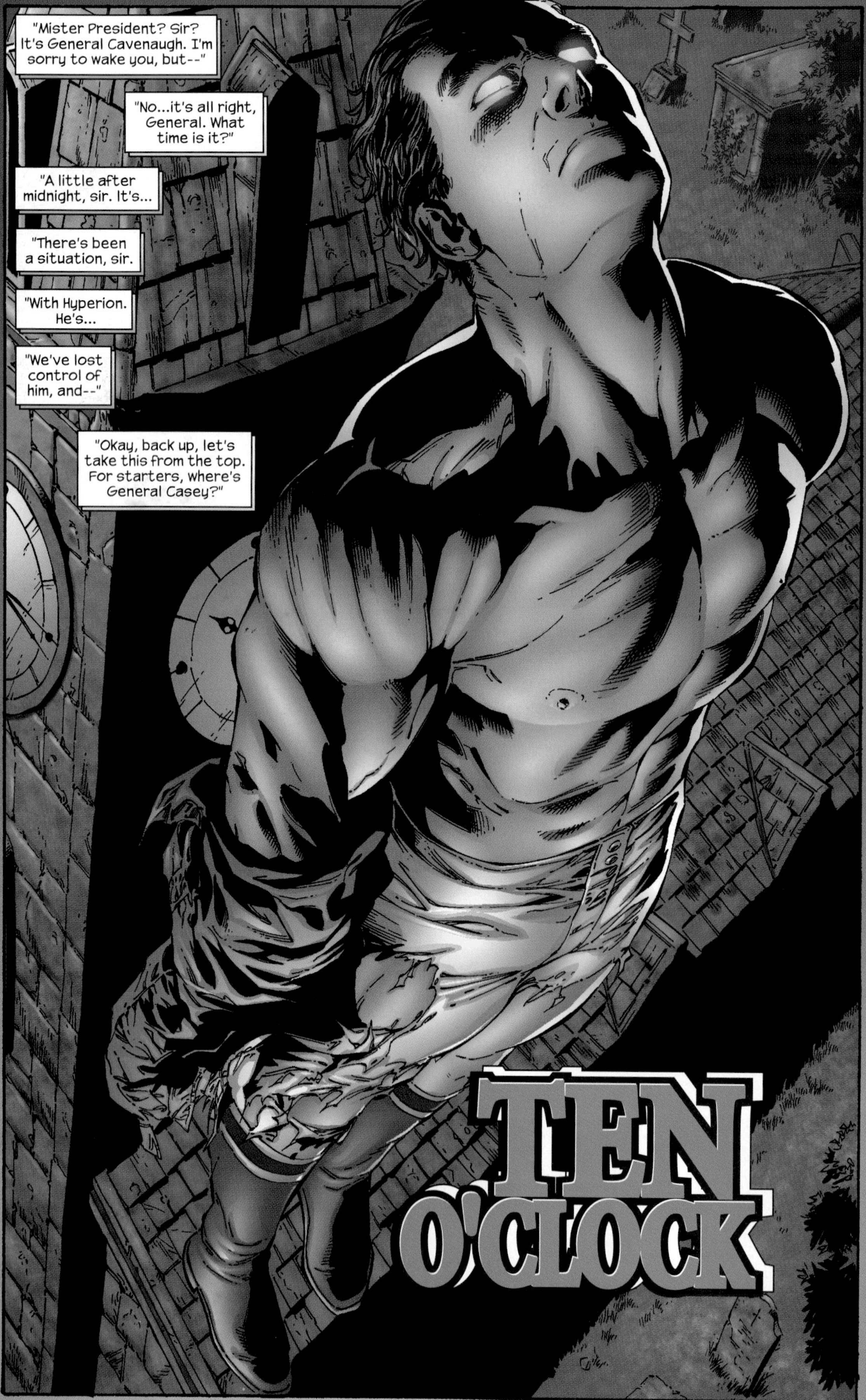
"Mister President? Sir? It's General Cavenaugh. I'm sorry to wake you, but--"
"No...it's all right, General. What time is it?"
"A little after midnight, sir. It's...
"There's been a situation, sir.
"With Hyperion. He's...
"We've lost control of him, and--"
"Okay, back up, let's take this from the top. For starters, where's General Casey?"
TEN O'CLOCK

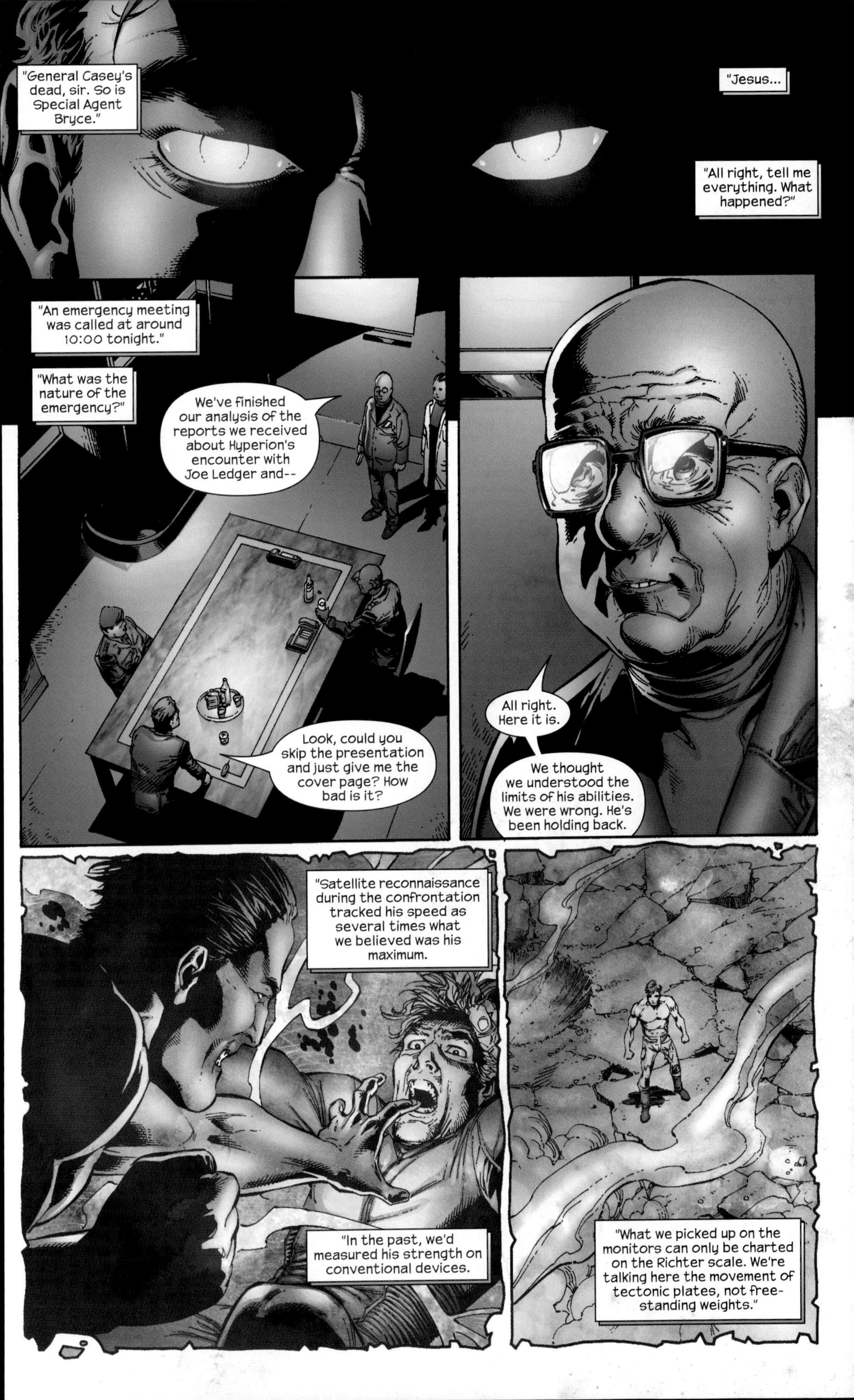
"General Casey's dead, sir. So is Special Agent Bryce."
"Jesus...
"All right, tell me everything. What happened?"
"An emergency meeting was called at around 10:00 tonight."
"What was the nature of the emergency?"
We've finished our analysis of the reports we received about Hyperion's encounter with Joe Ledger and--
Look, could you skip the presentation and just give me the cover page? How bad is it?
All right. Here it is.
We thought we understood the limits of his abilities. We were wrong. He's been holding back.
"Satellite reconnaissance during the confrontation tracked his speed as several times what we believed was his maximum.
"In the past, we'd measured his strength on conventional devices.
"What we picked up on the monitors can only be charted on the Richter scale. We're talking here the movement of tectonic plates, not free-standing weights."

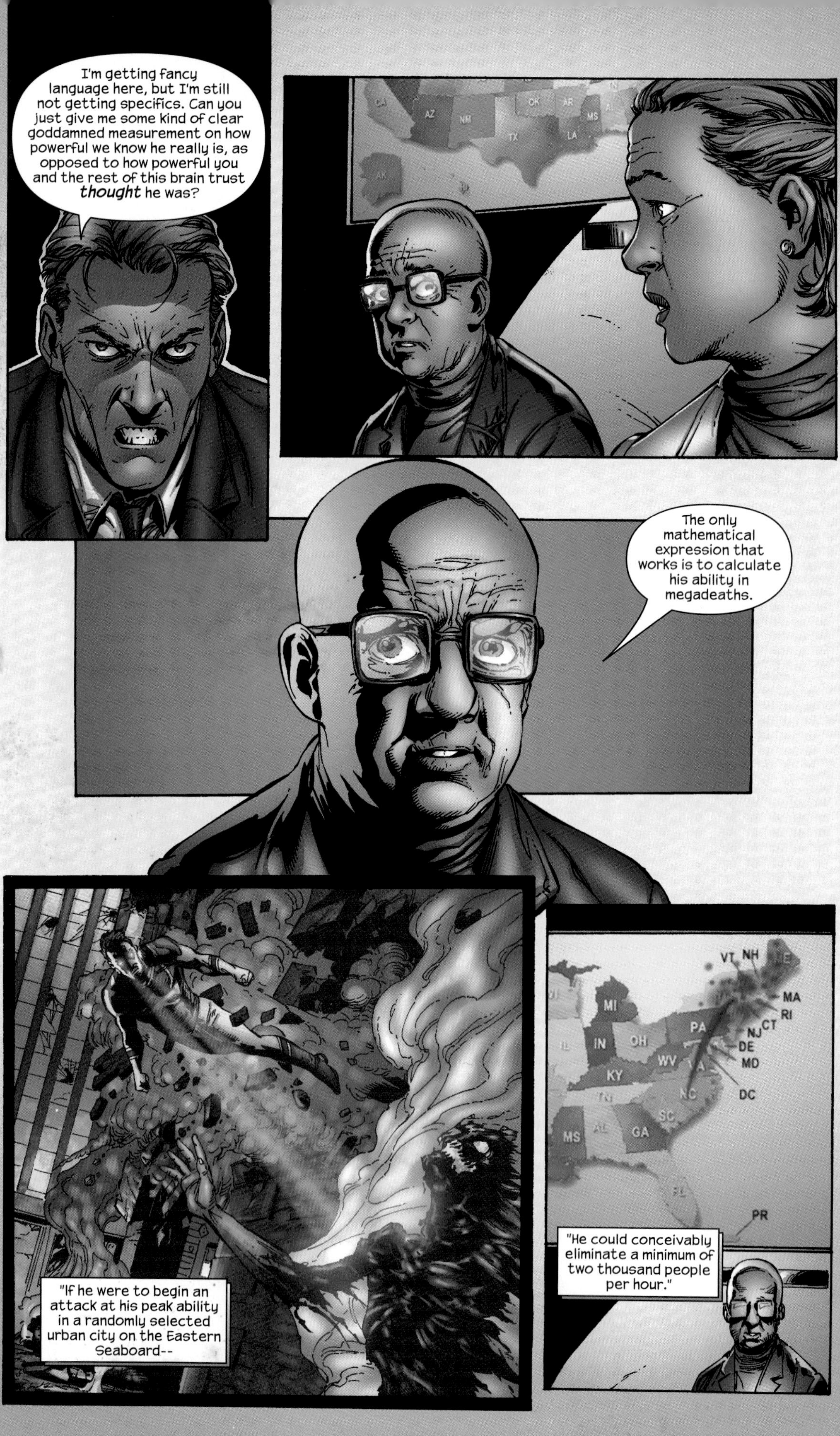
I'm getting fancy language here, but I'm still not getting specifics. Can you just give me some kind of clear goddamned measurement on how powerful we know he really is, as opposed to how powerful you and the rest of this brain trust *thought* he was?
CA AZ NM OK AR MS AL TX LA AK
The only mathematical expression that works is to calculate his ability in megadeaths.
"If he were to begin an attack at his peak ability in a randomly selected urban city on the Eastern Seaboard--
VT NH MA RI CT NJ DE MD DC MI PA IN OH WV KY NC SC GA AL MS PR
"He could conceivably eliminate a minimum of two thousand people per hour."

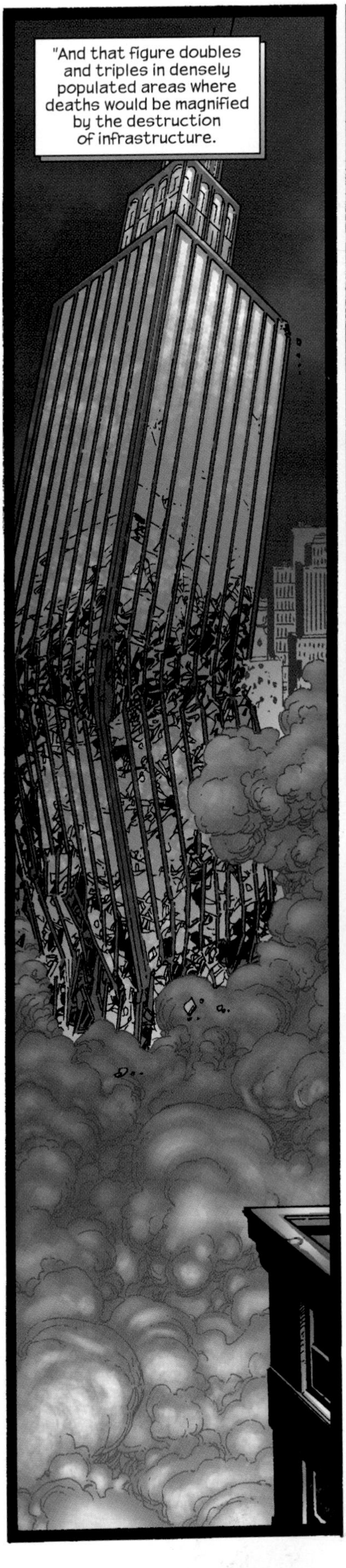
"And that figure doubles and triples in densely populated areas where deaths would be magnified by the destruction of infrastructure.

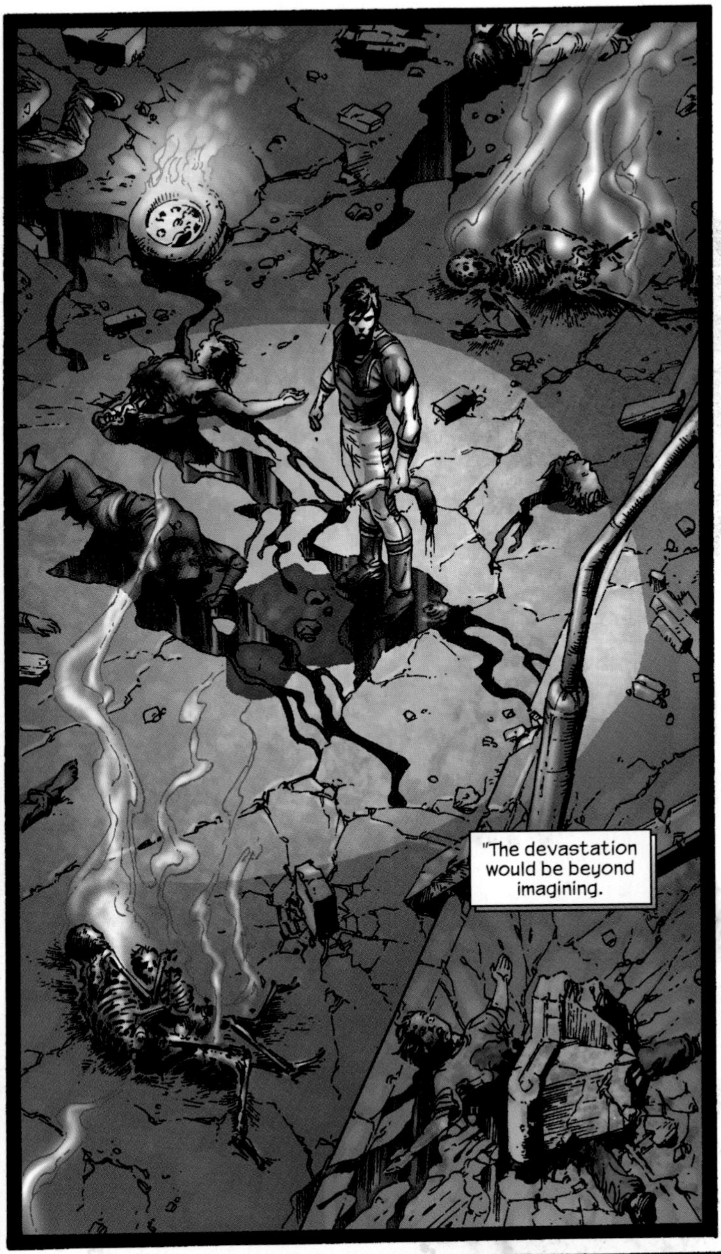
"The devastation would be beyond imagining.

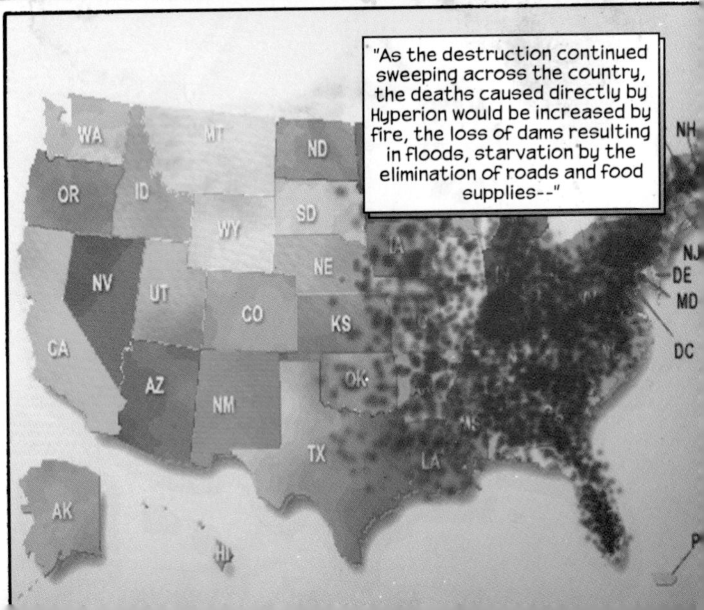
"As the destruction continued sweeping across the country, the deaths caused directly by Hyperion would be increased by fire, the loss of dams resulting in floods, starvation by the elimination of roads and food supplies--"
WA
MT
ND
OR
ID
SD
WY
NE
NV
UT
CO
KS
CA
AZ
NM
OK
TX
LA
AK
HI
NH
NJ
DE
MD
DC

At an average of two thousand five hundred deaths per hour, his potential is a kill-rate of one million deaths every 16.6 days.

Jesus Christ... Jesus Christ...Jesus, Jesus, Jesus...

What do we do?

We?

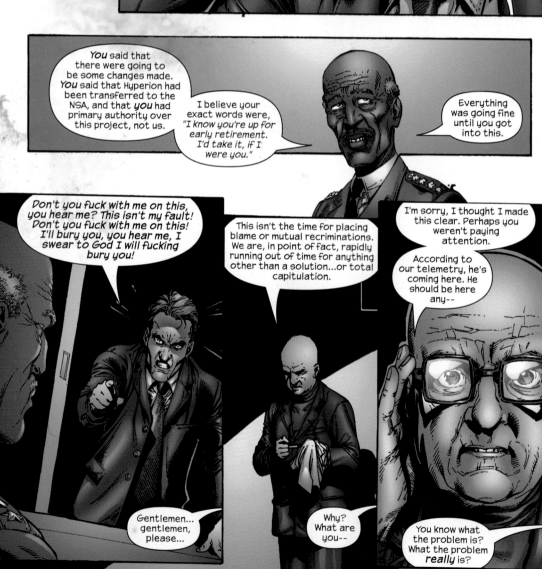

You said that there were going to be some changes made. *You* said that Hyperion had been transferred to the NSA, and that *you* had primary authority over this project, not us.

I believe your exact words were, *"I know you're up for early retirement. I'd take it, if I were you."*

Everything was going fine until you got into this.

Don't you fuck with me on this, you hear me? This isn't my fault! Don't you fuck with me on this! I'll bury you, you hear me, I swear to God I will fucking bury you!

This isn't the time for placing blame or mutual recriminations. We are, in point of fact, rapidly running out of time for anything other than a solution...or total capitulation.

I'm sorry, I thought I made this clear. Perhaps you weren't paying attention.

According to our telemetry, he's coming here. He should be here any--

Gentlemen... gentlemen, please...

Why? What are you--

You know what the problem is? What the problem *really* is?

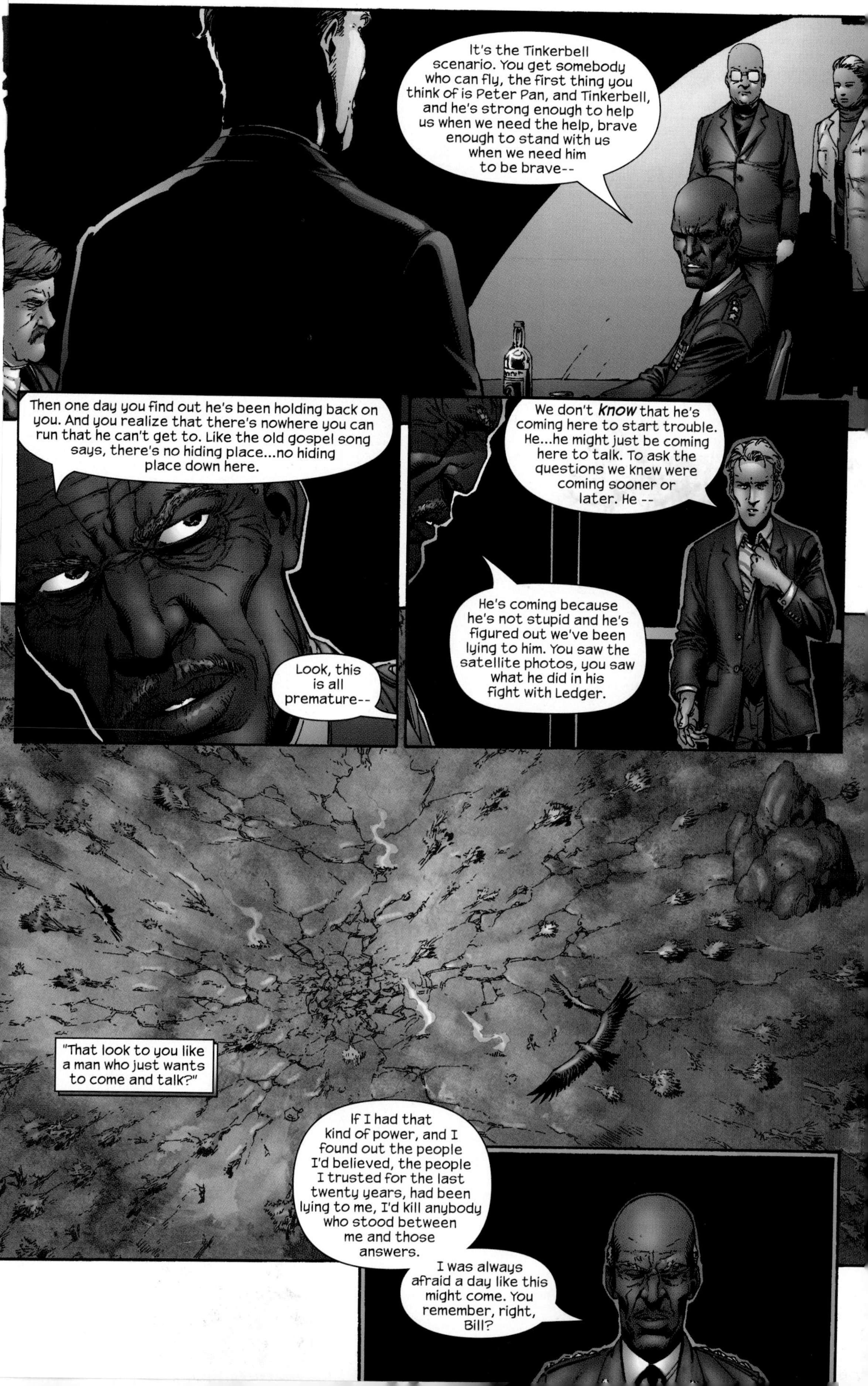
It's the Tinkerbell scenario. You get somebody who can fly, the first thing you think of is Peter Pan, and Tinkerbell, and he's strong enough to help us when we need the help, brave enough to stand with us when we need him to be brave--
Then one day you find out he's been holding back on you. And you realize that there's nowhere you can run that he can't get to. Like the old gospel song says, there's no hiding place...no hiding place down here.
Look, this is all premature--
We don't KNOW that he's coming here to start trouble. He...he might just be coming here to talk. To ask the questions we knew were coming sooner or later. He --
He's coming because he's not stupid and he's figured out we've been lying to him. You saw the satellite photos, you saw what he did in his fight with Ledger.
"That look to you like a man who just wants to come and talk?"
If I had that kind of power, and I found out the people I'd believed, the people I trusted for the last twenty years, had been lying to me, I'd kill anybody who stood between me and those answers.
I was always afraid a day like this might come. You remember, right, Bill?

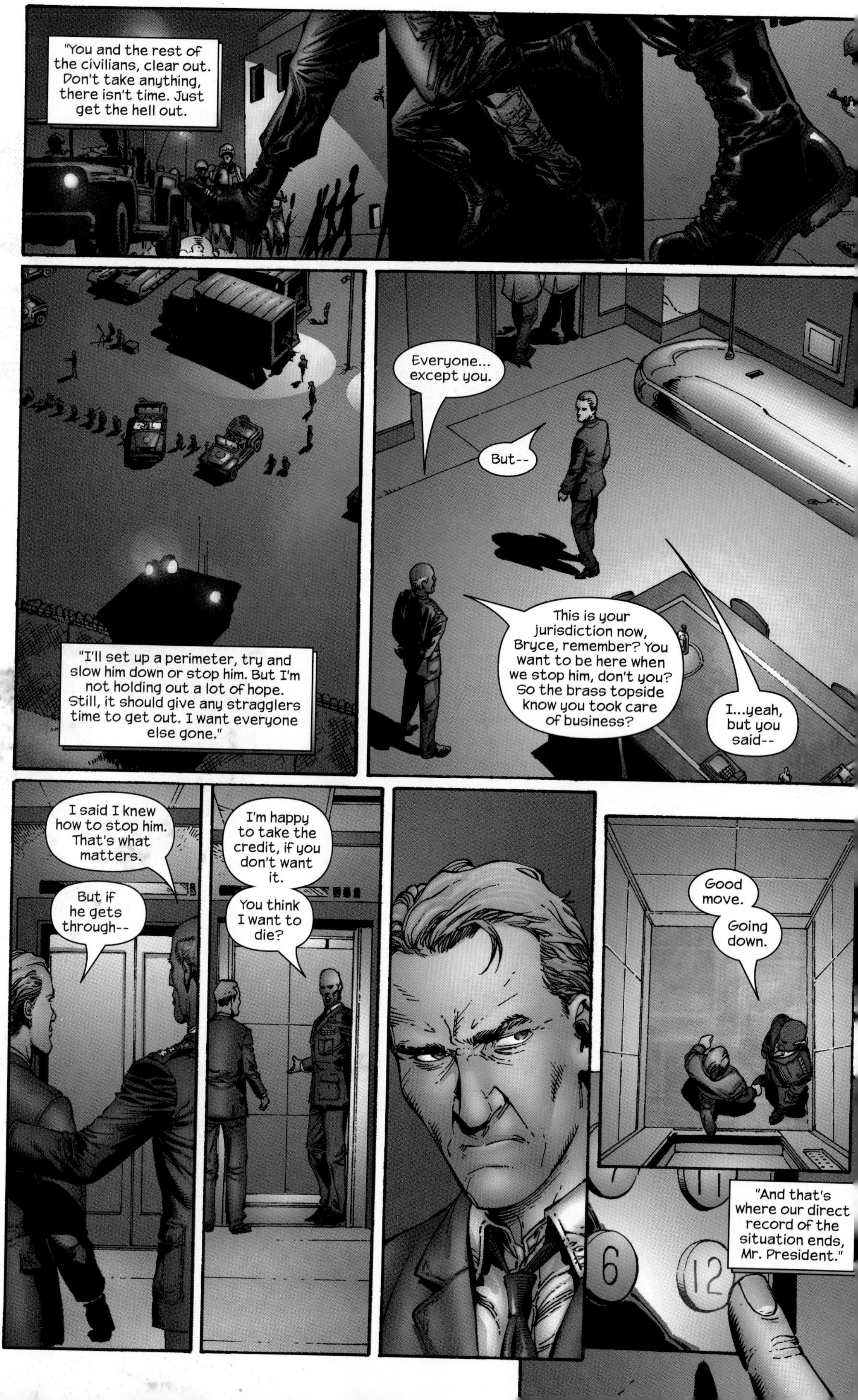
"You and the rest of the civilians, clear out. Don't take anything, there isn't time. Just get the hell out.
"I'll set up a perimeter, try and slow him down or stop him. But I'm not holding out a lot of hope. Still, it should give any stragglers time to get out. I want everyone else gone."
Everyone... except you.
But--
This is your jurisdiction now, Bryce, remember? You want to be here when we stop him, don't you? So the brass topside know you took care of business?
I...yeah, but you said--
I said I knew how to stop him. That's what matters.
But if he gets through--
I'm happy to take the credit, if you don't want it.
You think I want to die?
Good move.
Going down.
"And that's where our direct record of the situation ends, Mr. President."

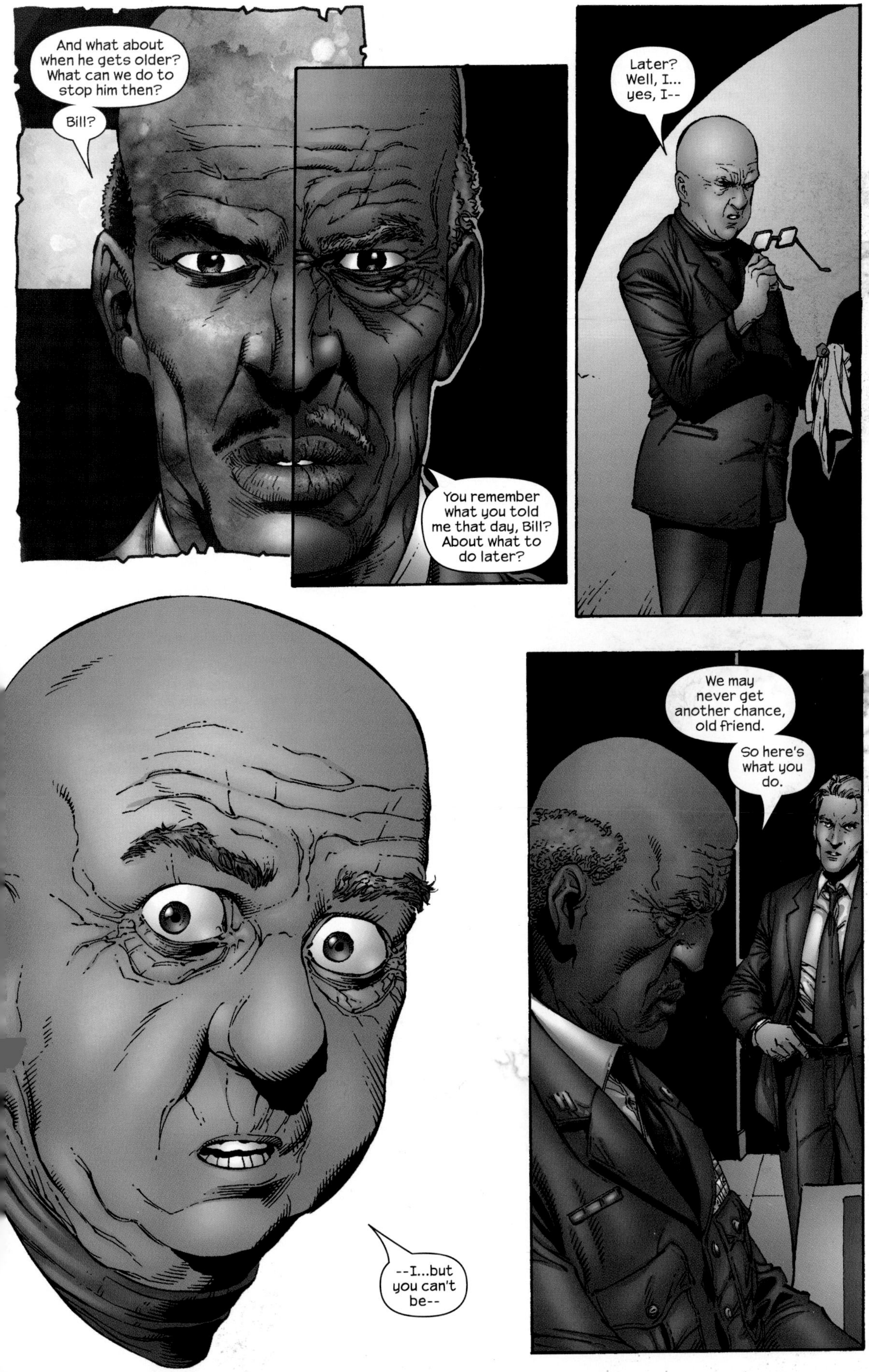
And what about when he gets older? What can we do to stop him then?
Bill?
You remember what you told me that day, Bill? About what to do later?
Later? Well, I... yes, I--
We may never get another chance, old friend.
So here's what you do.
--I...but you can't be--

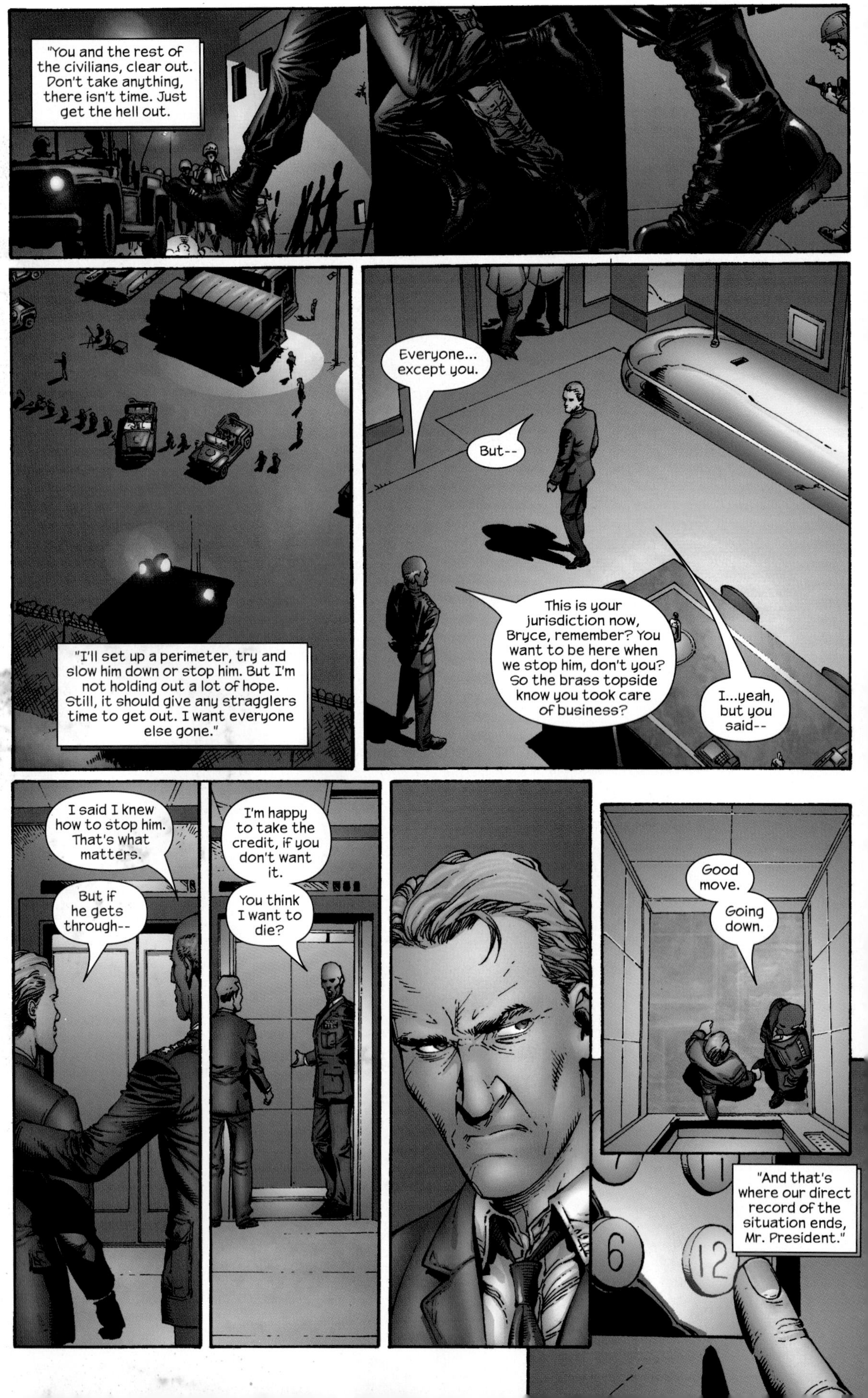
"You and the rest of the civilians, clear out. Don't take anything, there isn't time. Just get the hell out.
"I'll set up a perimeter, try and slow him down or stop him. But I'm not holding out a lot of hope. Still, it should give any stragglers time to get out. I want everyone else gone."
Everyone... except you.
But--
This is your jurisdiction now, Bryce, remember? You want to be here when we stop him, don't you? So the brass topside know you took care of business?
I...yeah, but you said--
I said I knew how to stop him. That's what matters.
But if he gets through--
I'm happy to take the credit, if you don't want it.
You think I want to die?
Good move.
Going down.
"And that's where our direct record of the situation ends, Mr. President."

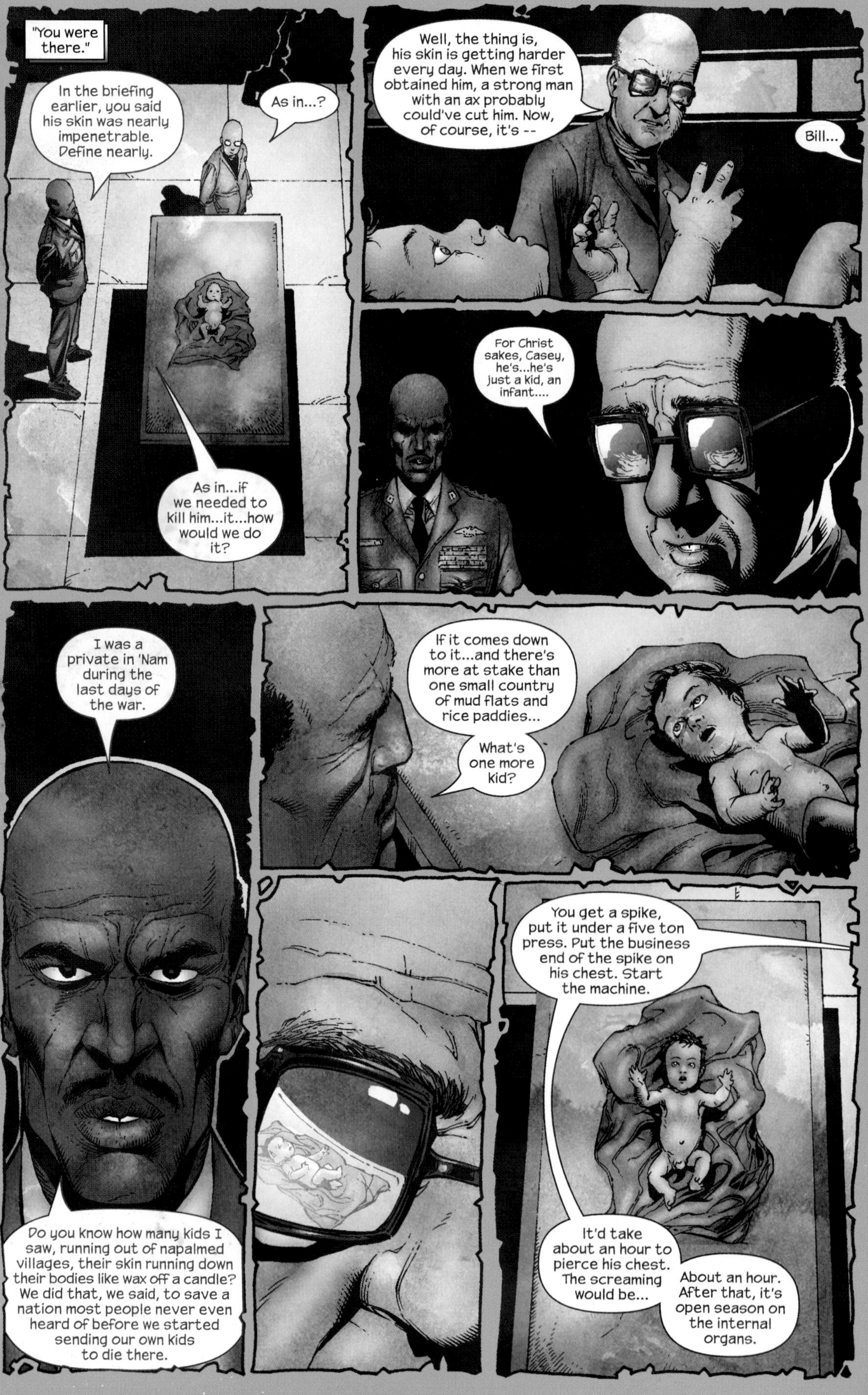
"You were there."
In the briefing earlier, you said his skin was nearly impenetrable. Define nearly.
As in...?
As in...if we needed to kill him...it...how would we do it?
Well, the thing is, his skin is getting harder every day. When we first obtained him, a strong man with an ax probably could've cut him. Now, of course, it's --
Bill...
For Christ sakes, Casey, he's...he's just a kid, an infant....
I was a private in 'Nam during the last days of the war.
Do you know how many kids I saw, running out of napalmed villages, their skin running down their bodies like wax off a candle? We did that, we said, to save a nation most people never even heard of before we started sending our own kids to die there.
If it comes down to it...and there's more at stake than one small country of mud flats and rice paddies...
What's one more kid?
You get a spike, put it under a five ton press. Put the business end of the spike on his chest. Start the machine.
It'd take about an hour to pierce his chest. The screaming would be...
About an hour. After that, it's open season on the internal organs.

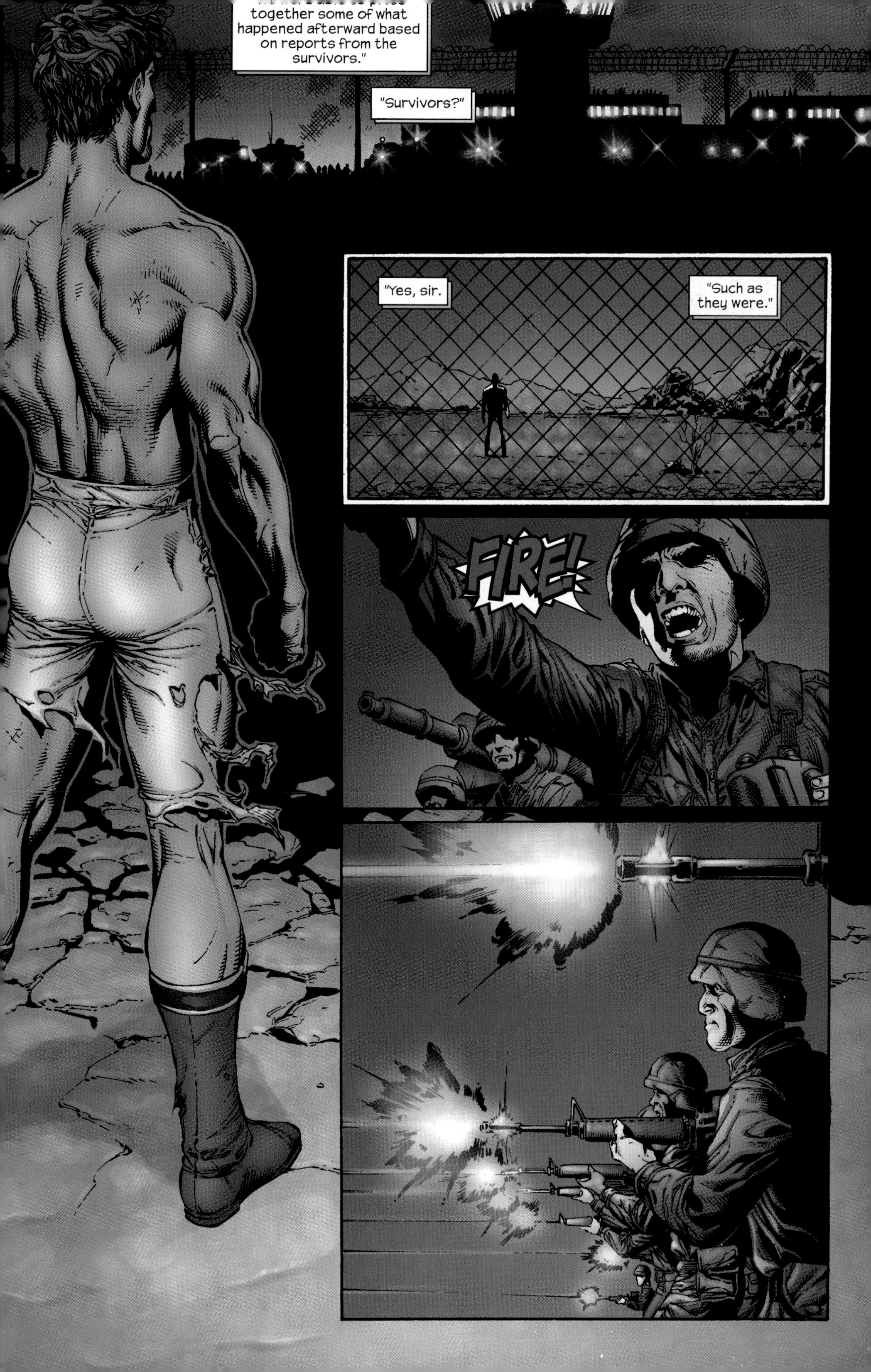
together some of what happened afterward based on reports from the survivors."
"Survivors?"
"Yes, sir.
"Such as they were."
FIRE!

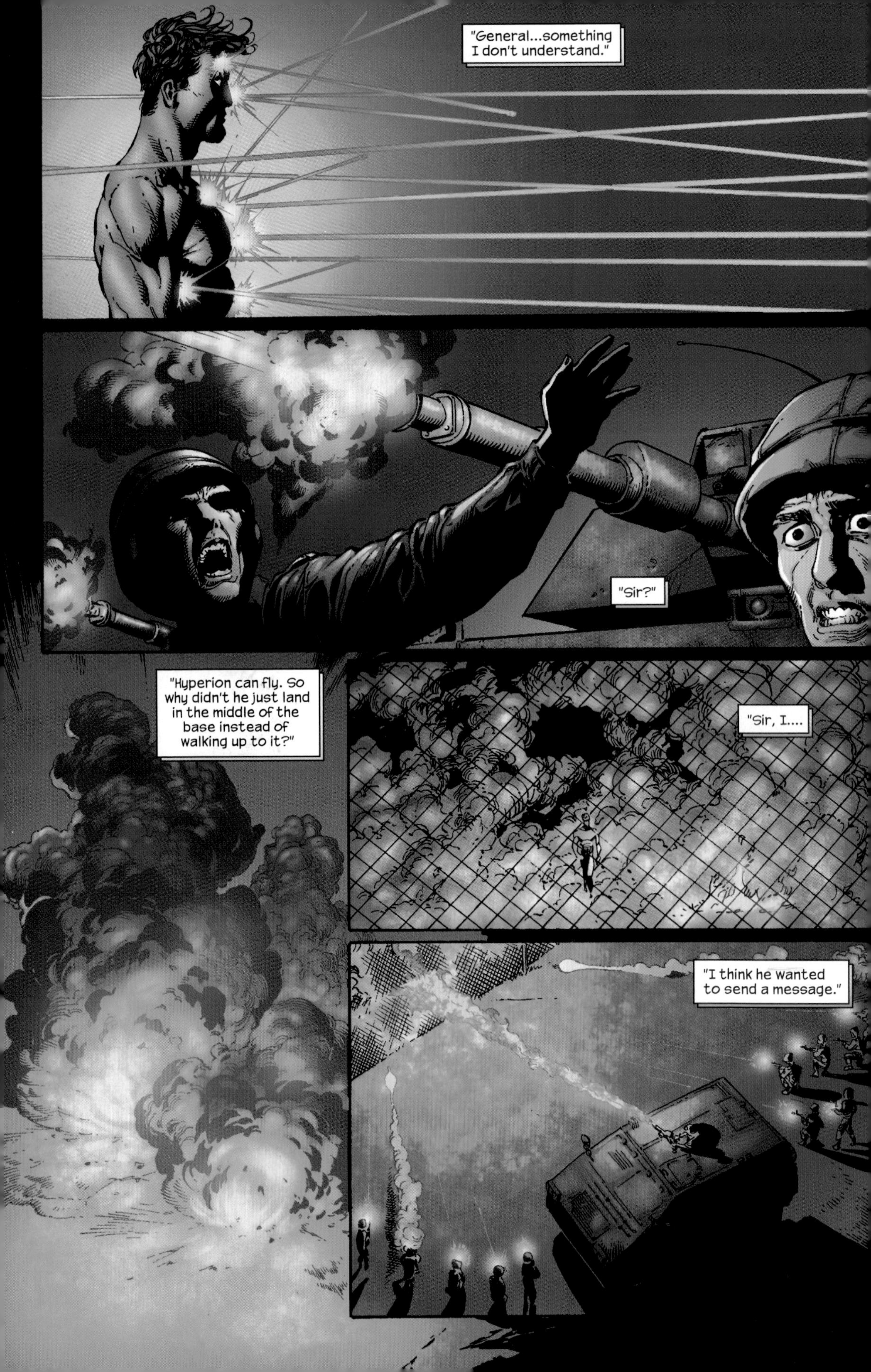
"General...something I don't understand."
"Sir?"
"Hyperion can fly. So why didn't he just land in the middle of the base instead of walking up to it?"
"Sir, I....
"I think he wanted to send a message."

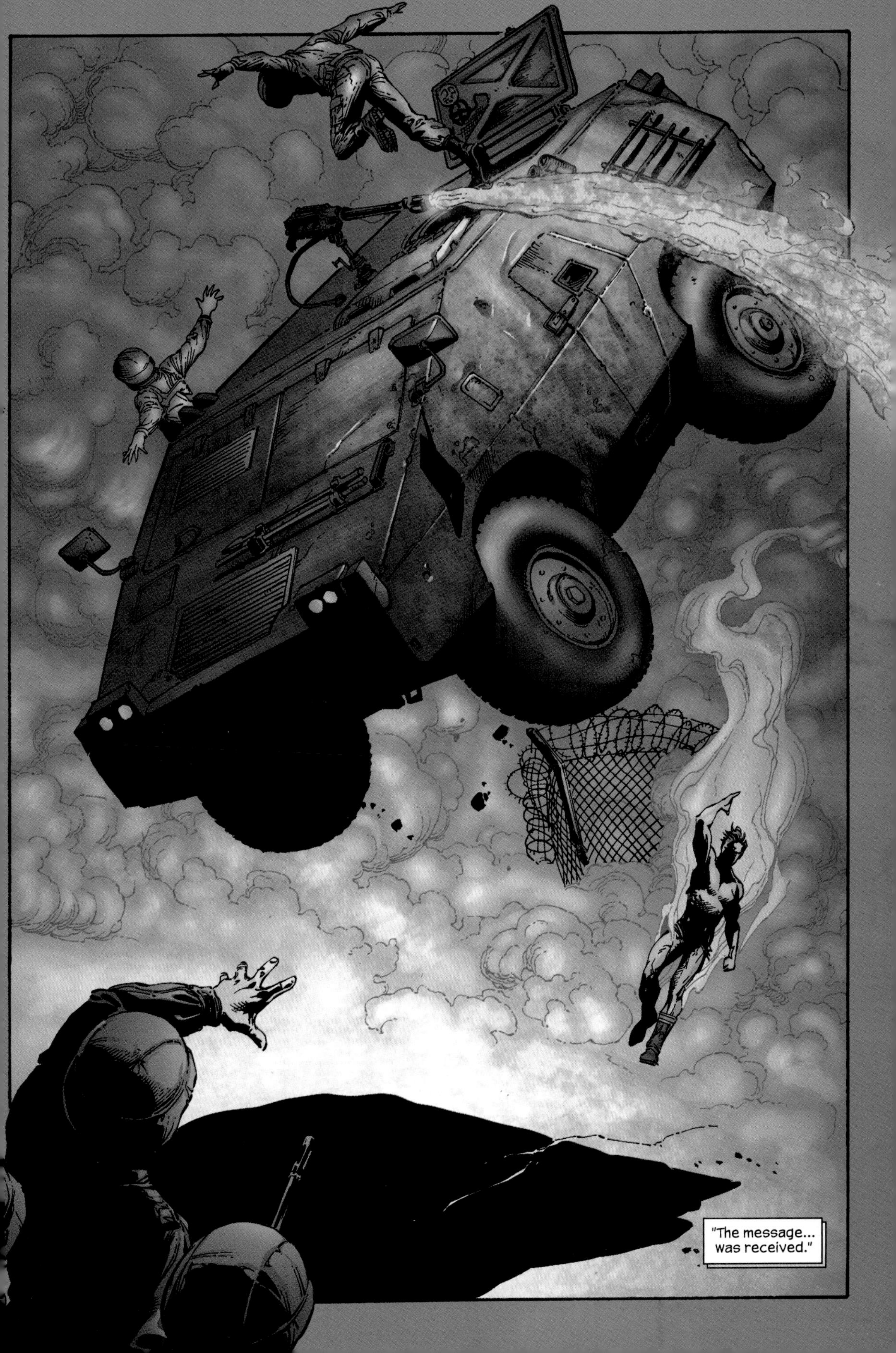
"The message...
was received."

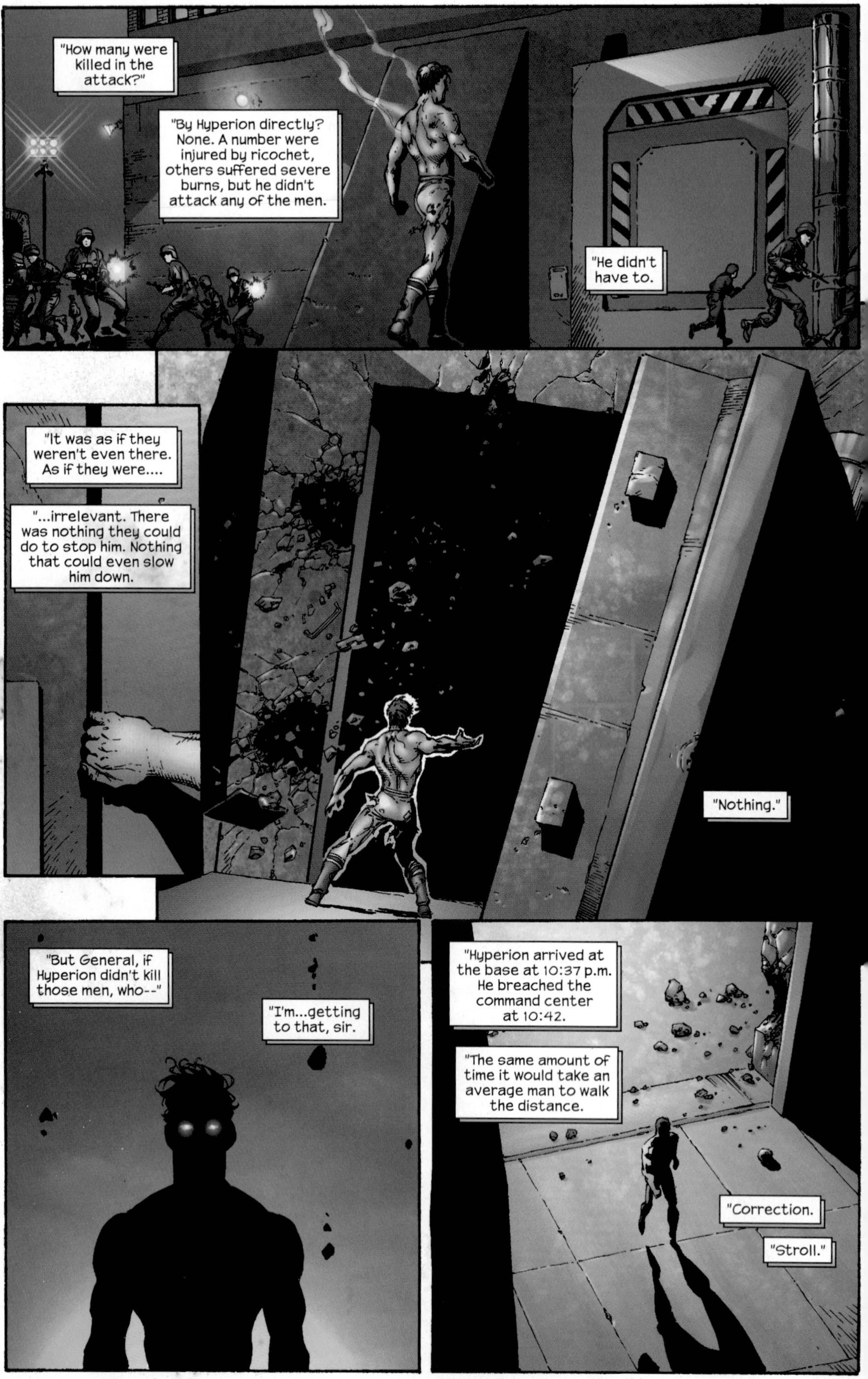
"How many were killed in the attack?"
"By Hyperion directly? None. A number were injured by ricochet, others suffered severe burns, but he didn't attack any of the men.
"He didn't have to.
"It was as if they weren't even there. As if they were....
"...irrelevant. There was nothing they could do to stop him. Nothing that could even slow him down.
"Nothing."
"But General, if Hyperion didn't kill those men, who--"
"I'm...getting to that, sir.
"Hyperion arrived at the base at 10:37 p.m. He breached the command center at 10:42.
"The same amount of time it would take an average man to walk the distance.
"Correction.
"Stroll."

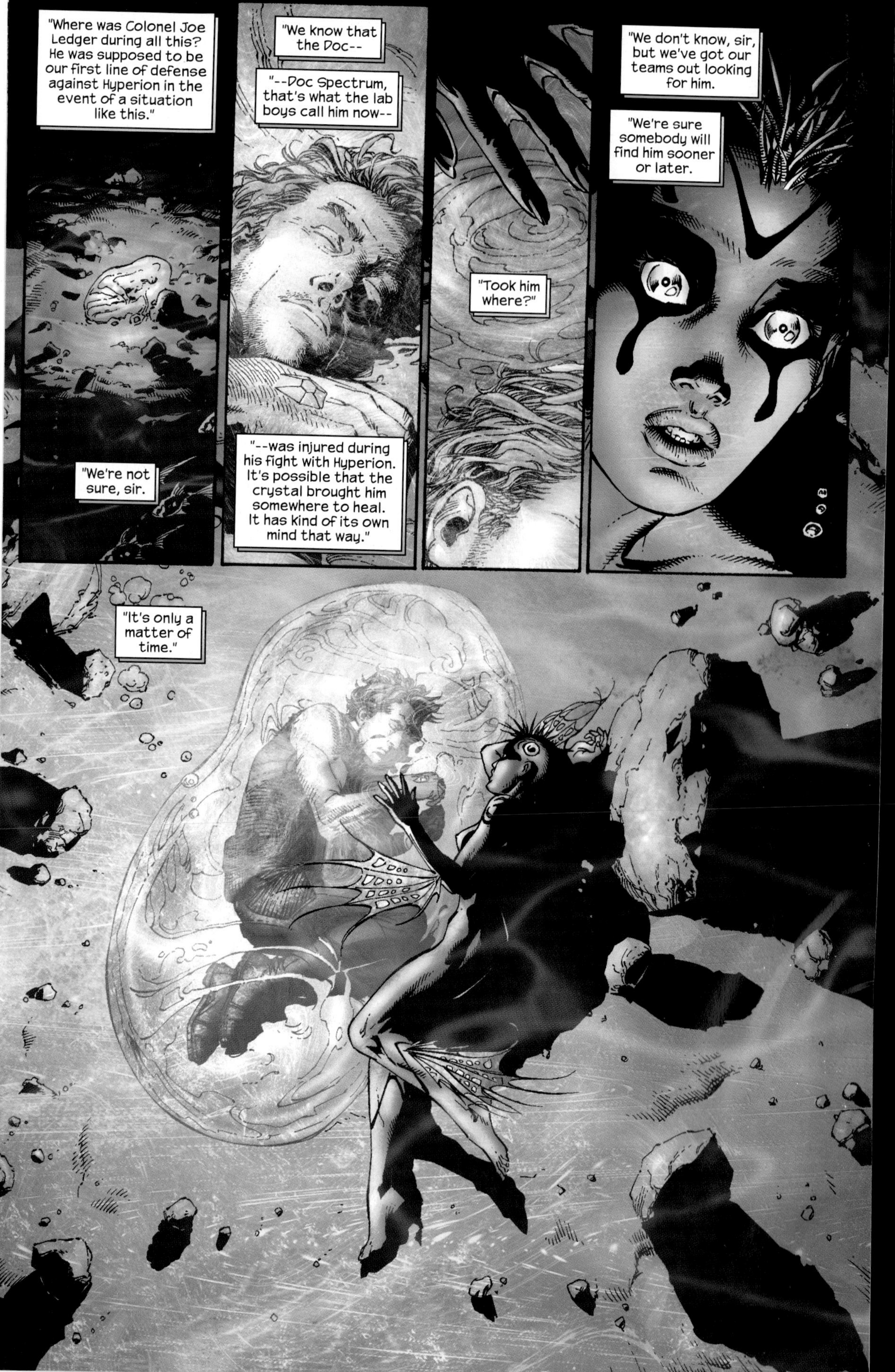
"Where was Colonel Joe Ledger during all this? He was supposed to be our first line of defense against Hyperion in the event of a situation like this."
"We're not sure, sir.
"We know that the Doc--
"--Doc Spectrum, that's what the lab boys call him now--
"--was injured during his fight with Hyperion. It's possible that the crystal brought him somewhere to heal. It has kind of its own mind that way."
"Took him where?"
"We don't know, sir, but we've got our teams out looking for him.
"We're sure somebody will find him sooner or later.
"It's only a matter of time."

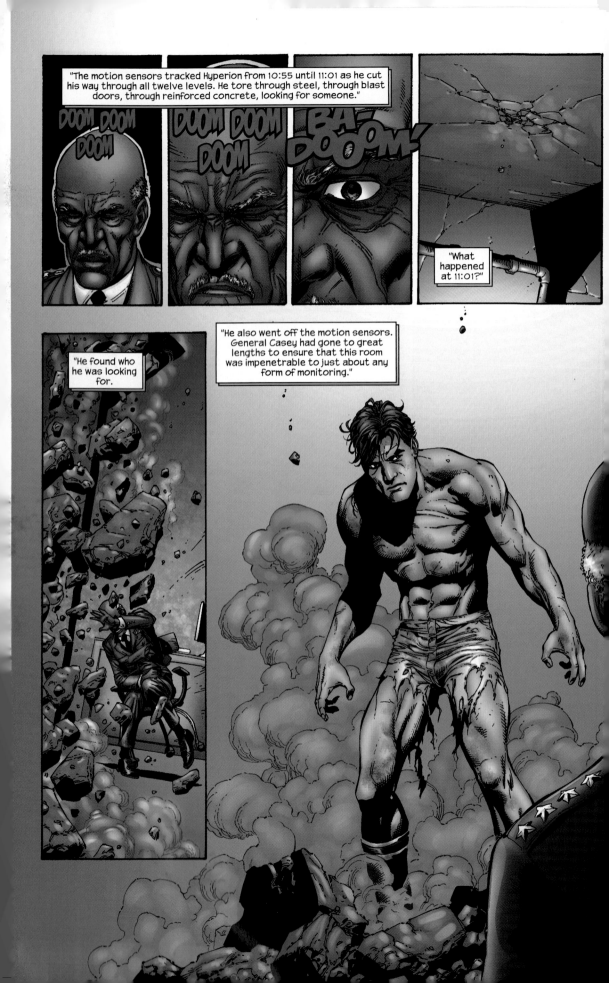

"The motion sensors tracked Hyperion from 10:55 until 11:01 as he cut his way through all twelve levels. He tore through steel, through blast doors, through reinforced concrete, looking for someone."

DOOM DOOM DOOM

DOOM DOOM DOOM

BA DOOOM!

"What happened at 11:01?"

"He also went off the motion sensors. General Casey had gone to great lengths to ensure that this room was impenetrable to just about any form of monitoring."

"He found who he was looking for.

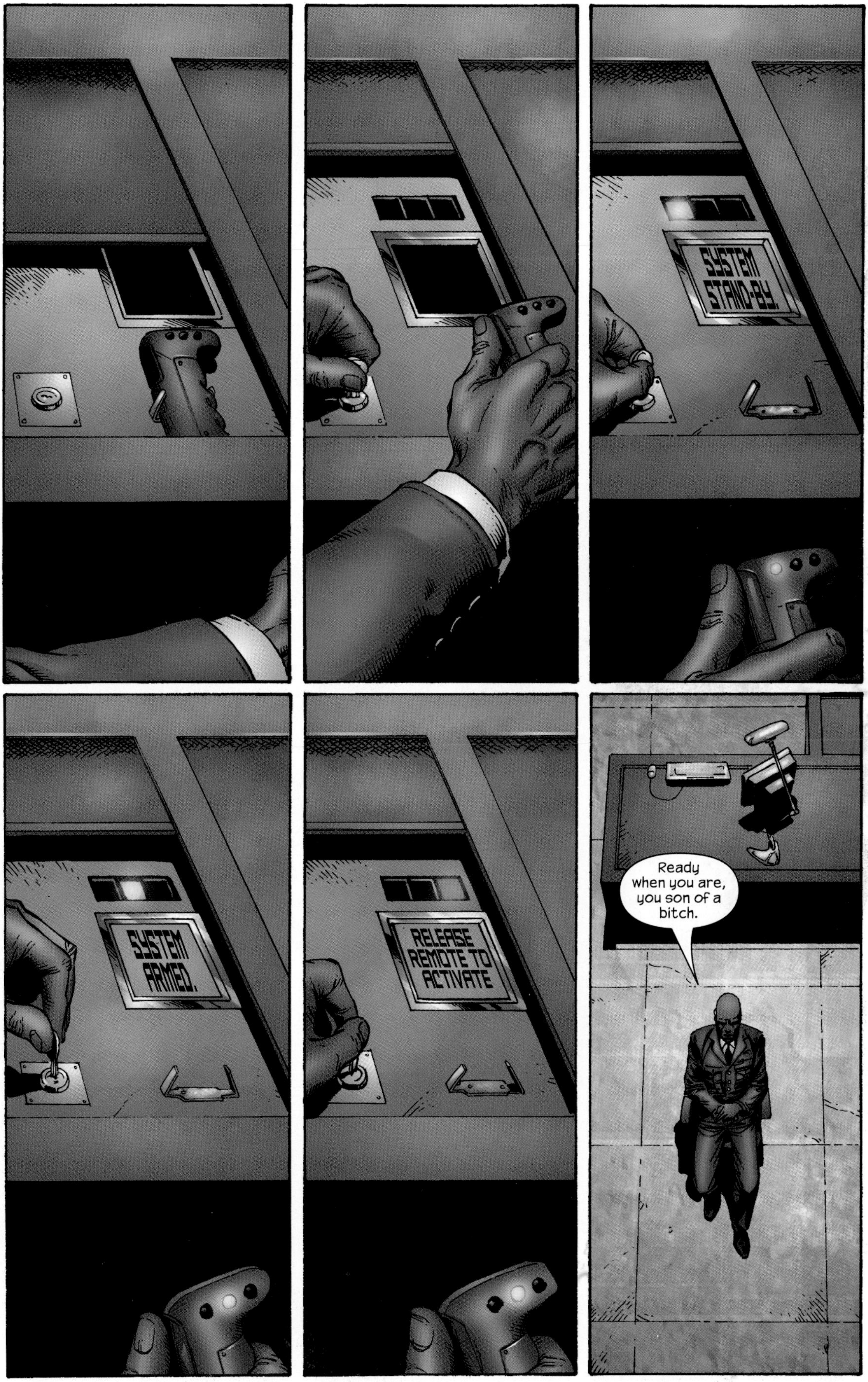
SYSTEM STAND-BY.
SYSTEM ARMED.
RELEASE REMOTE TO ACTIVATE
Ready when you are, you son of a bitch.

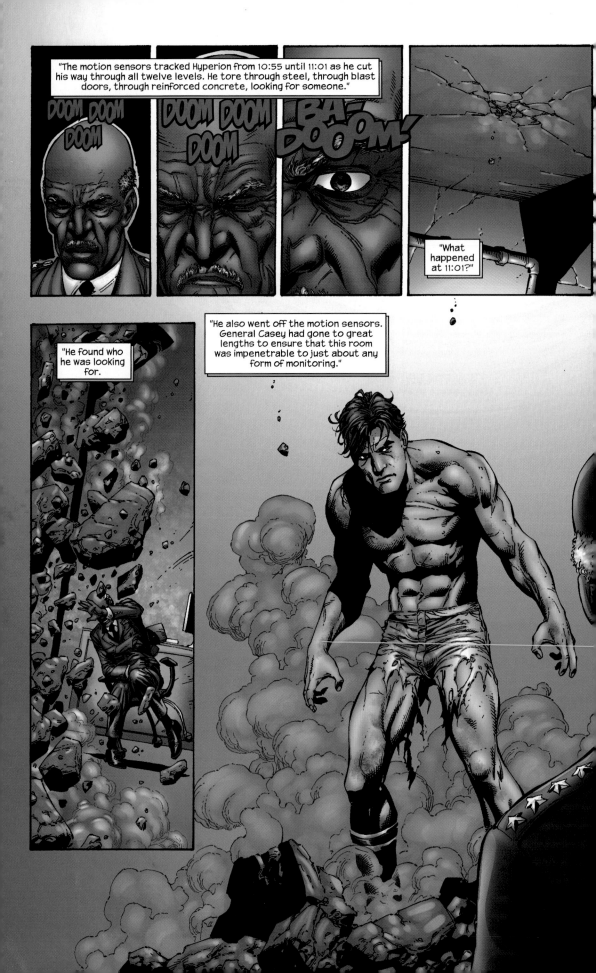

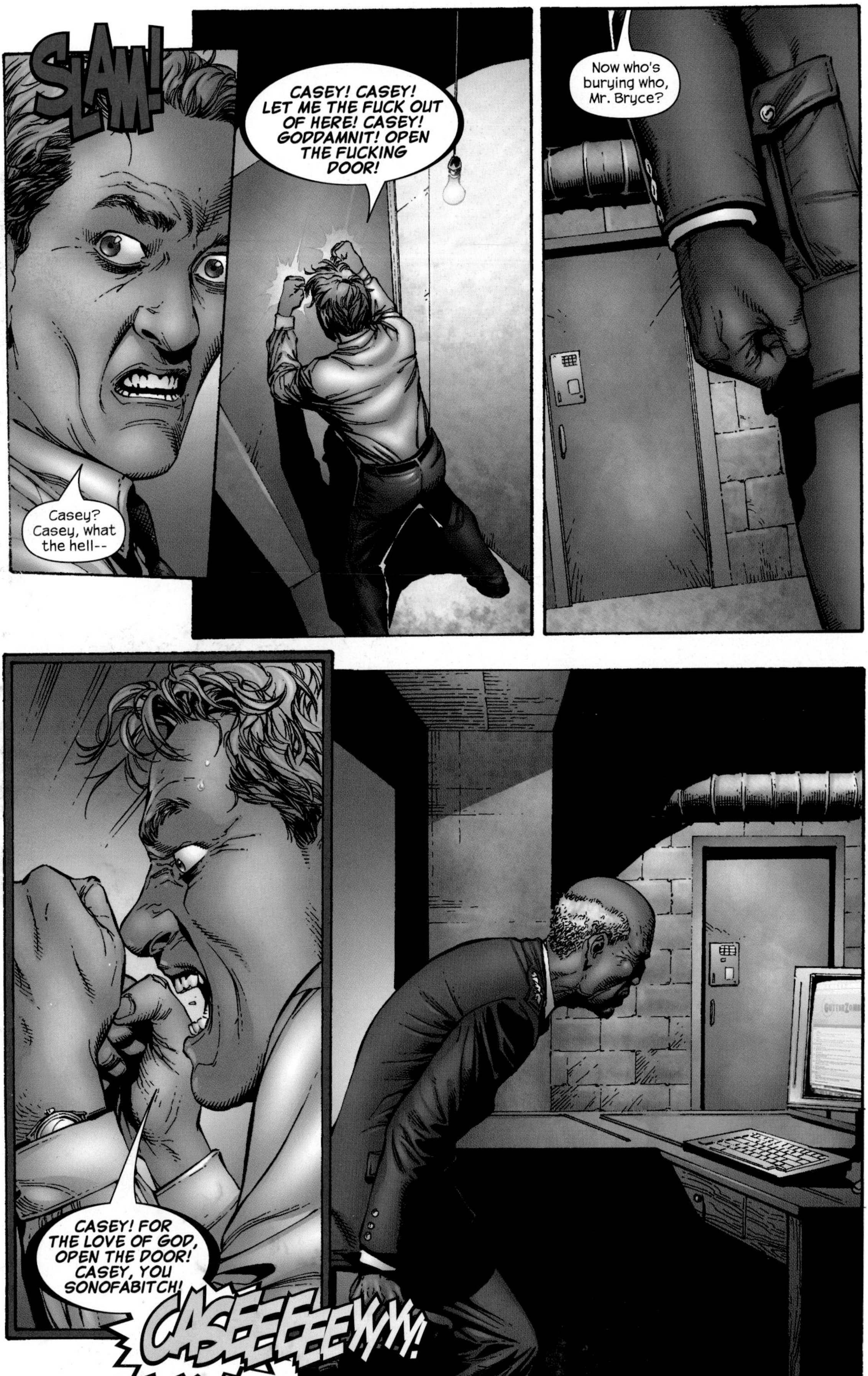
SLAM!
Casey? Casey, what the hell--
CASEY! CASEY! LET ME THE FUCK OUT OF HERE! CASEY! GODDAMNIT! OPEN THE FUCKING DOOR!
Now who's burying who, Mr. Bryce?
CASEY! FOR THE LOVE OF GOD, OPEN THE DOOR! CASEY, YOU SONOFABITCH!
CASEEEEEYYYY!

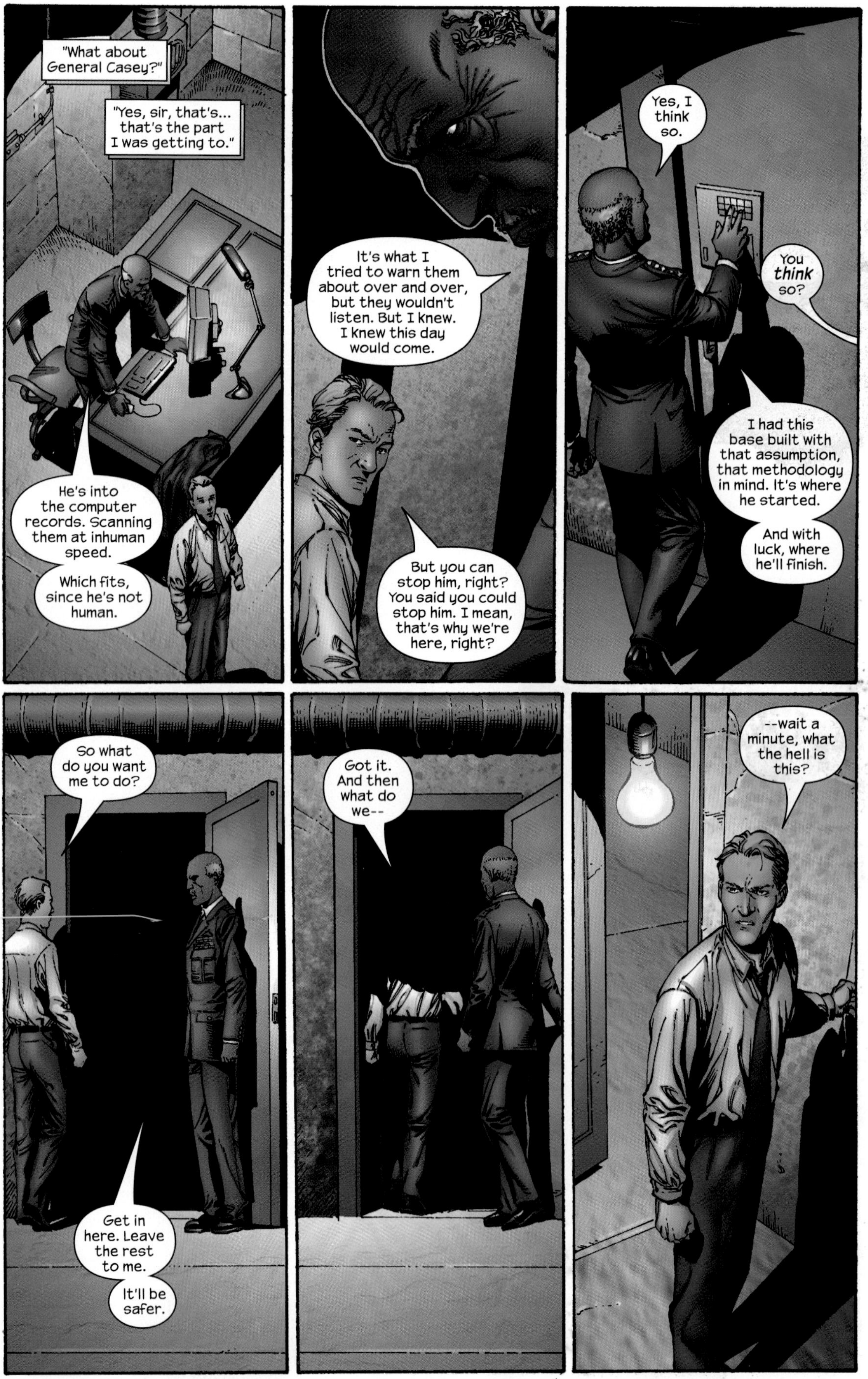
"What about General Casey?"
"Yes, sir, that's... that's the part I was getting to."
He's into the computer records. Scanning them at inhuman speed.
Which fits, since he's not human.
It's what I tried to warn them about over and over, but they wouldn't listen. But I knew. I knew this day would come.
But you can stop him, right? You said you could stop him. I mean, that's why we're here, right?
Yes, I think so.
You *think* so?
I had this base built with that assumption, that methodology in mind. It's where he started.
And with luck, where he'll finish.
So what do you want me to do?
Get in here. Leave the rest to me.
It'll be safer.
Got it. And then what do we--
--wait a minute, what the hell is this?

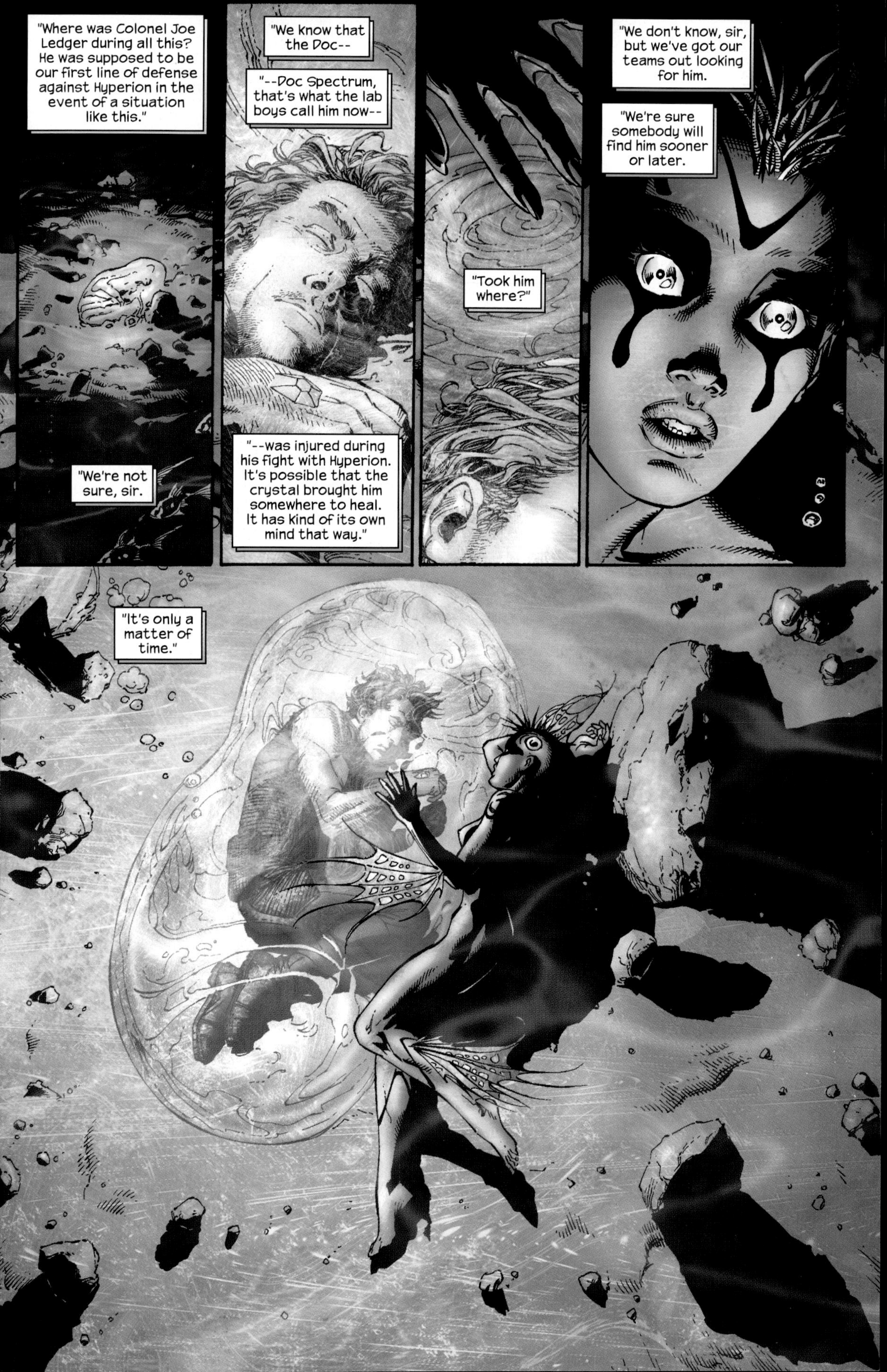
"Where was Colonel Joe Ledger during all this? He was supposed to be our first line of defense against Hyperion in the event of a situation like this."
"We're not sure, sir.
"We know that the Doc--
"--Doc Spectrum, that's what the lab boys call him now--
"--was injured during his fight with Hyperion. It's possible that the crystal brought him somewhere to heal. It has kind of its own mind that way."
"Took him where?"
"We don't know, sir, but we've got our teams out looking for him.
"We're sure somebody will find him sooner or later.
"It's only a matter of time."

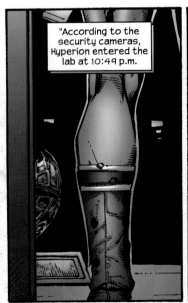

"According to the security cameras, Hyperion entered the lab at 10:49 p.m."

"He found the ship at 10:51."

"The ship? He found--"

"--Jesus Christ--"

"--why the hell wasn't it taken away? Why didn't somebody hide it?"

"Sir...

"Where could we hide it...that he could not find it?"

"Do you think...is it your opinion that he knew what it was, that he now knows that this was where he came from?"

"Yes, sir.

"He knows."

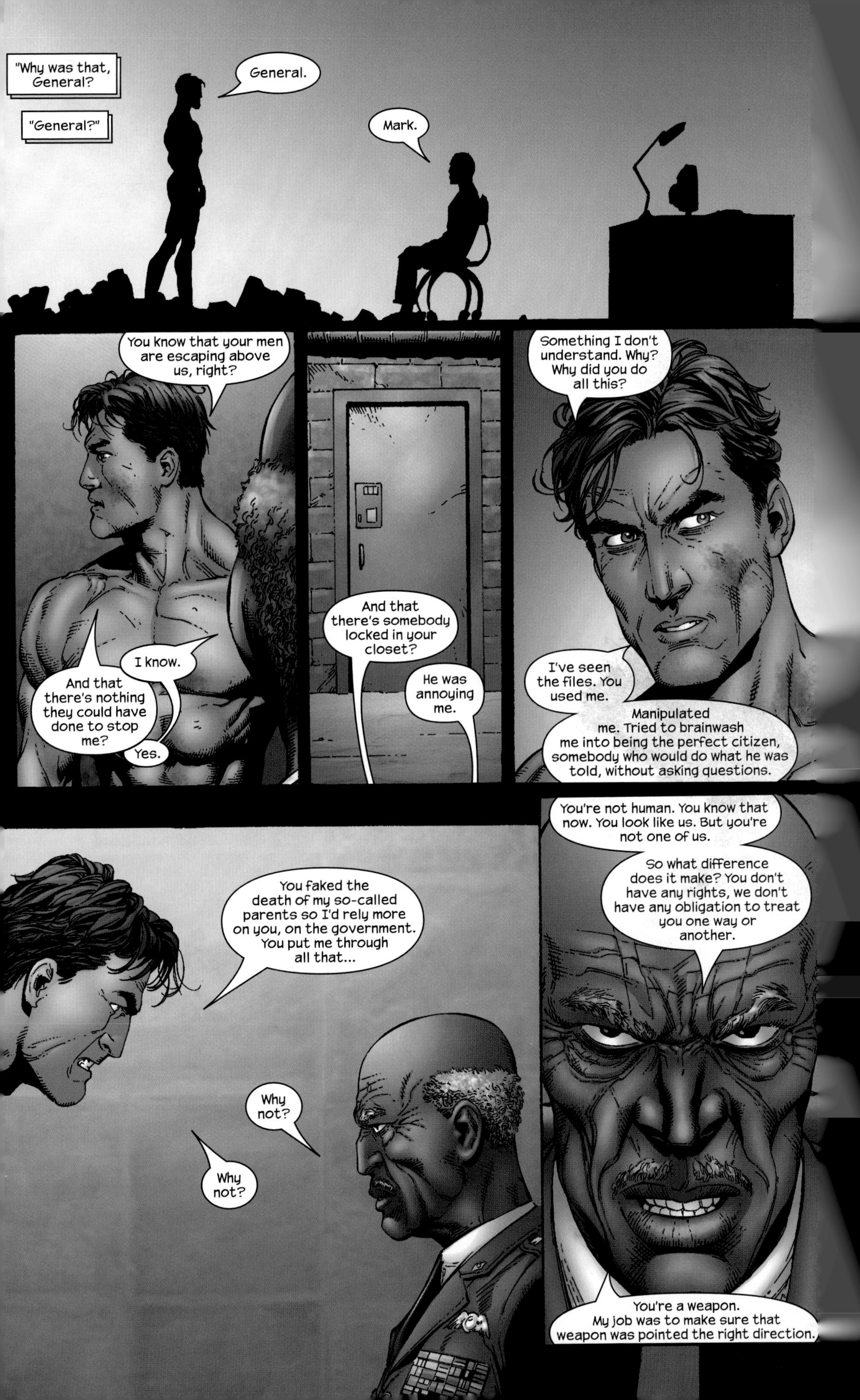
"Why was that, General?
"General?"
General.
Mark.
You know that your men are escaping above us, right?
I know.
And that there's nothing they could have done to stop me?
Yes.
And that there's somebody locked in your closet?
He was annoying me.
Something I don't understand. Why? Why did you do all this?
I've seen the files. You used me.
Manipulated me. Tried to brainwash me into being the perfect citizen, somebody who would do what he was told, without asking questions.
You faked the death of my so-called parents so I'd rely more on you, on the government. You put me through all that...
Why not?
Why not?
You're not human. You know that now. You look like us. But you're not one of us.
So what difference does it make? You don't have any rights, we don't have any obligation to treat you one way or another.
You're a weapon. My job was to make sure that weapon was pointed the right direction.

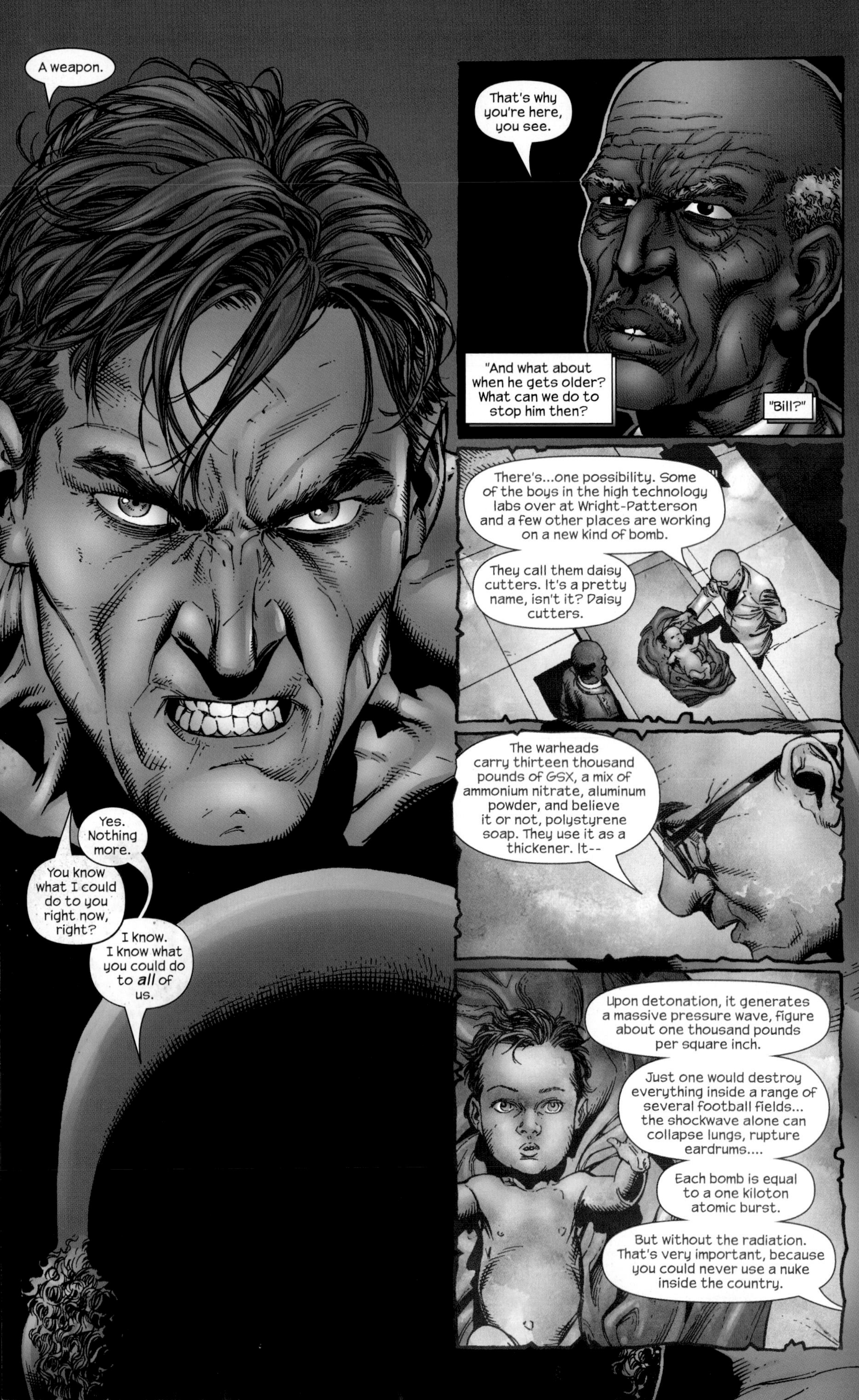
A weapon.
That's why you're here, you see.
"And what about when he gets older? What can we do to stop him then?
"Bill?"
There's...one possibility. Some of the boys in the high technology labs over at Wright-Patterson and a few other places are working on a new kind of bomb.
They call them daisy cutters. It's a pretty name, isn't it? Daisy cutters.
The warheads carry thirteen thousand pounds of GSX, a mix of ammonium nitrate, aluminum powder, and believe it or not, polystyrene soap. They use it as a thickener. It--
Upon detonation, it generates a massive pressure wave, figure about one thousand pounds per square inch.
Just one would destroy everything inside a range of several football fields... the shockwave alone can collapse lungs, rupture eardrums....
Each bomb is equal to a one kiloton atomic burst.
But without the radiation. That's very important, because you could never use a nuke inside the country.
Yes. Nothing more.
You know what I could do to you right now, right?
I know. I know what you could do to *all* of us.

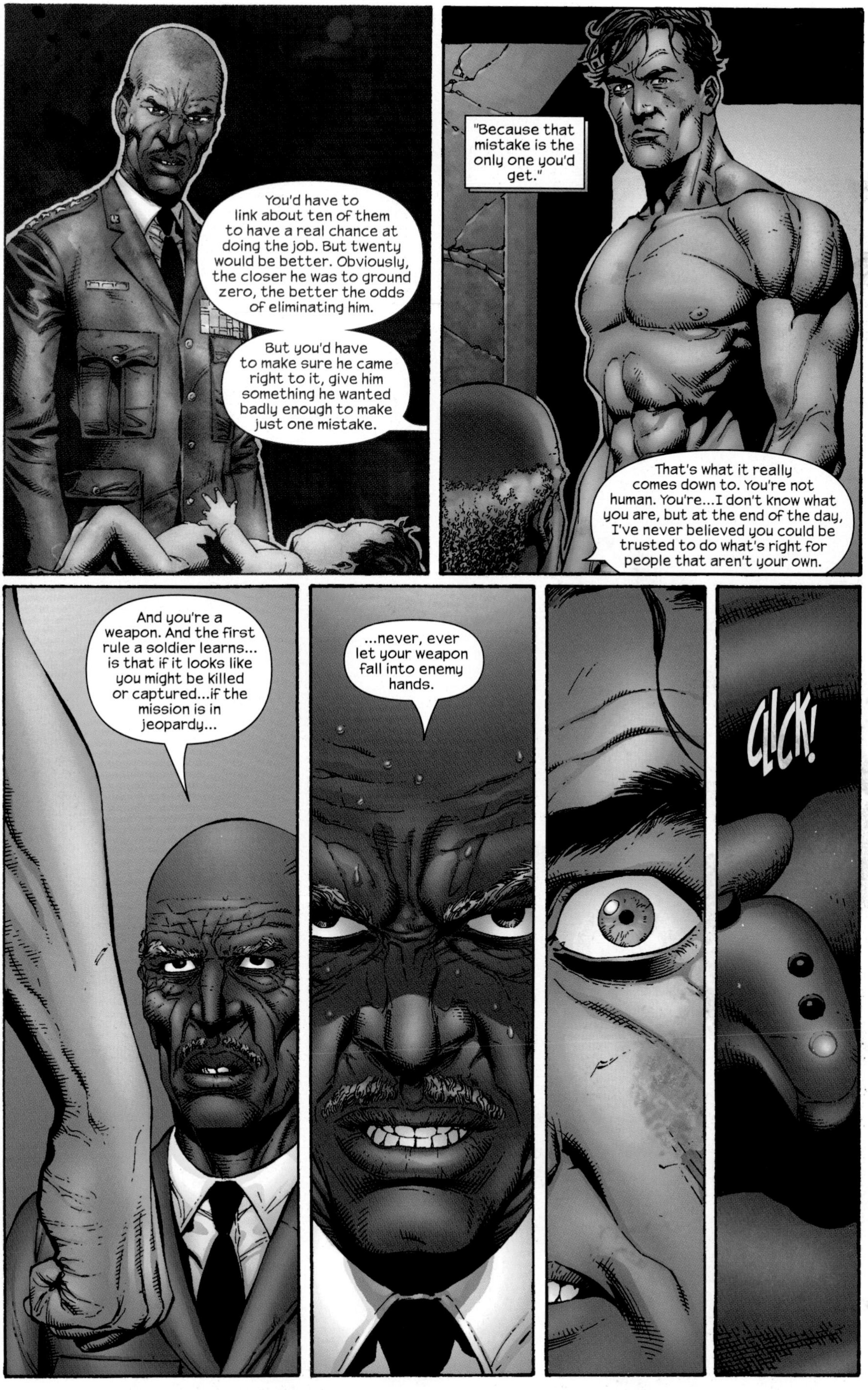
You'd have to link about ten of them to have a real chance at doing the job. But twenty would be better. Obviously, the closer he was to ground zero, the better the odds of eliminating him.
But you'd have to make sure he came right to it, give him something he wanted badly enough to make just one mistake.
"Because that mistake is the only one you'd get."
That's what it really comes down to. You're not human. You're...I don't know what you are, but at the end of the day, I've never believed you could be trusted to do what's right for people that aren't your own.
And you're a weapon. And the first rule a soldier learns... is that if it looks like you might be killed or captured...if the mission is in jeopardy...
...never, ever let your weapon fall into enemy hands.
CLICK!

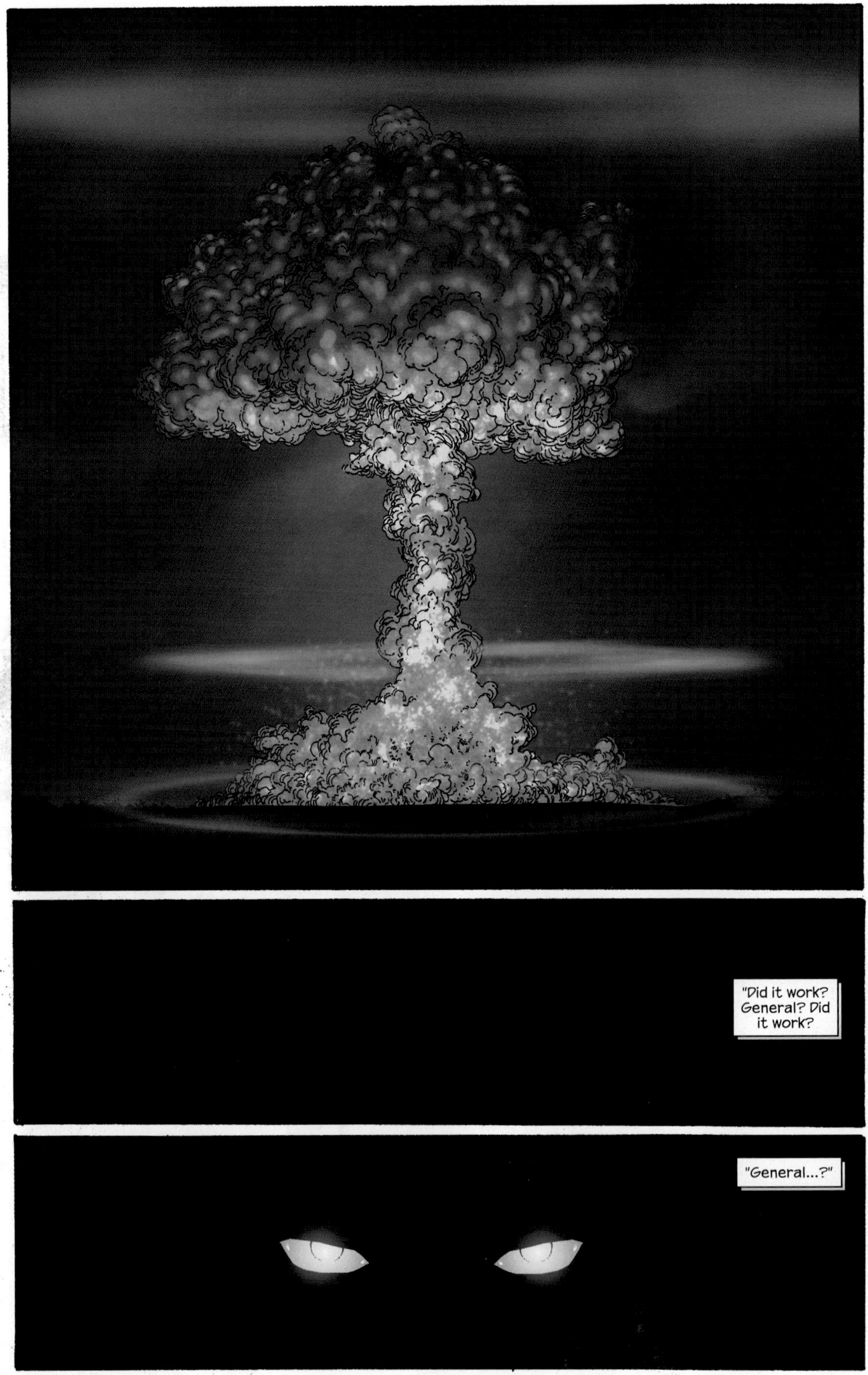
"Did it work? General? Did it work?
"General...?"

#10

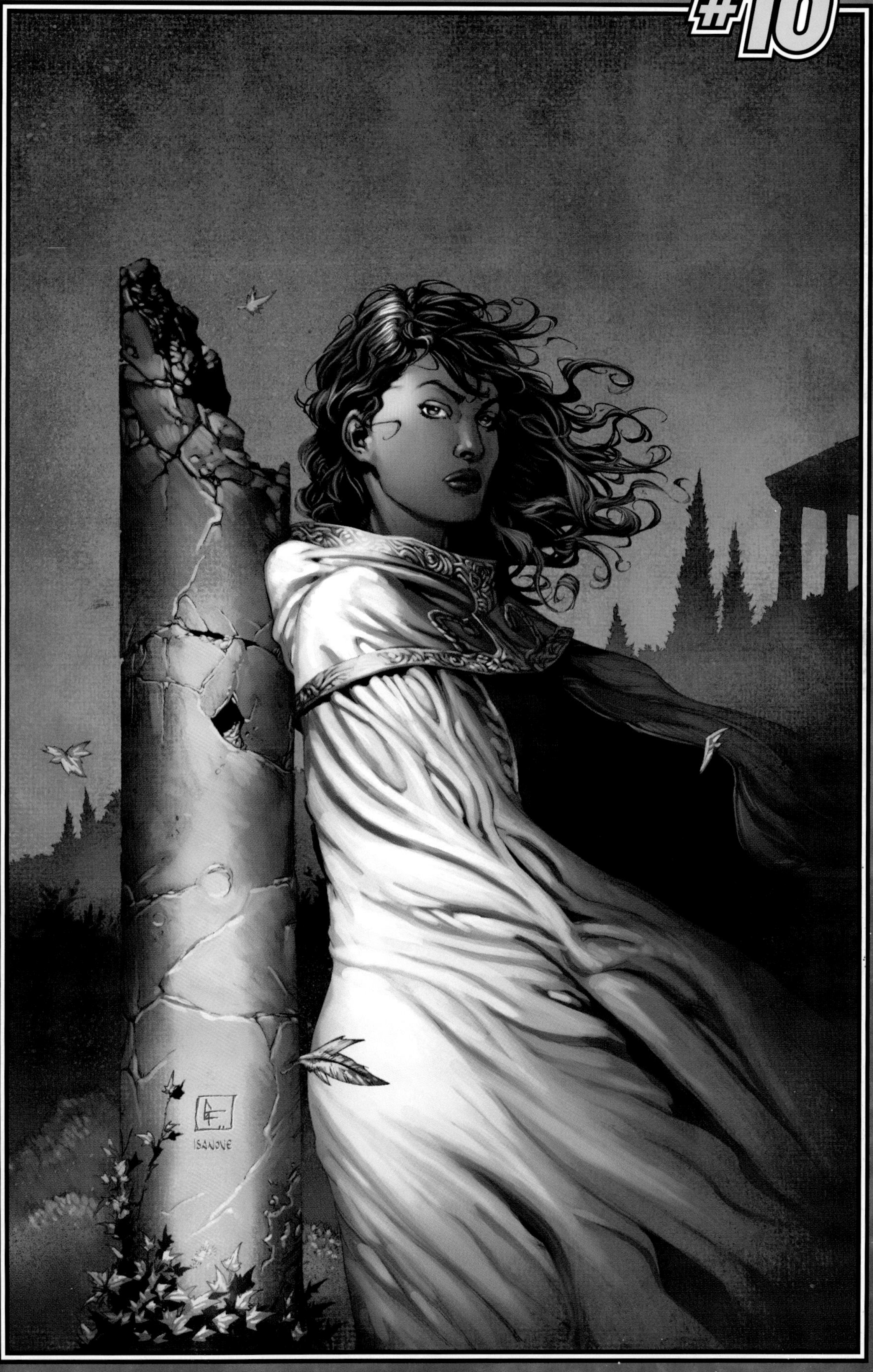
ISANOVE

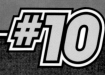

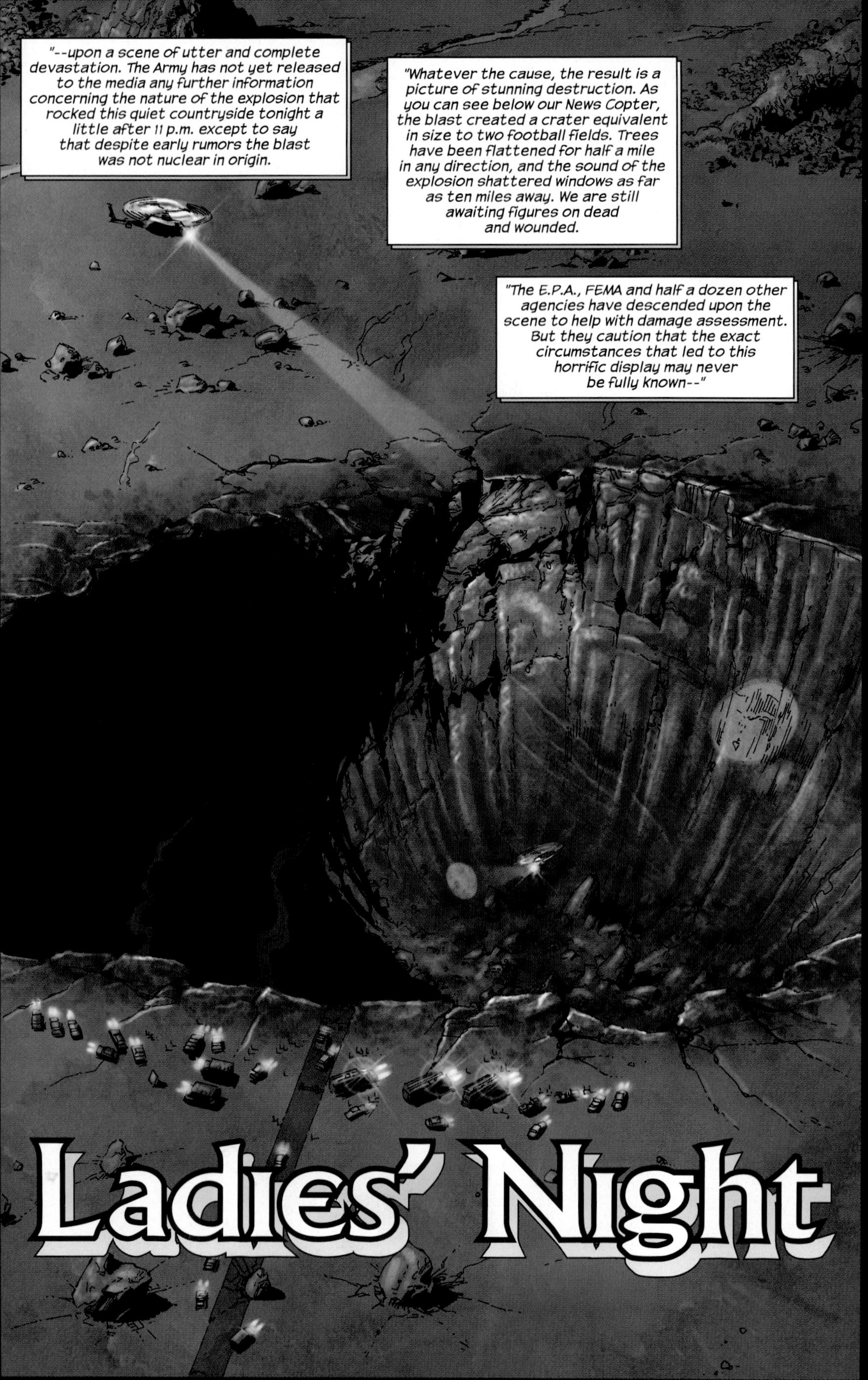
"--upon a scene of utter and complete devastation. The Army has not yet released to the media any further information concerning the nature of the explosion that rocked this quiet countryside tonight a little after 11 p.m. except to say that despite early rumors the blast was not nuclear in origin.
"Whatever the cause, the result is a picture of stunning destruction. As you can see below our News Copter, the blast created a crater equivalent in size to two football fields. Trees have been flattened for half a mile in any direction, and the sound of the explosion shattered windows as far as ten miles away. We are still awaiting figures on dead and wounded.
"The E.P.A., FEMA and half a dozen other agencies have descended upon the scene to help with damage assessment. But they caution that the exact circumstances that led to this horrific display may never be fully known--"
Ladies' Night

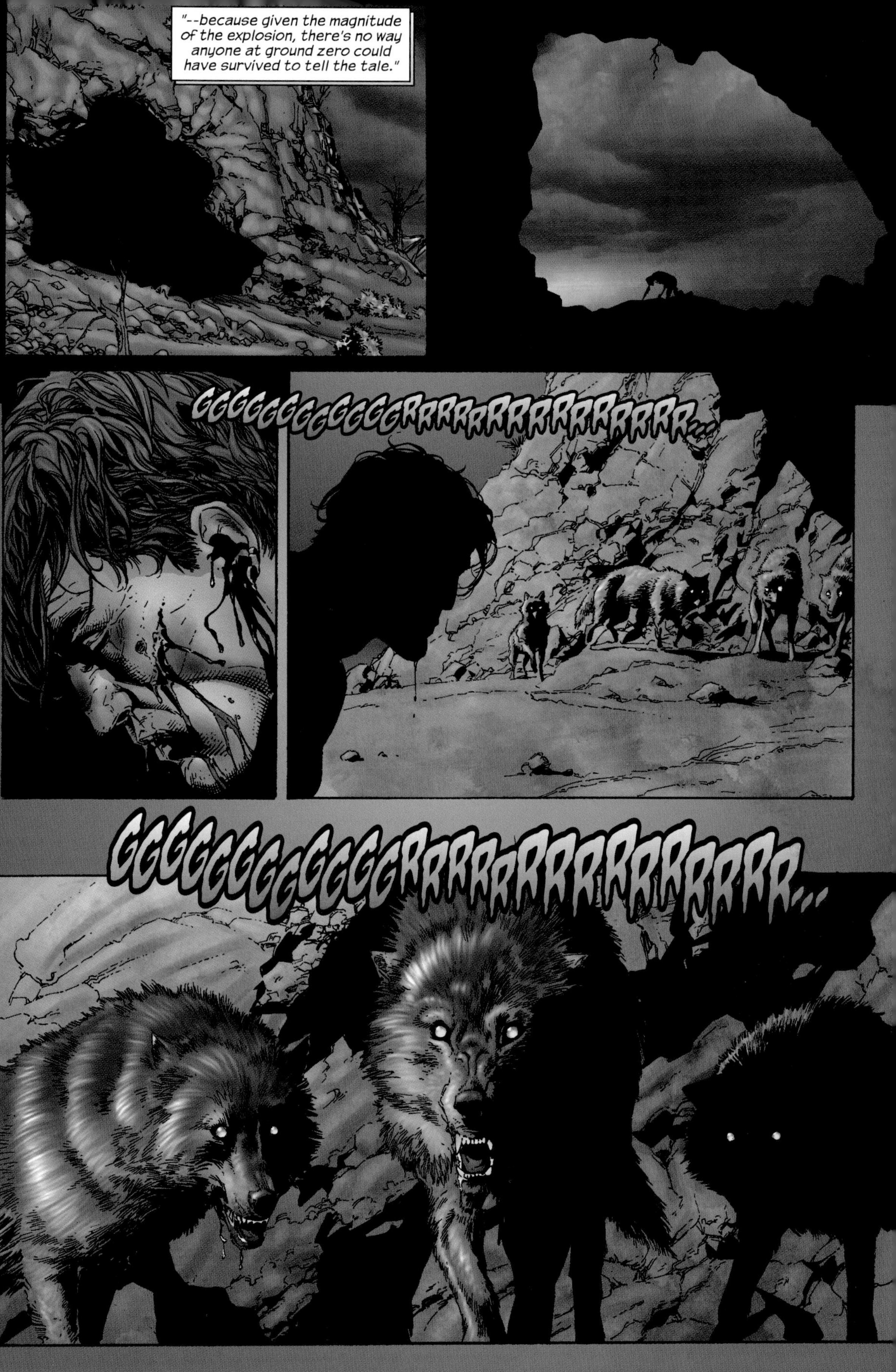
"--because given the magnitude of the explosion, there's no way anyone at ground zero could have survived to tell the tale."
GGGGGGGGGGGGRRRRRRRRRRRRRRRR...
GGGGGGGGGGGGGRRRRRRRRRRRRRRRRR...

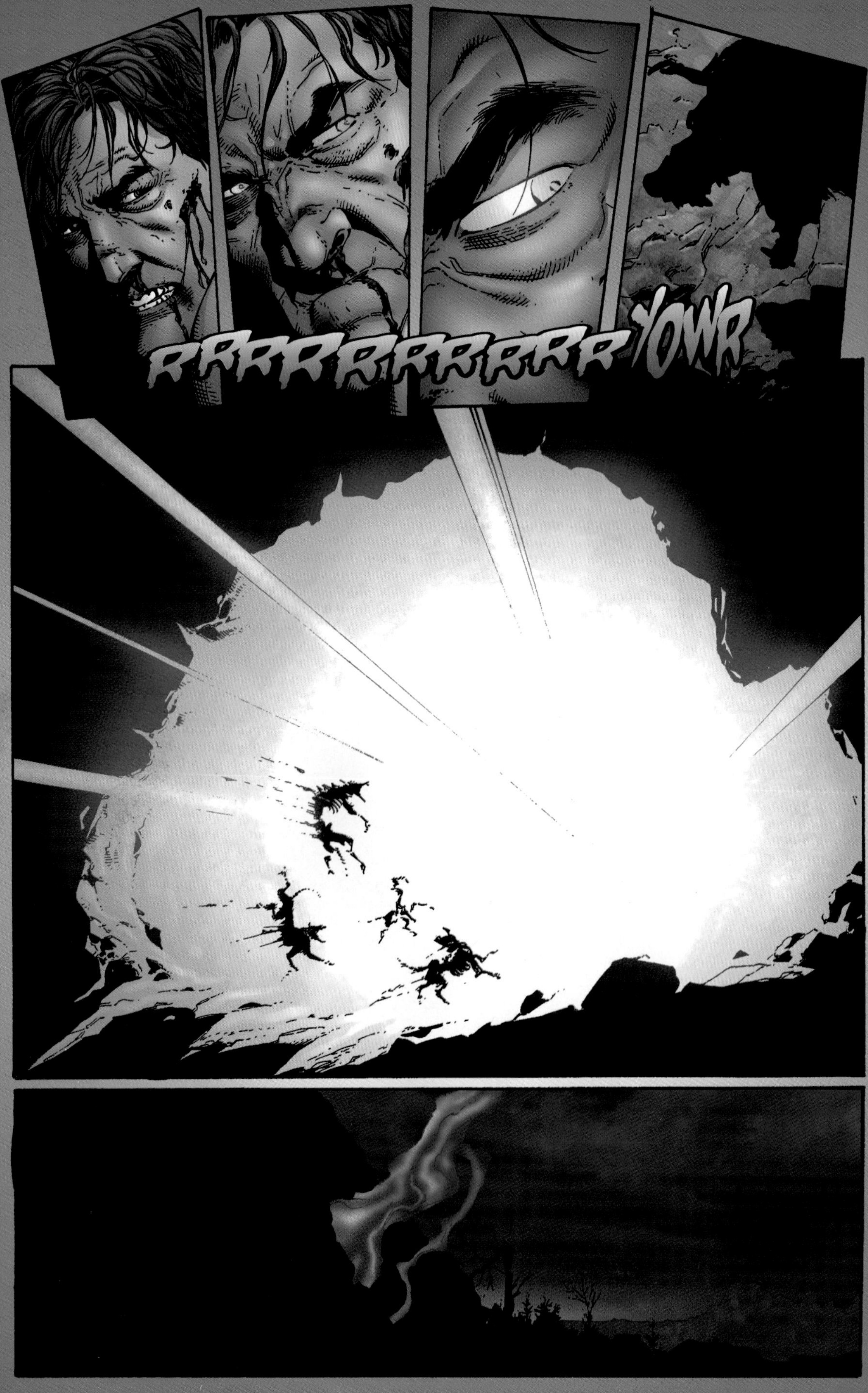
RRRRRRRRRRRYOWR

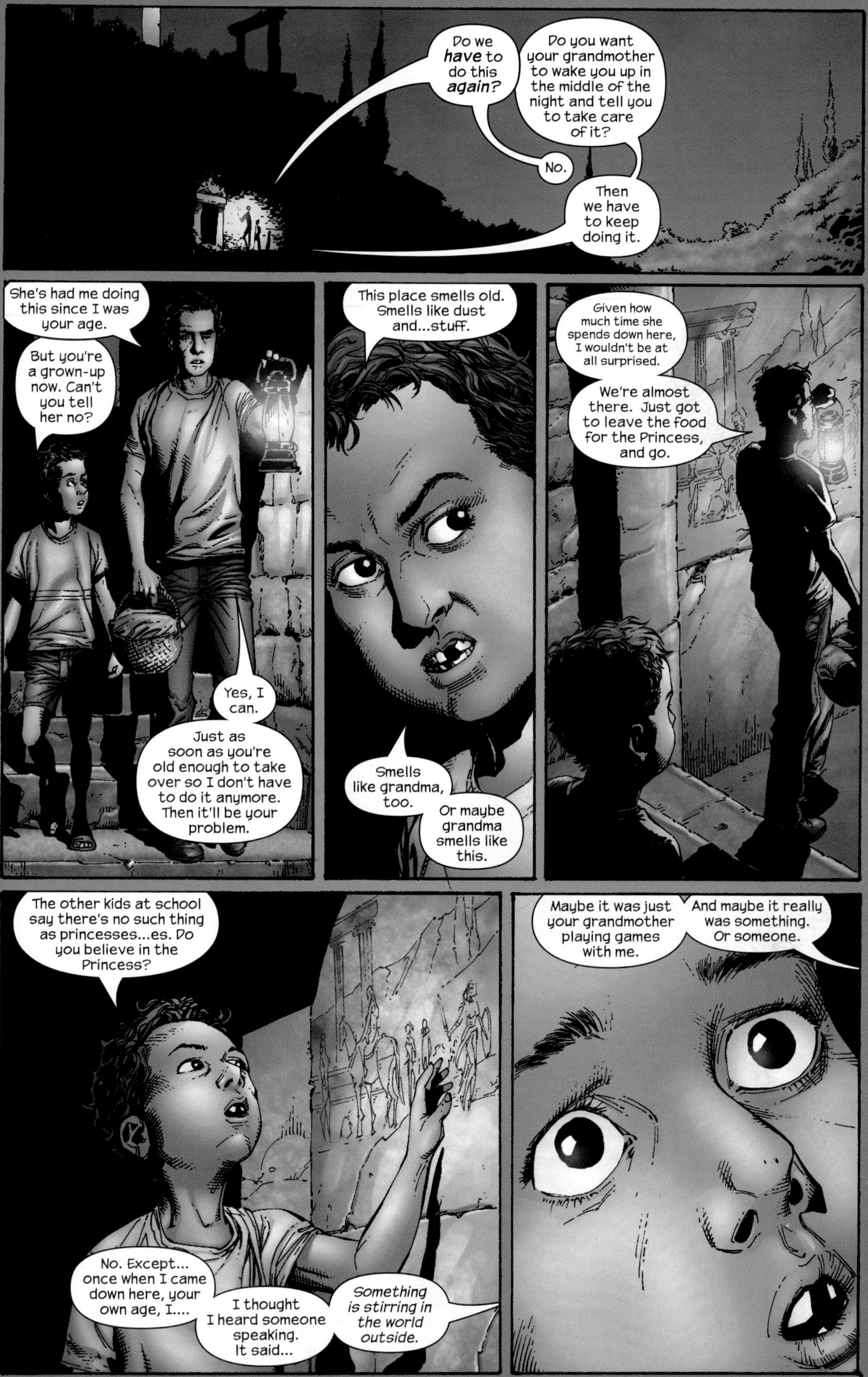

Do we *have* to do this *again?*
Do you want your grandmother to wake you up in the middle of the night and tell you to take care of it?
No.
Then we have to keep doing it.
She's had me doing this since I was your age.
But you're a grown-up now. Can't you tell her no?
Yes, I can.
Just as soon as you're old enough to take over so I don't have to do it anymore. Then it'll be your problem.
This place smells old. Smells like dust and...stuff.
Smells like grandma, too.
Or maybe grandma smells like this.
Given how much time she spends down here, I wouldn't be at all surprised.
We're almost there. Just got to leave the food for the Princess, and go.
The other kids at school say there's no such thing as princesses...es. Do you believe in the Princess?
No. Except... once when I came down here, your own age, I....
I thought I heard someone speaking. It said...
Something is stirring in the world outside.
Maybe it was just your grandmother playing games with me.
And maybe it really was something. Or someone.

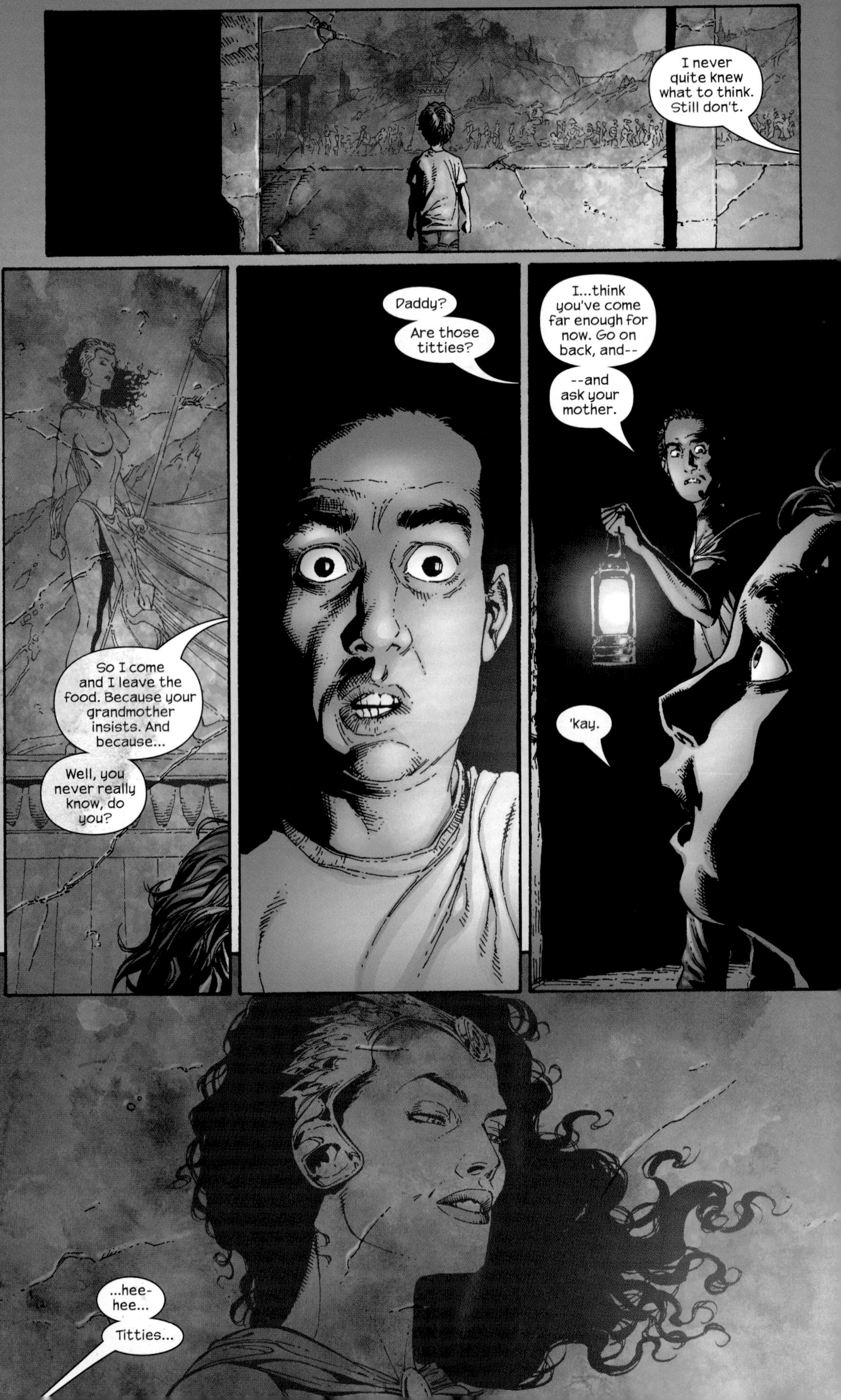

I never quite knew what to think. Still don't.
So I come and I leave the food. Because your grandmother insists. And because...
Well, you never really know, do you?
Daddy?
Are those titties?
I...think you've come far enough for now. Go on back, and--
--and ask your mother.
'Kay.
...hee-hee...
Titties...

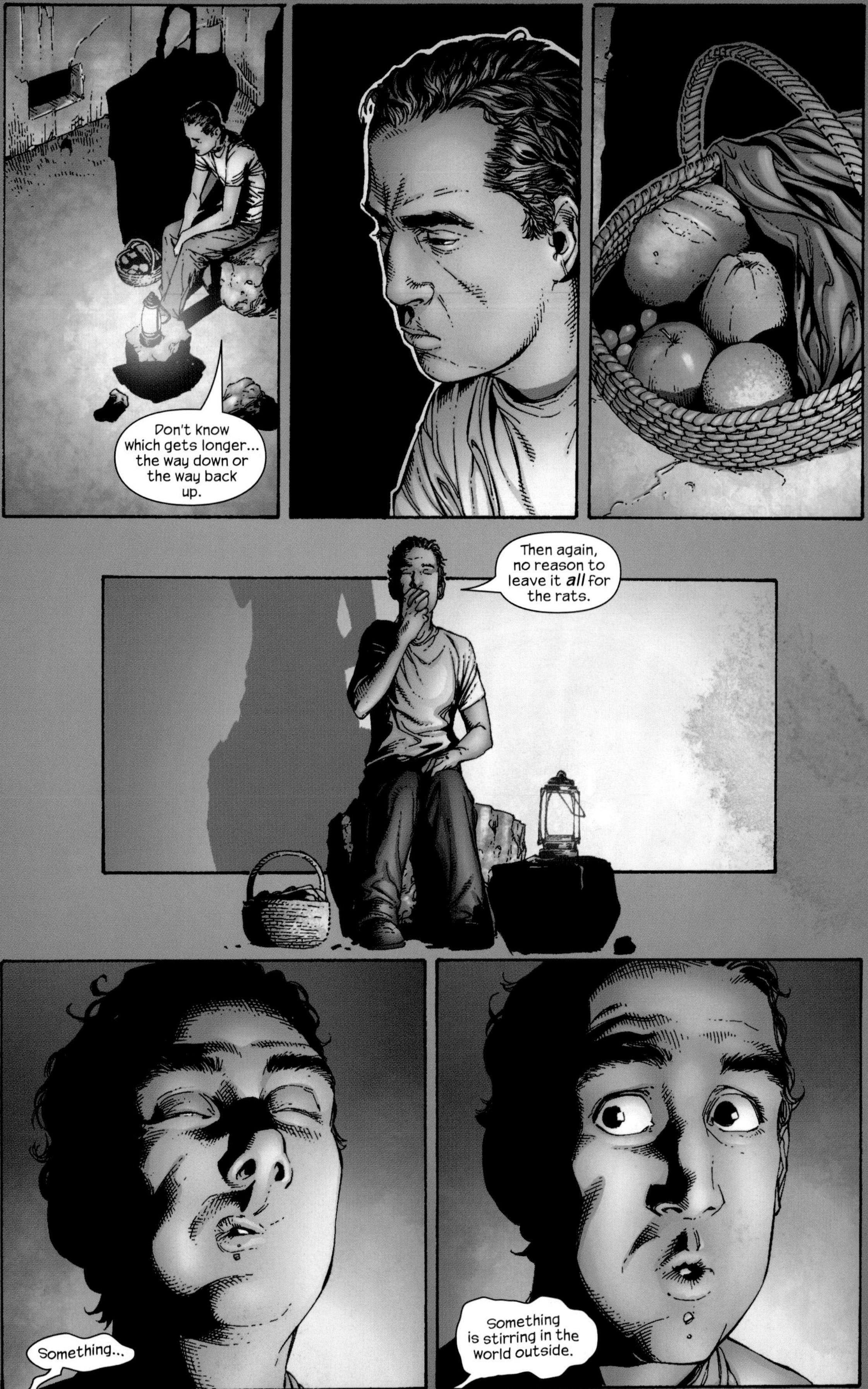
Don't know which gets longer... the way down or the way back up.
Then again, no reason to leave it *all* for the rats.
Something...
Something is stirring in the world outside.

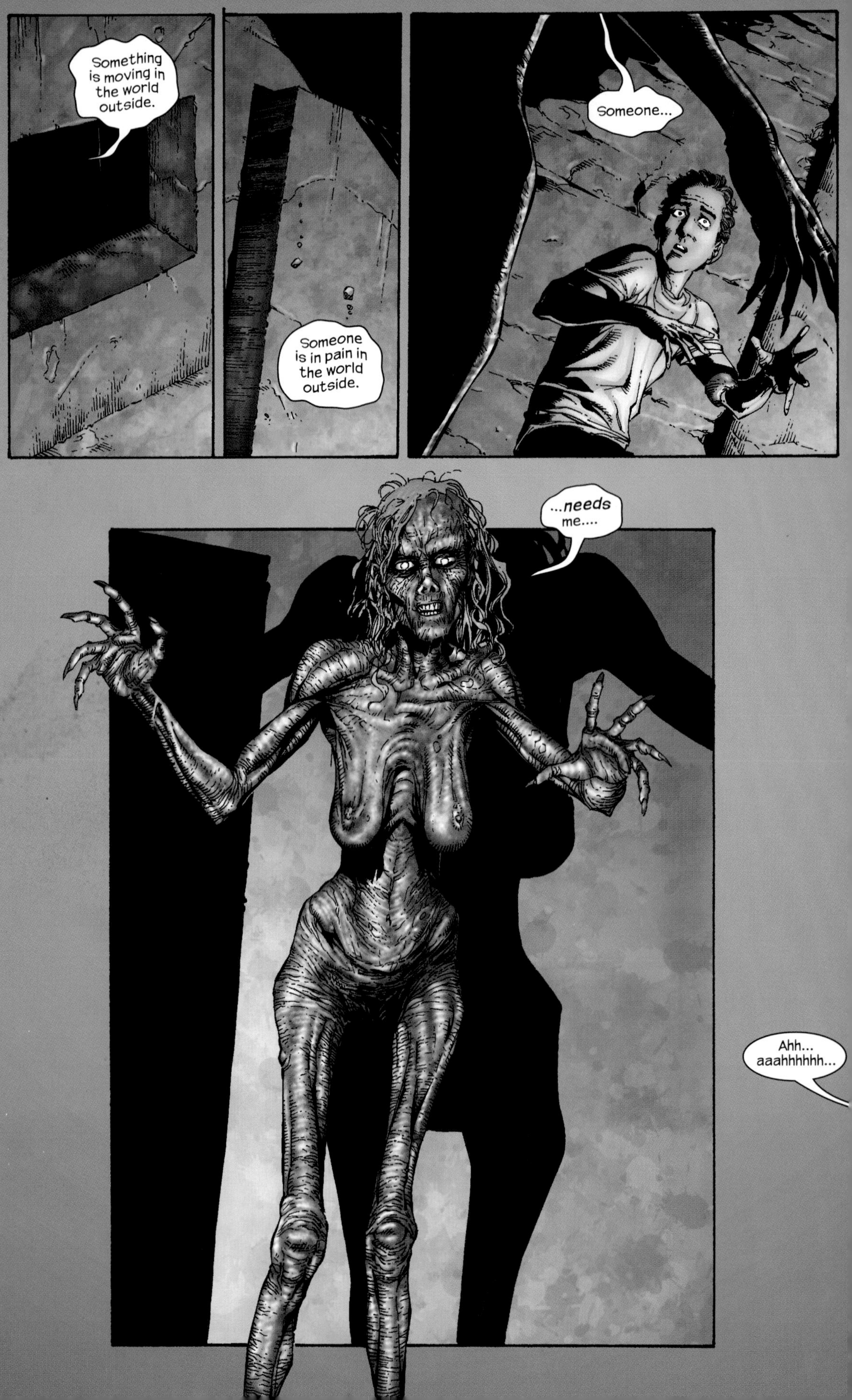
Something is moving in the world outside.
Someone is in pain in the world outside.
Someone...
...needs me....
Ahh... aaahhhhhh...

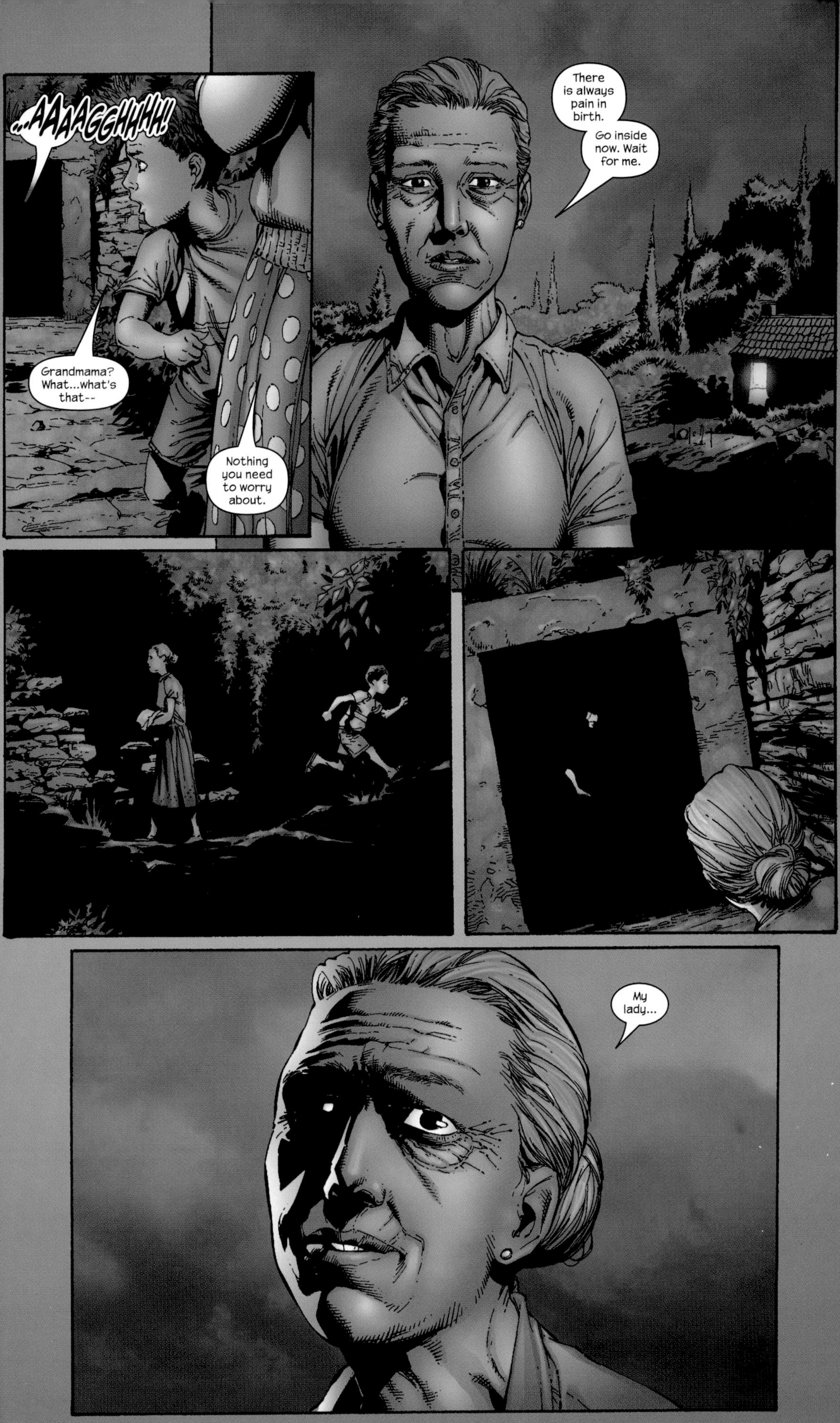

...AAAAGGHHHH!
Grandmama? What...what's that--
Nothing you need to worry about.
There is always pain in birth.
Go inside now. Wait for me.
My lady...

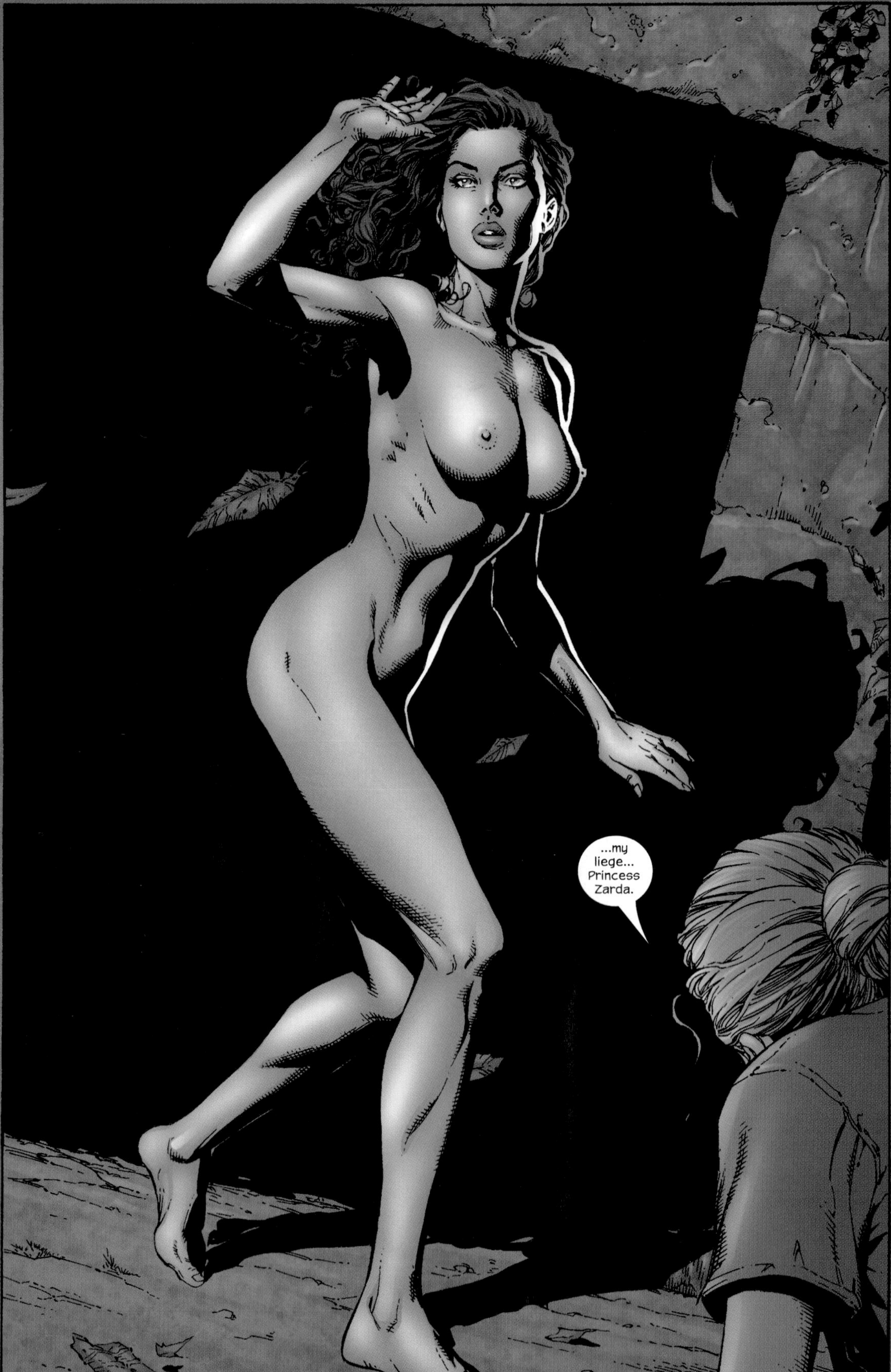
...my liege... Princess Zarda.

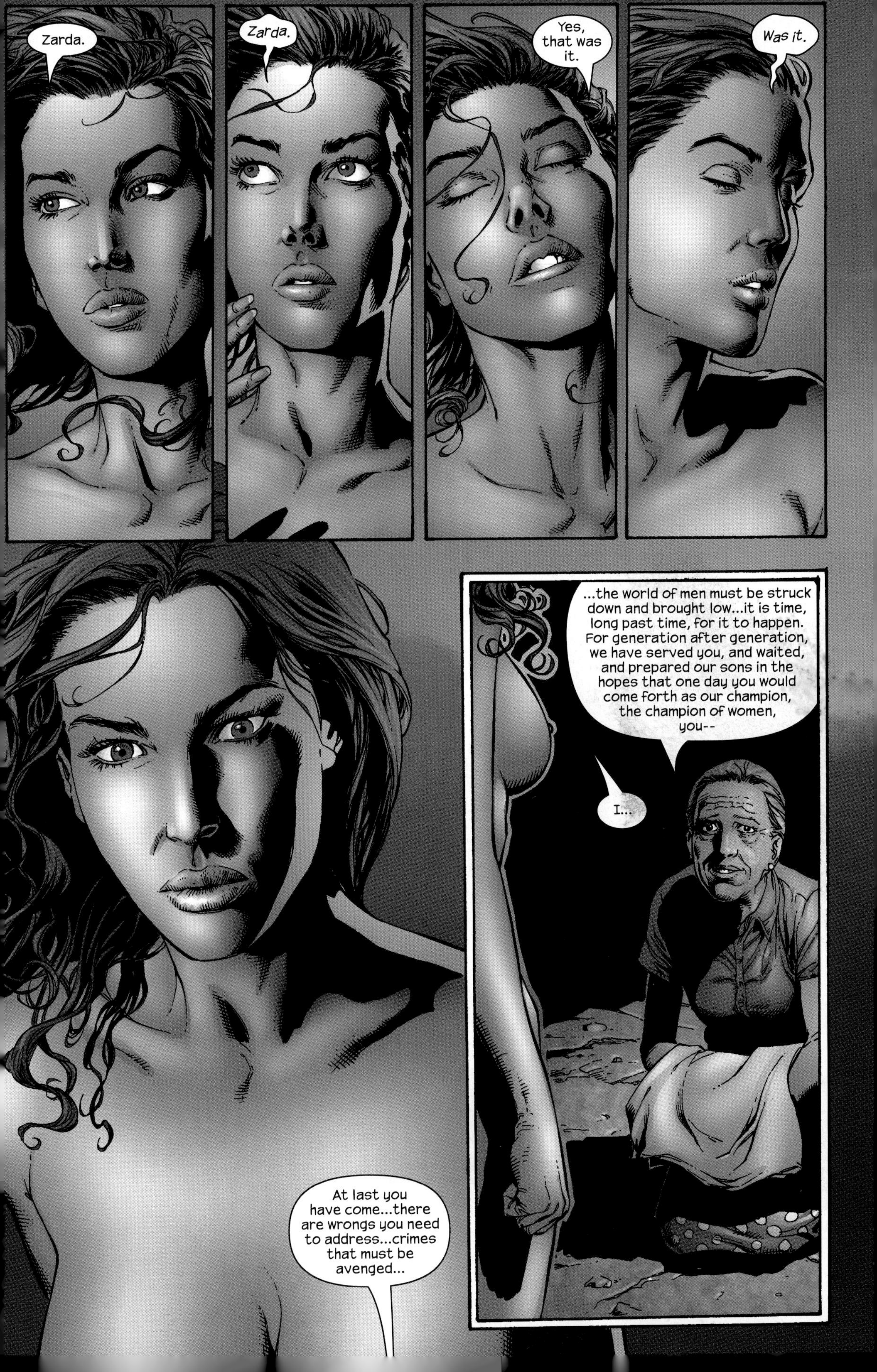
Zarda.
Zarda.
Yes, that was it.
Was it.
...the world of men must be struck down and brought low...it is time, long past time, for it to happen. For generation after generation, we have served you, and waited, and prepared our sons in the hopes that one day you would come forth as our champion, the champion of women, you--
I...
At last you have come...there are wrongs you need to address...crimes that must be avenged...

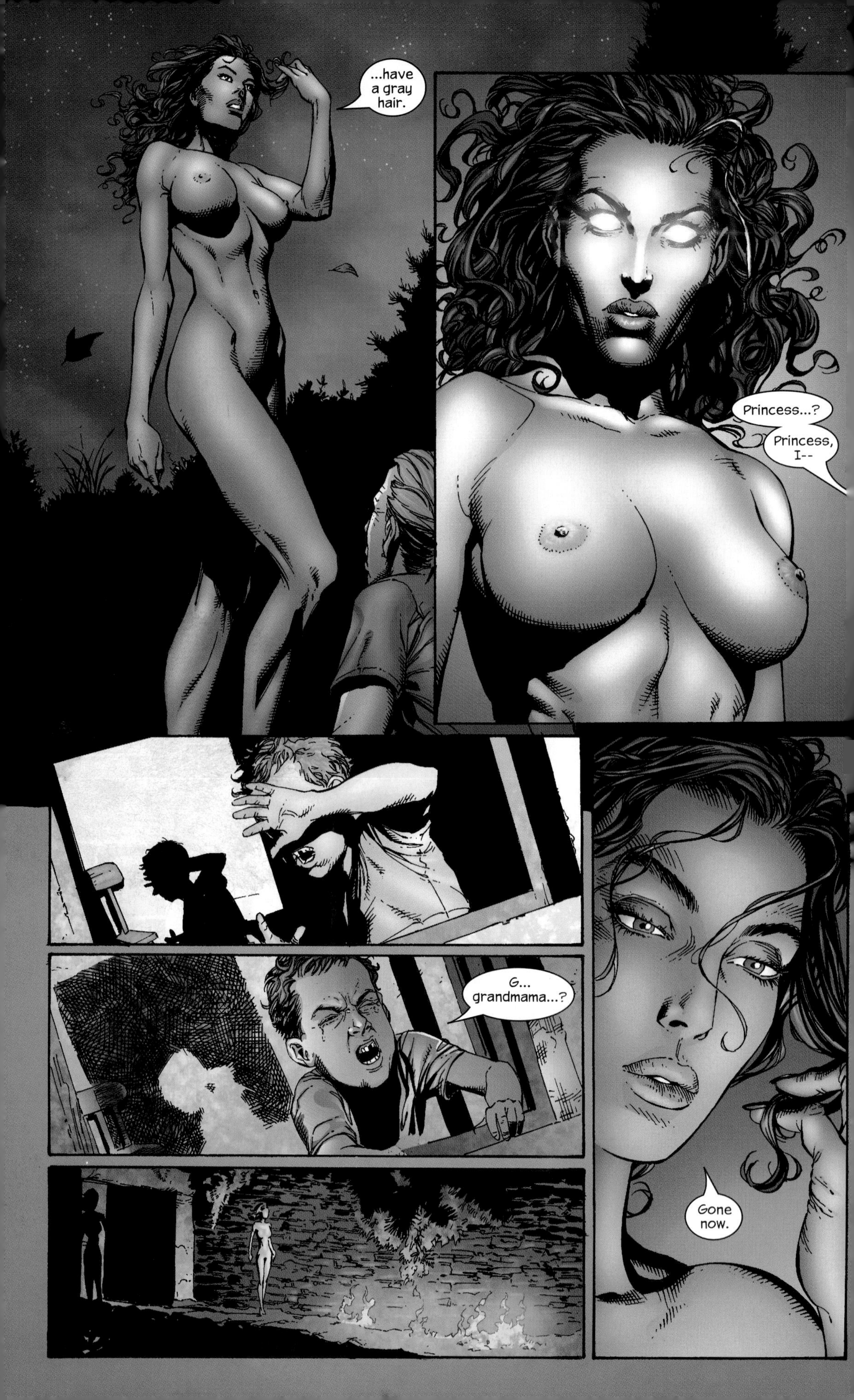
...have a gray hair.
Princess...?
Princess, I--
G... grandmama...?
Gone now.

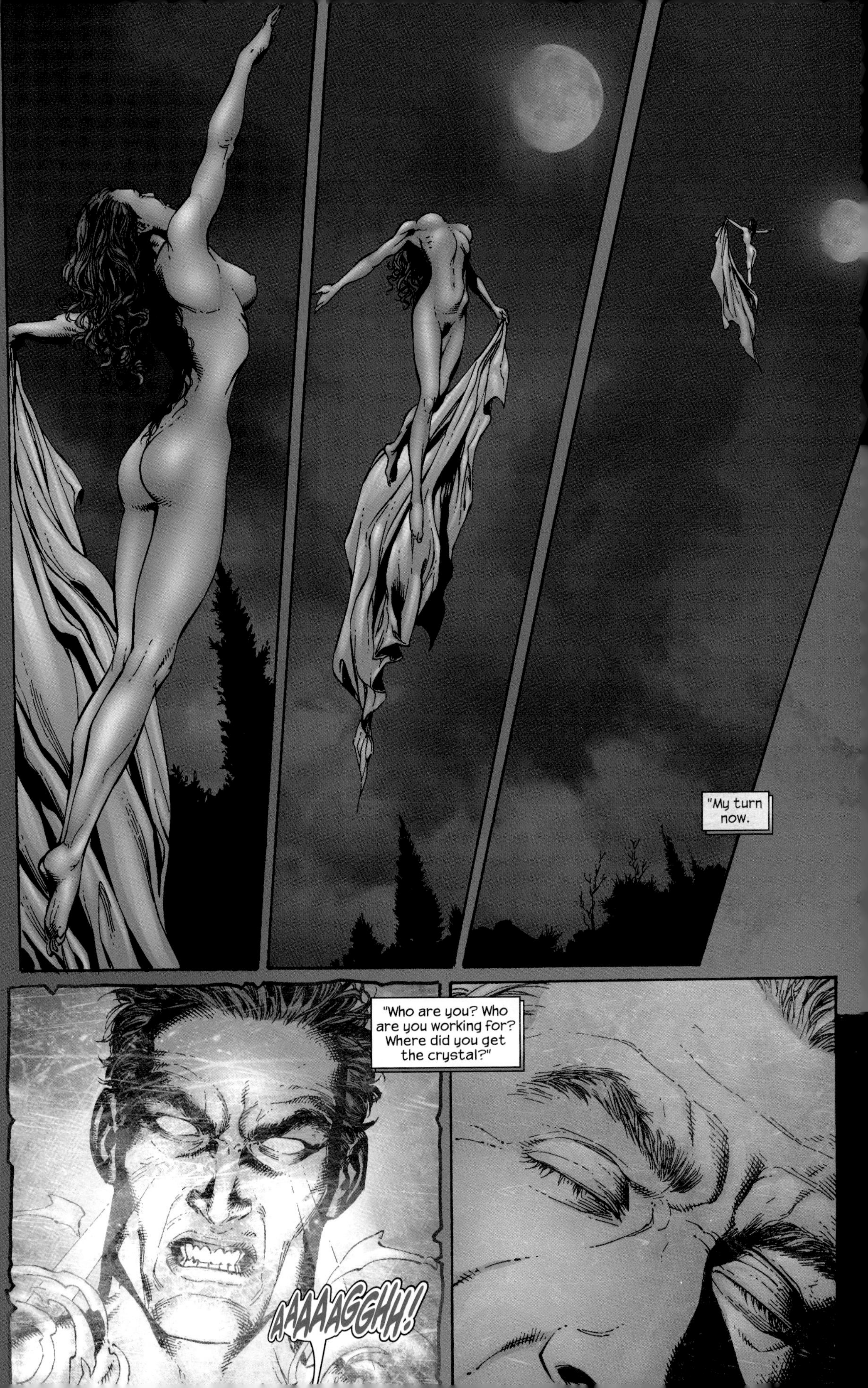
"My turn now.
"Who are you? Who are you working for? Where did you get the crystal?"
AAAAAGGHH!

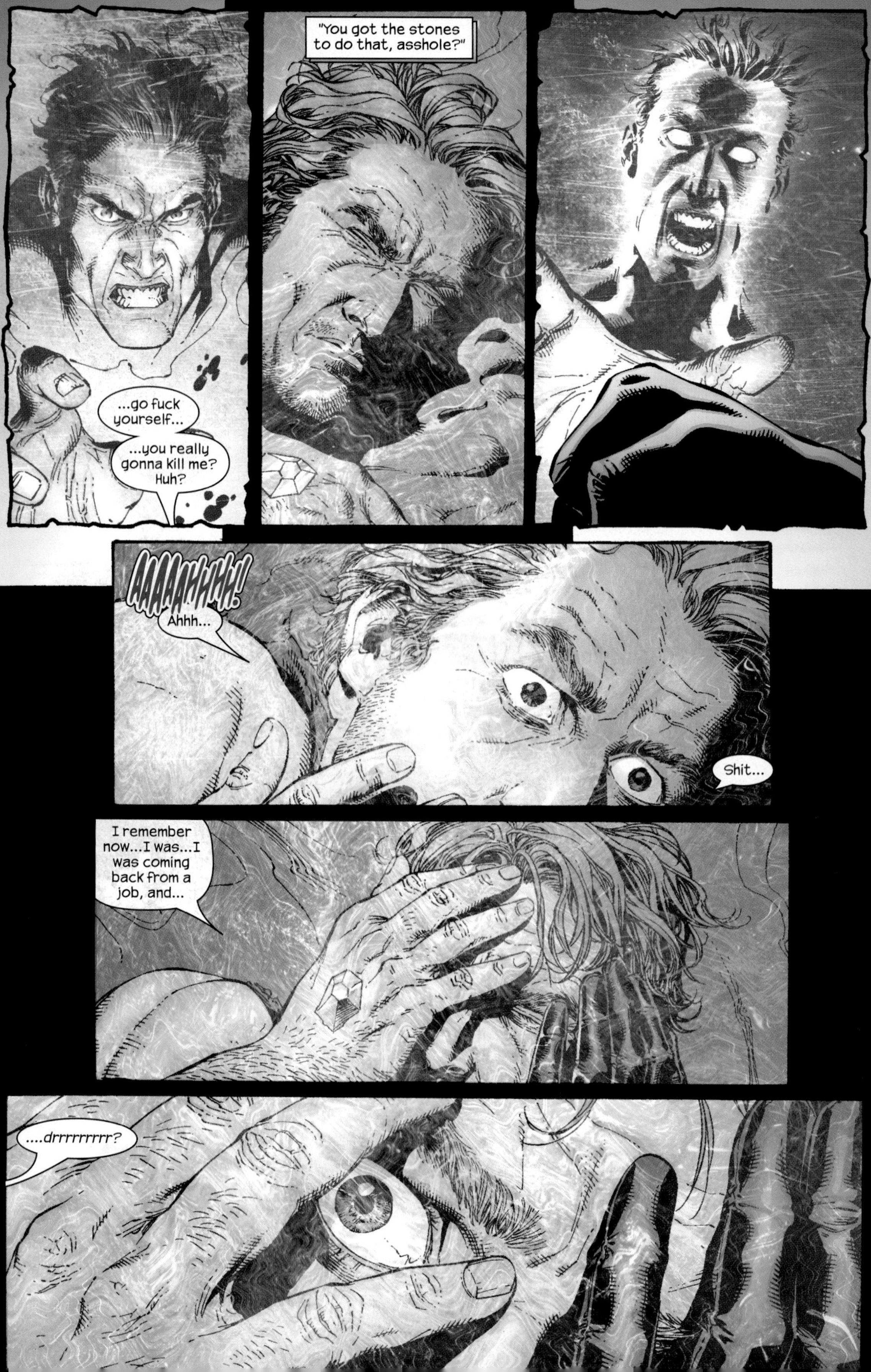
...go fuck yourself...
...you really gonna kill me? Huh?
"You got the stones to do that, asshole?"
AAAAAHHHH!
Ahhh...
Shit...
I remember now...I was...I was coming back from a job, and...
....drrrrrrrrr?

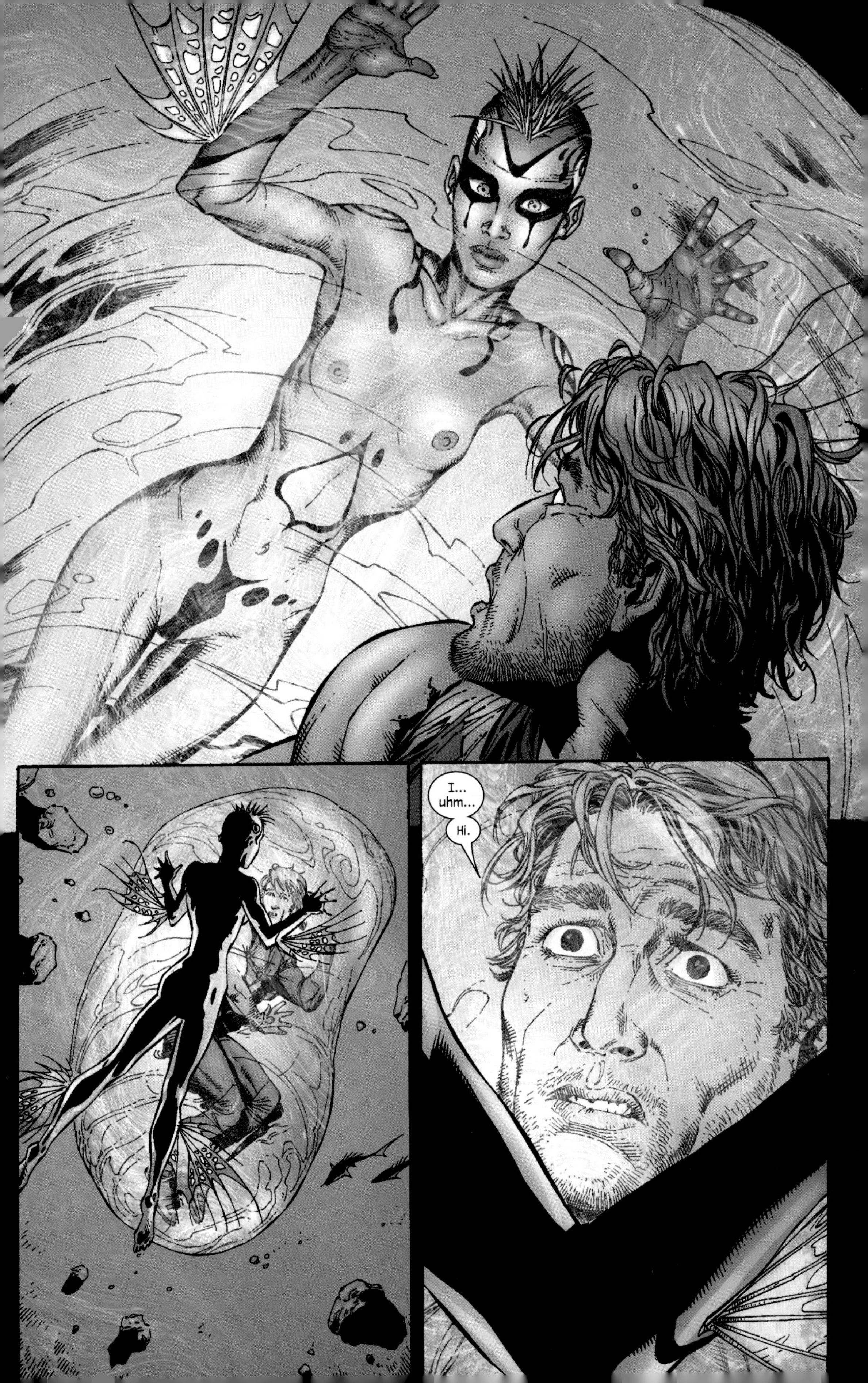
I... uhm...
Hi.

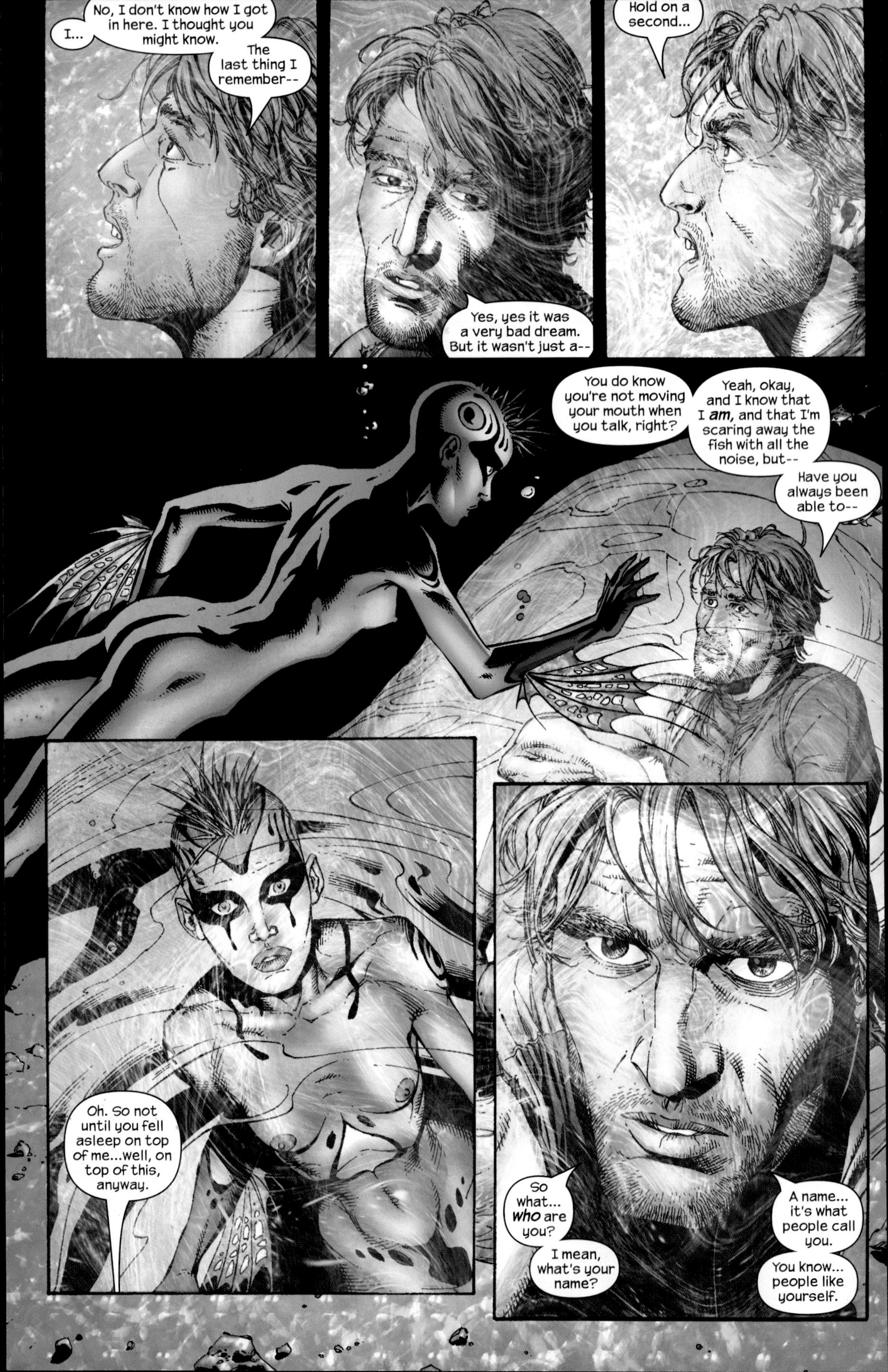
I...
No, I don't know how I got in here. I thought you might know.
The last thing I remember--
Yes, yes it was a very bad dream. But it wasn't just a--
Hold on a second...
You do know you're not moving your mouth when you talk, right?
Yeah, okay, and I know that I *am*, and that I'm scaring away the fish with all the noise, but--
Have you always been able to--
Oh. So not until you fell asleep on top of me...well, on top of this, anyway.
So what... *who* are you?
I mean, what's your name?
A name... it's what people call you.
You know... people like yourself.

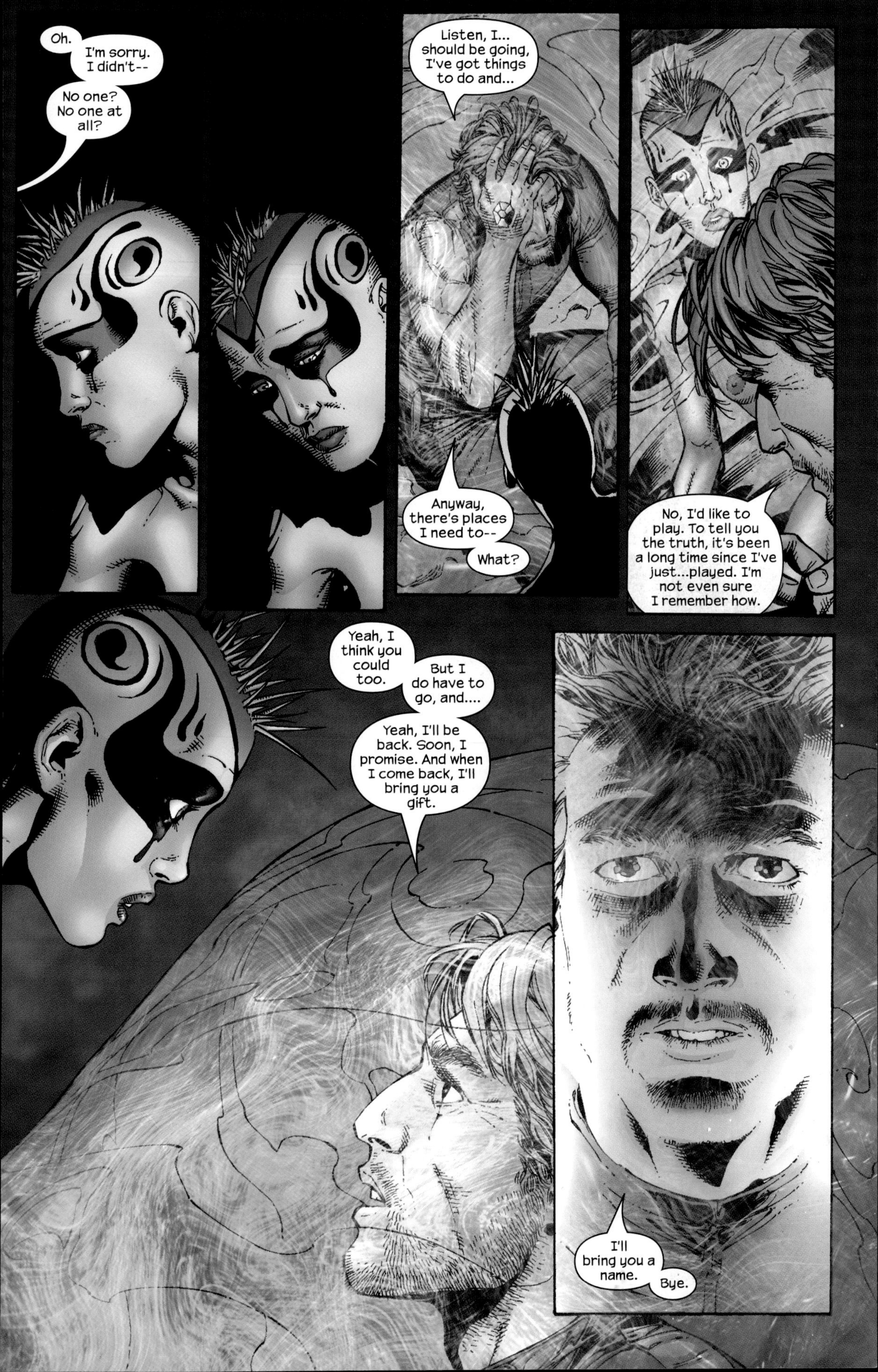

Oh.
I'm sorry. I didn't--
No one? No one at all?
Listen, I... should be going, I've got things to do and...
Anyway, there's places I need to--
What?
No, I'd like to play. To tell you the truth, it's been a long time since I've just...played. I'm not even sure I remember how.
Yeah, I think you could too.
But I do have to go, and....
Yeah, I'll be back. Soon, I promise. And when I come back, I'll bring you a gift.
I'll bring you a name.
Bye.

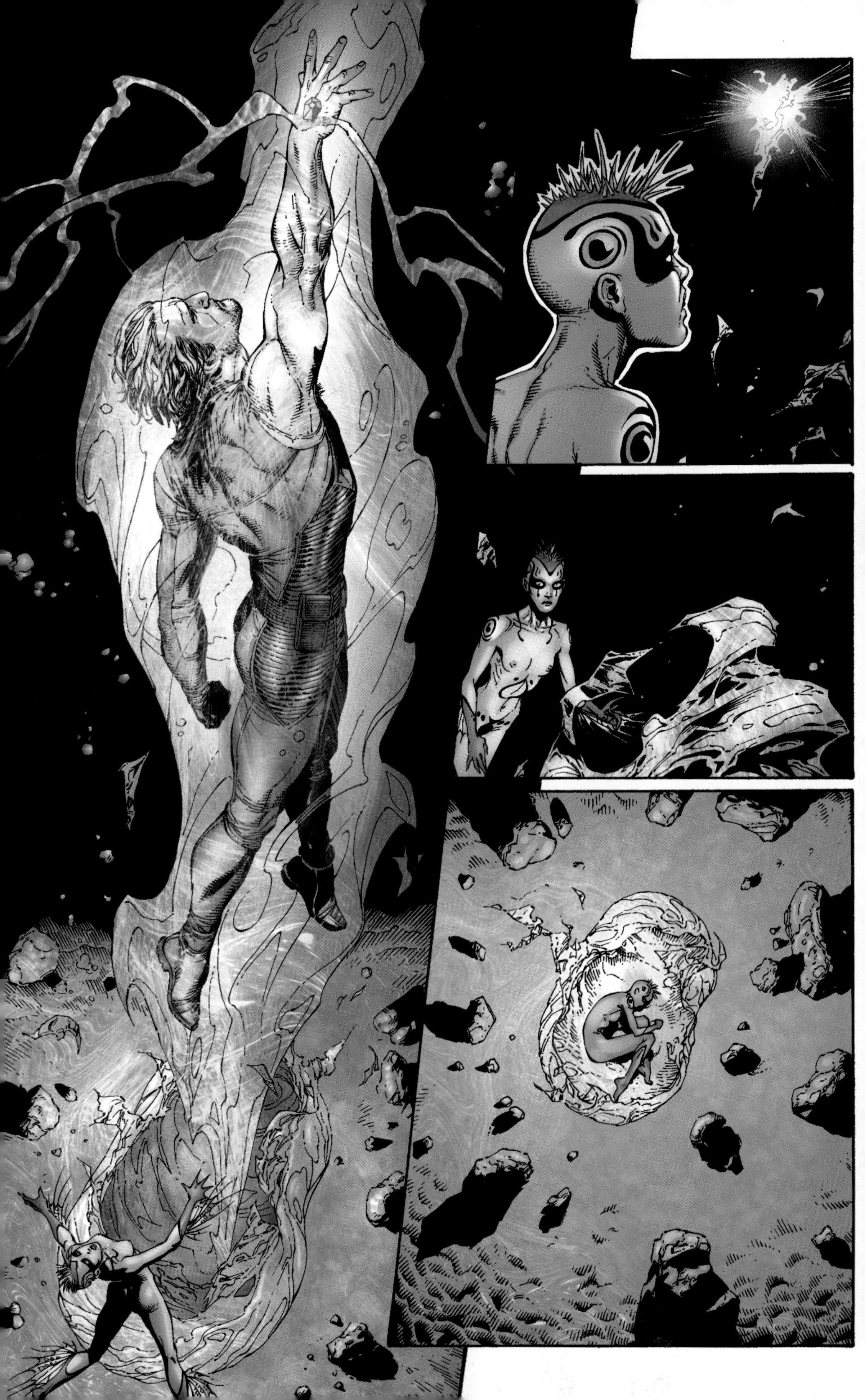

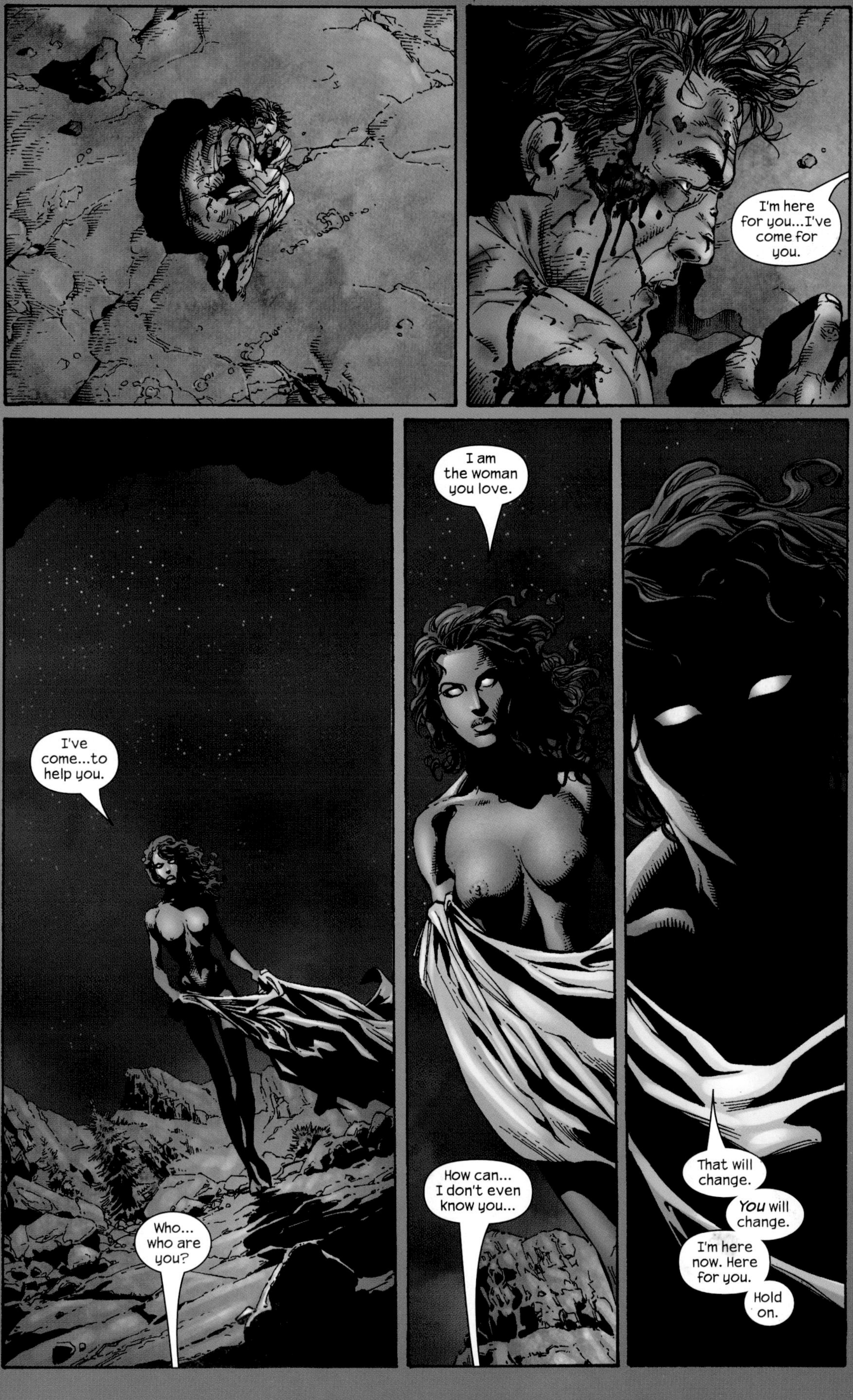
I'm here for you...I've come for you.
I've come...to help you.
Who... who are you?
I am the woman you love.
How can... I don't even know you...
That will change.
You will change.
I'm here now. Here for you.
Hold on.

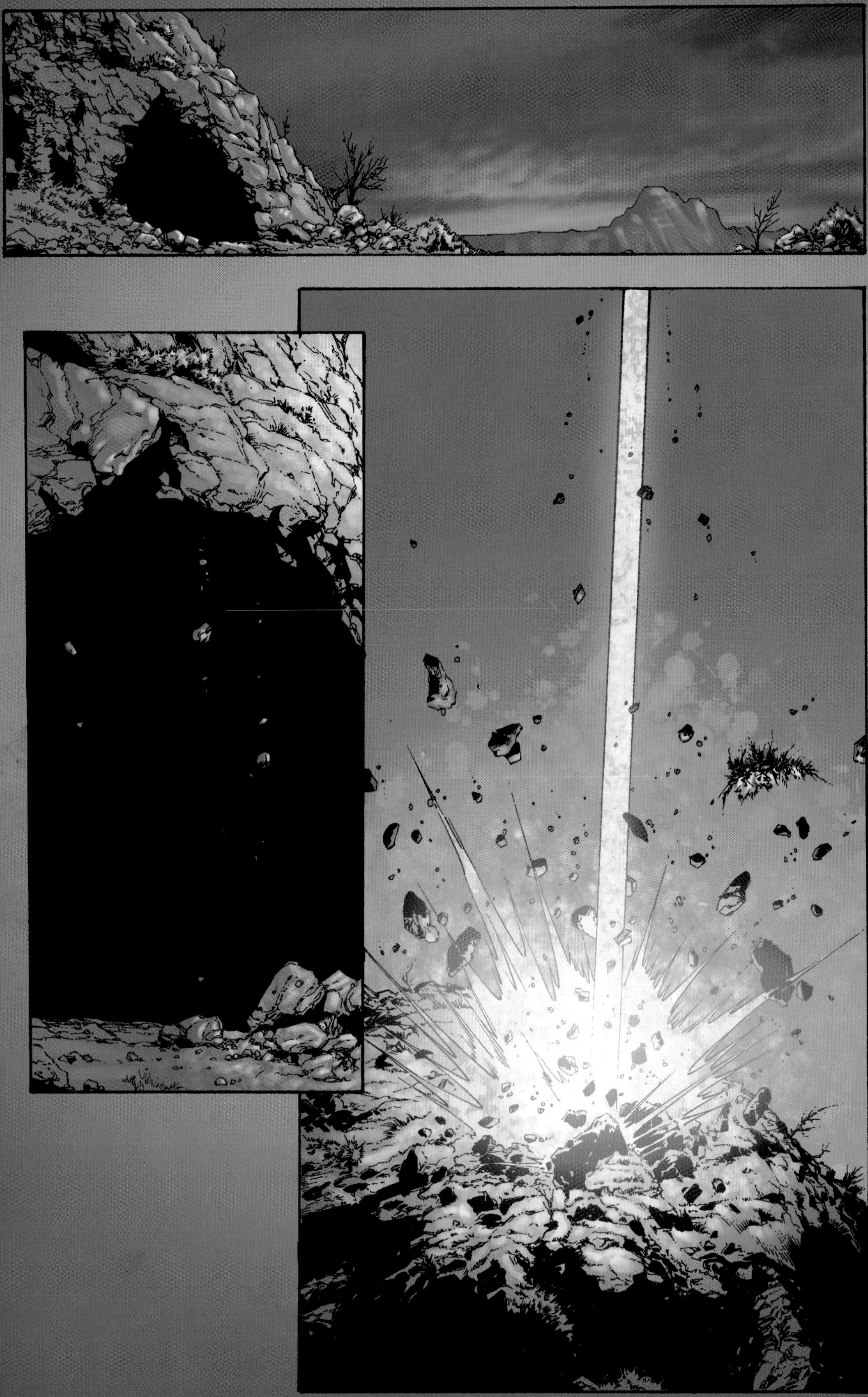

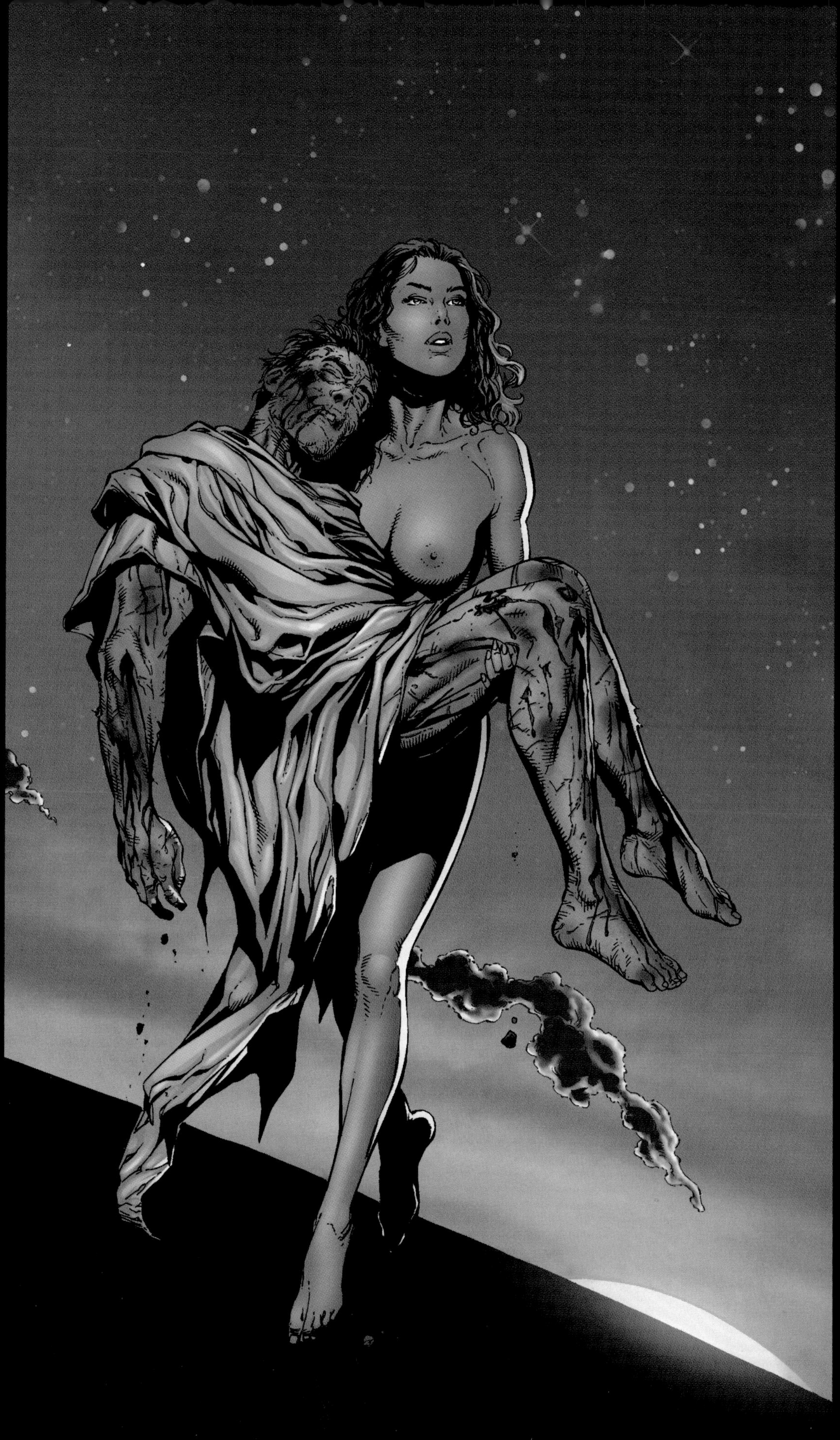

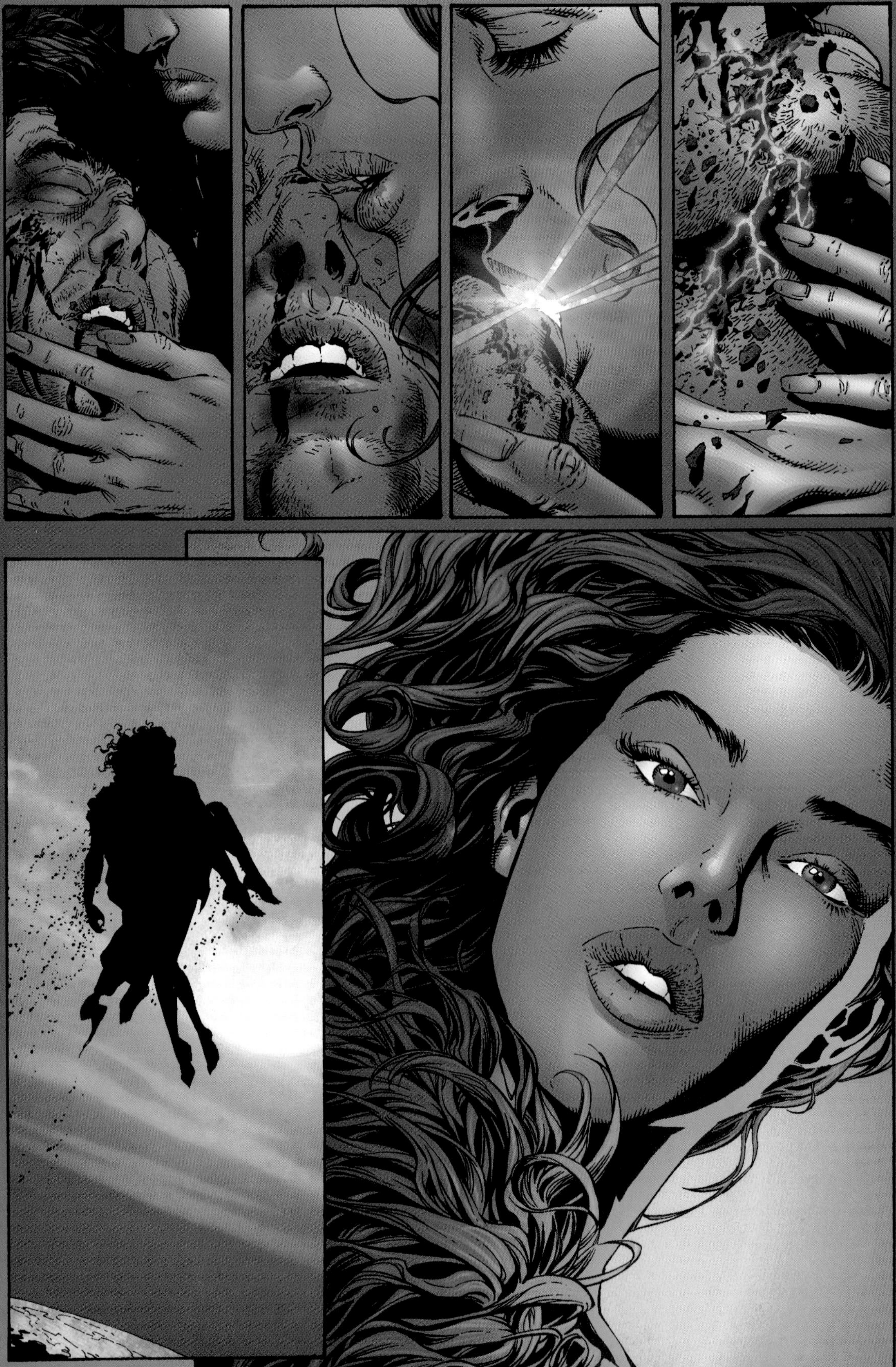

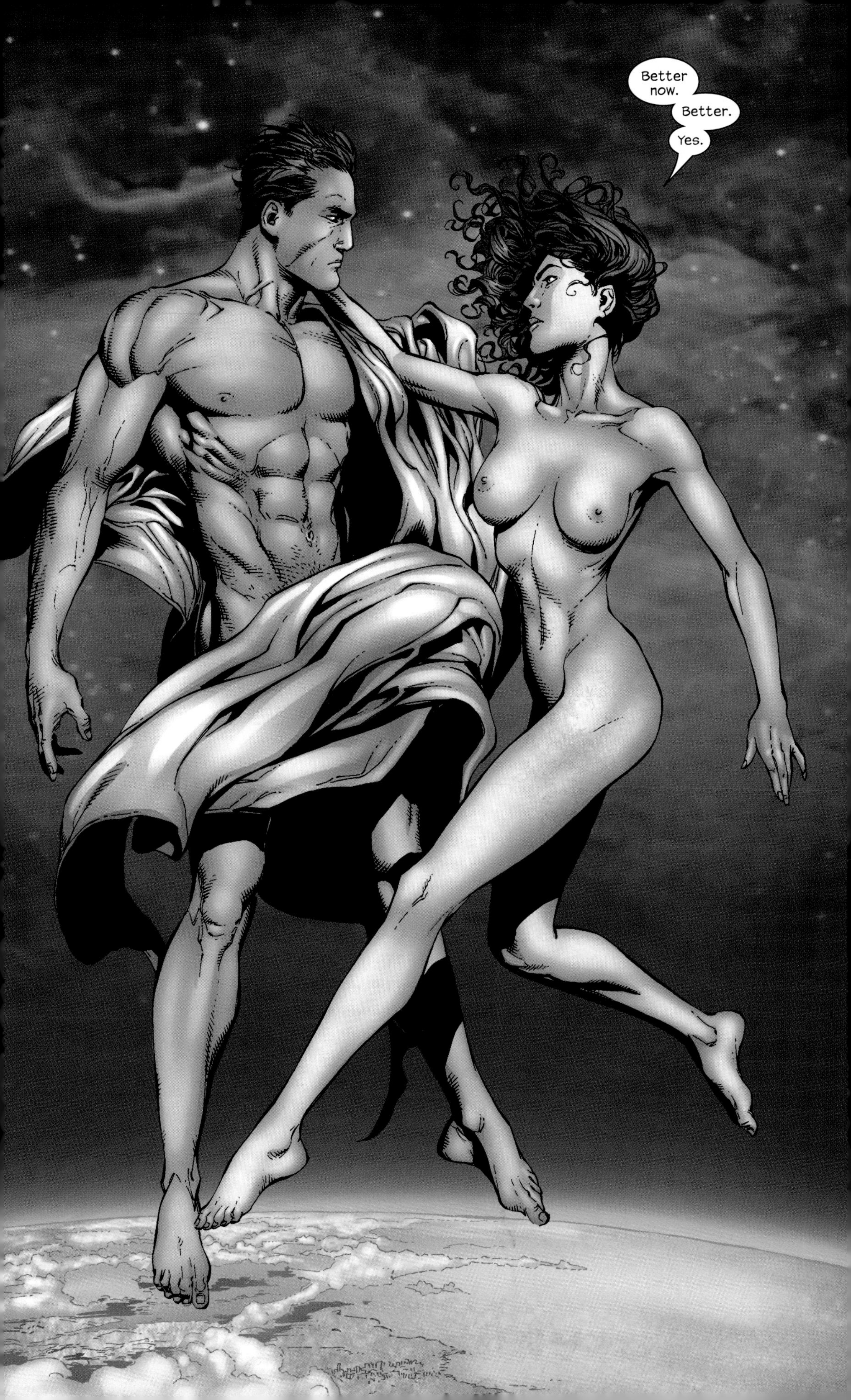
Better now.
Better.
Yes.

#11

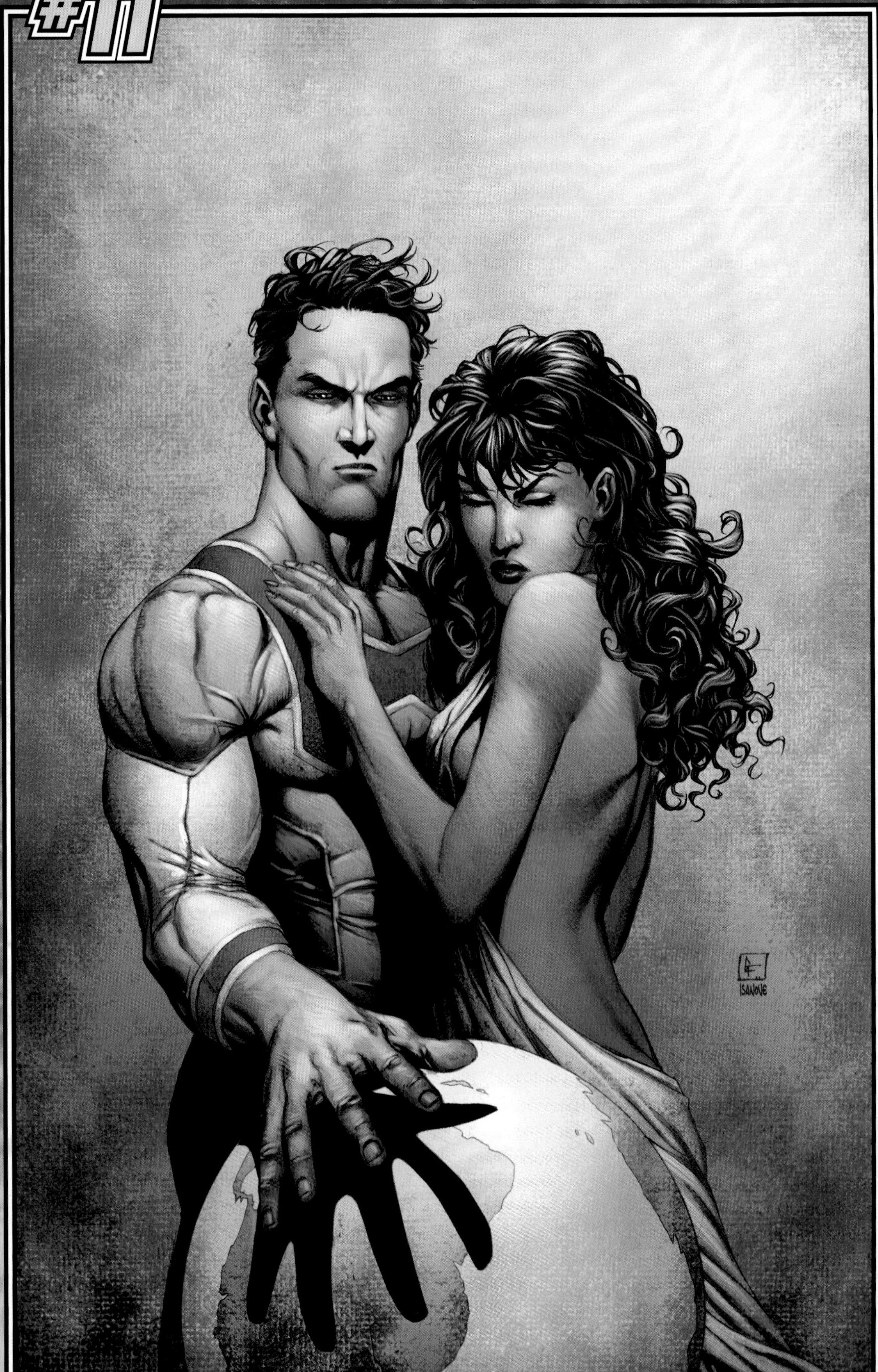
ISANOVE

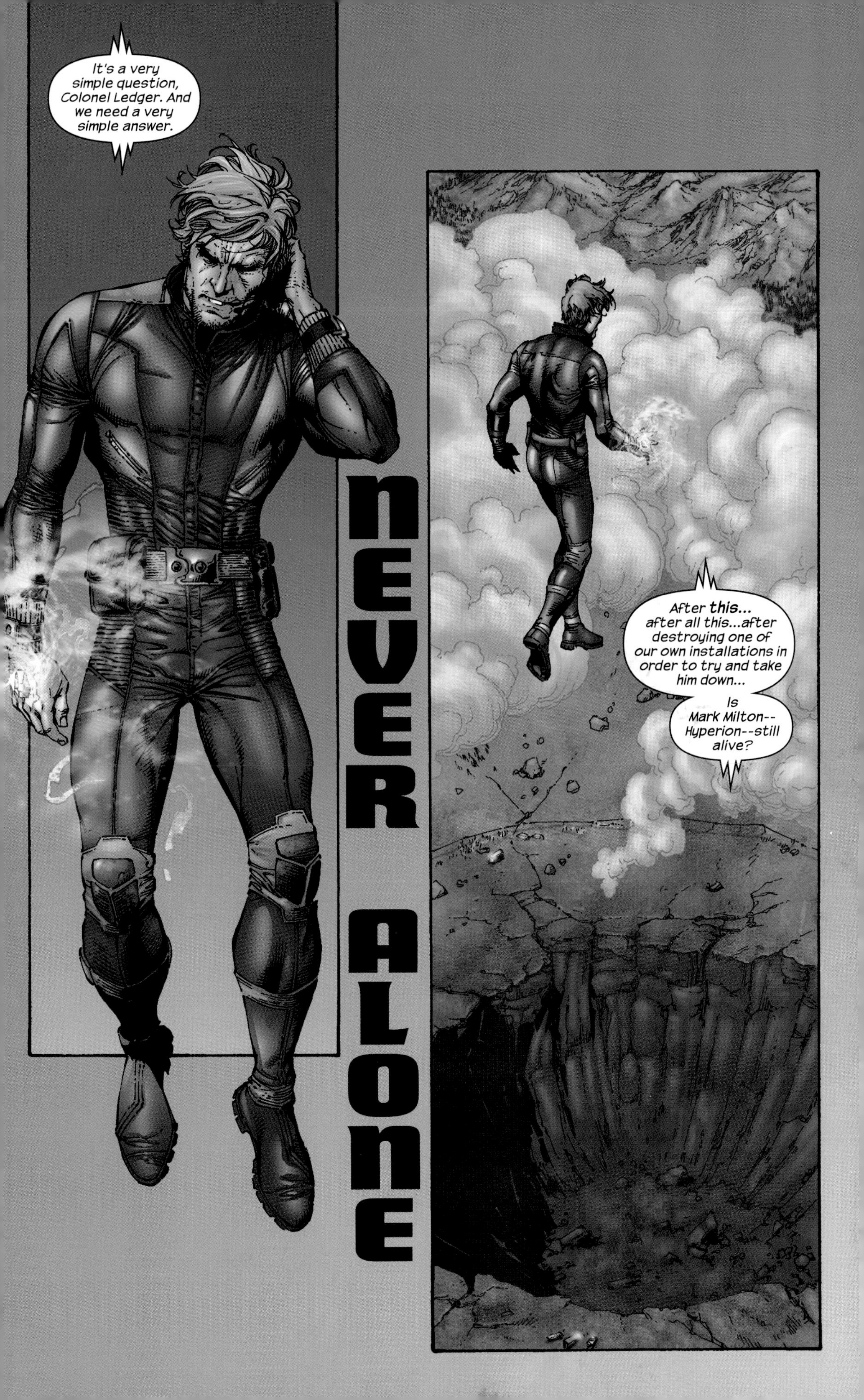
It's a very simple question, Colonel Ledger. And we need a very simple answer.
NEVER ALONE
After this... after all this...after destroying one of our own installations in order to try and take him down...
Is Mark Milton--Hyperion--still alive?

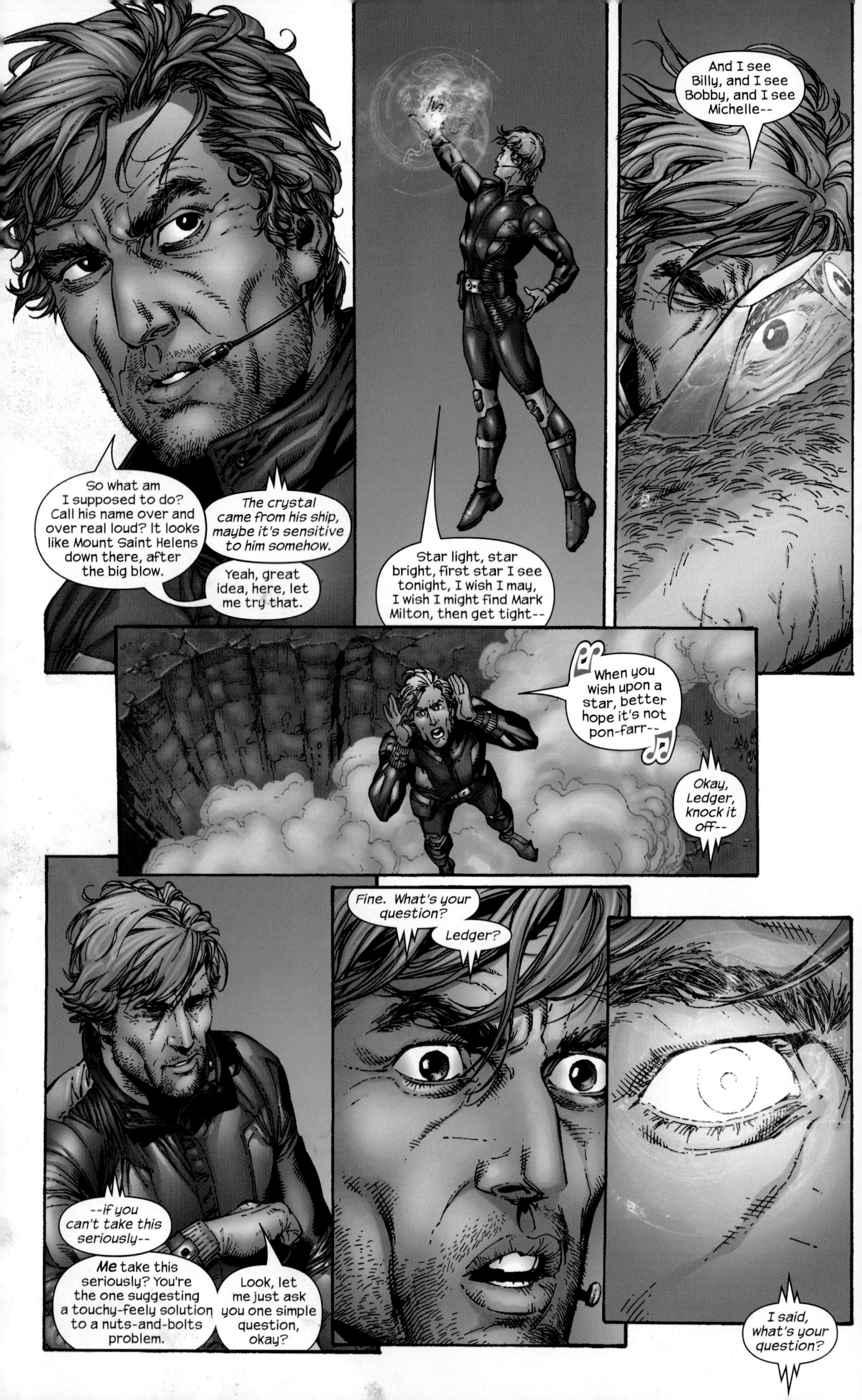
So what am I supposed to do? Call his name over and over real loud? It looks like Mount Saint Helens down there, after the big blow.
The crystal came from his ship, maybe it's sensitive to him somehow.
Yeah, great idea, here, let me try that.
Star light, star bright, first star I see tonight, I wish I may, I wish I might find Mark Milton, then get tight--
And I see Billy, and I see Bobby, and I see Michelle--
When you wish upon a star, better hope it's not pon-farr--
Okay, Ledger, knock it off--
--if you can't take this seriously--
Me take this seriously? You're the one suggesting a touchy-feely solution to a nuts-and-bolts problem.
Look, let me just ask you one simple question, okay?
Fine. What's your question?
Ledger?
I said, what's your question?

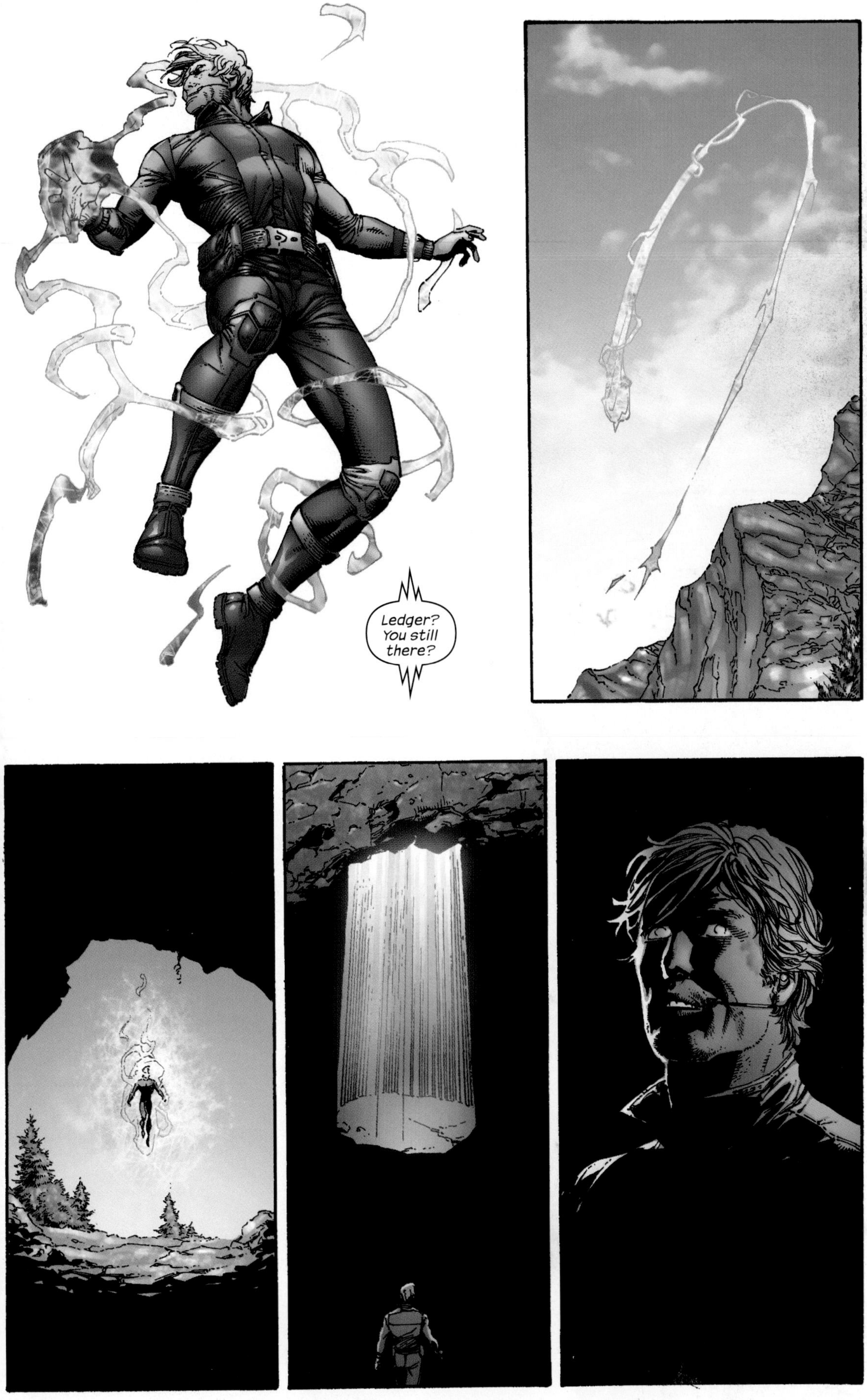
Ledger? You still there?

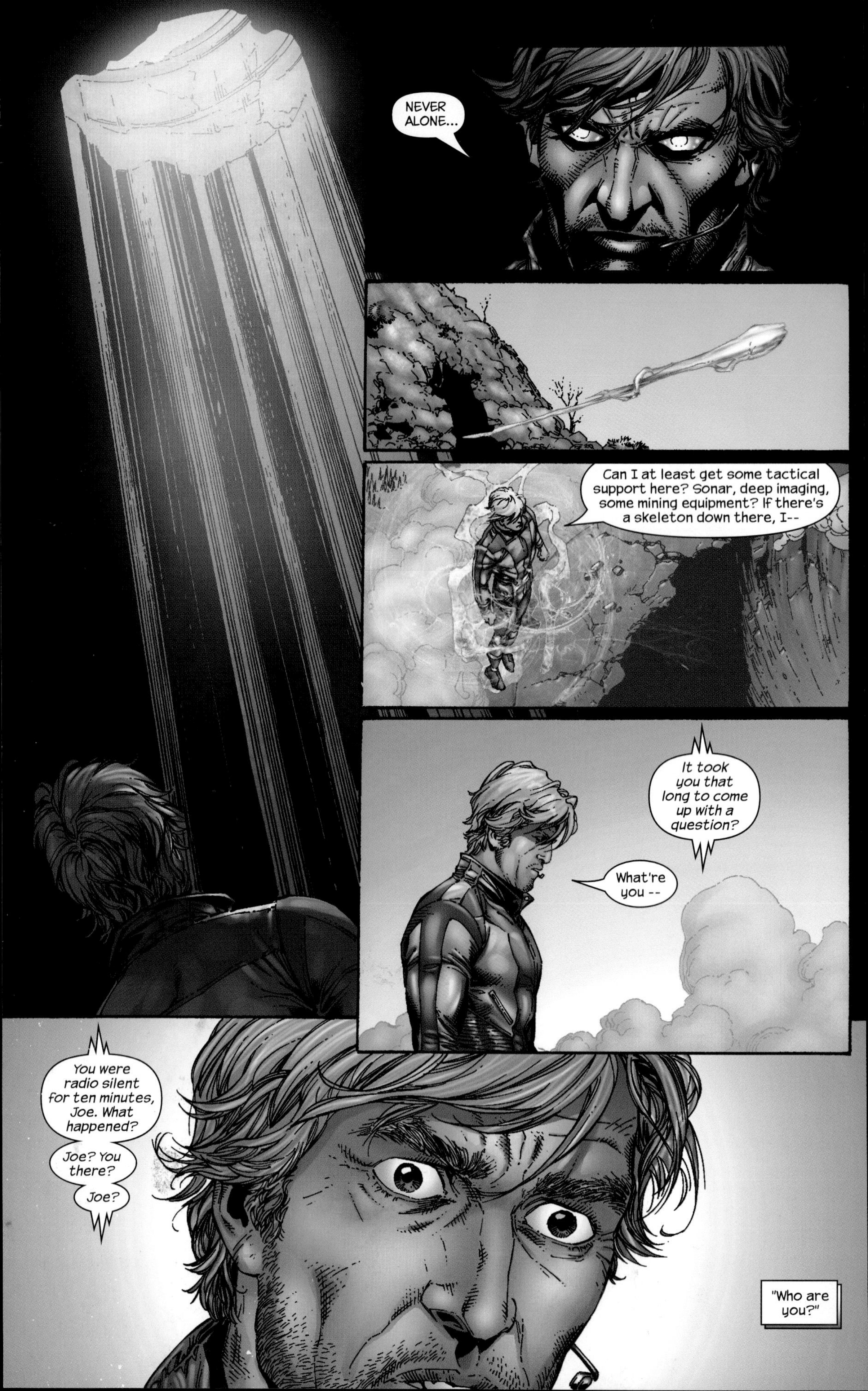

NEVER ALONE...
Can I at least get some tactical support here? Sonar, deep imaging, some mining equipment? If there's a skeleton down there, I--
It took you that long to come up with a question?
What're you --
You were radio silent for ten minutes, Joe. What happened?
Joe? You there?
Joe?
"Who are you?"

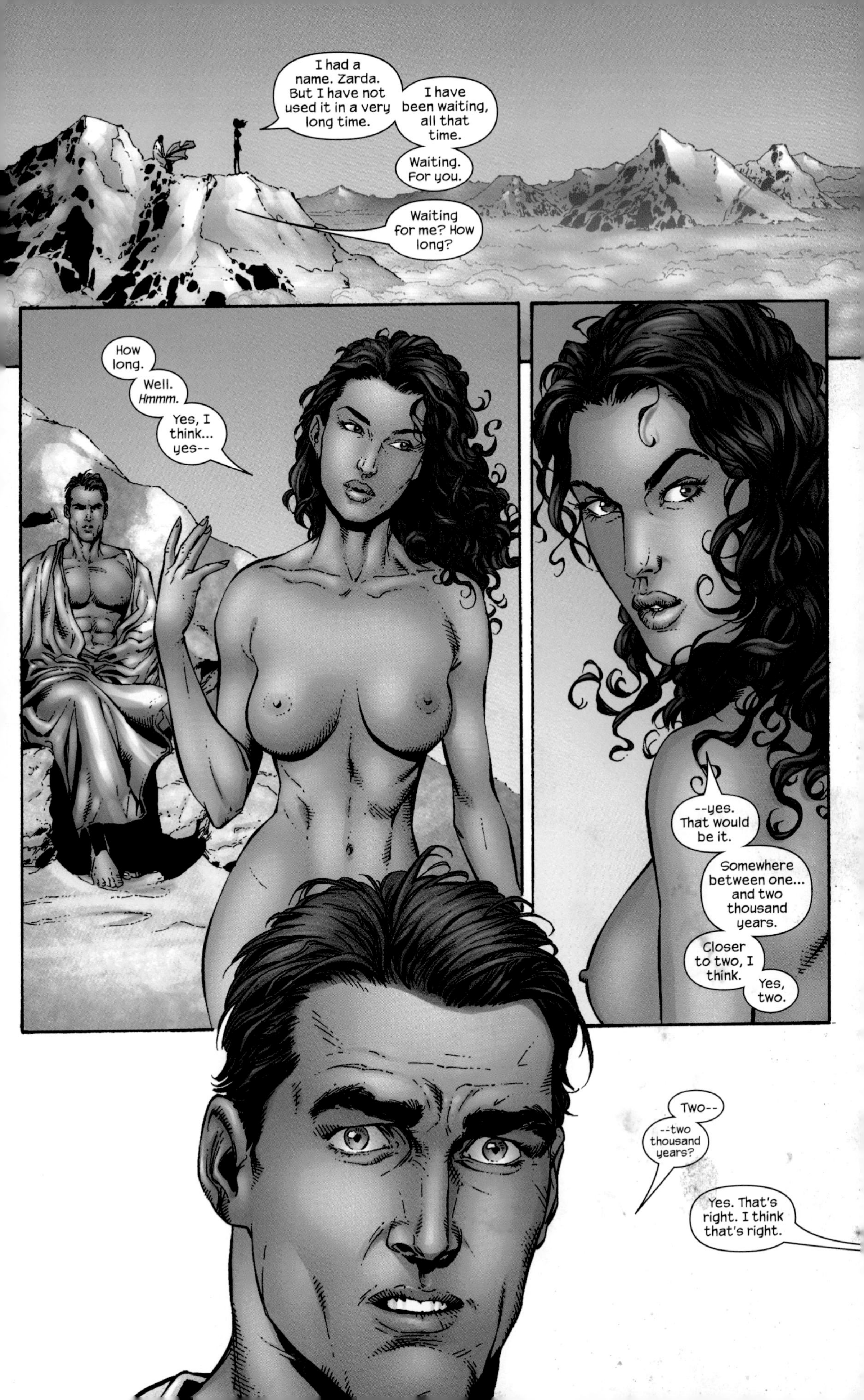
I had a name. Zarda. But I have not used it in a very long time.
I have been waiting, all that time.
Waiting. For you.
Waiting for me? How long?
How long.
Well. *Hmmm.*
Yes, I think... yes--
--yes. That would be it.
Somewhere between one... and two thousand years.
Closer to two, I think.
Yes, two.
Two--
--two thousand years?
Yes. That's right. I think that's right.

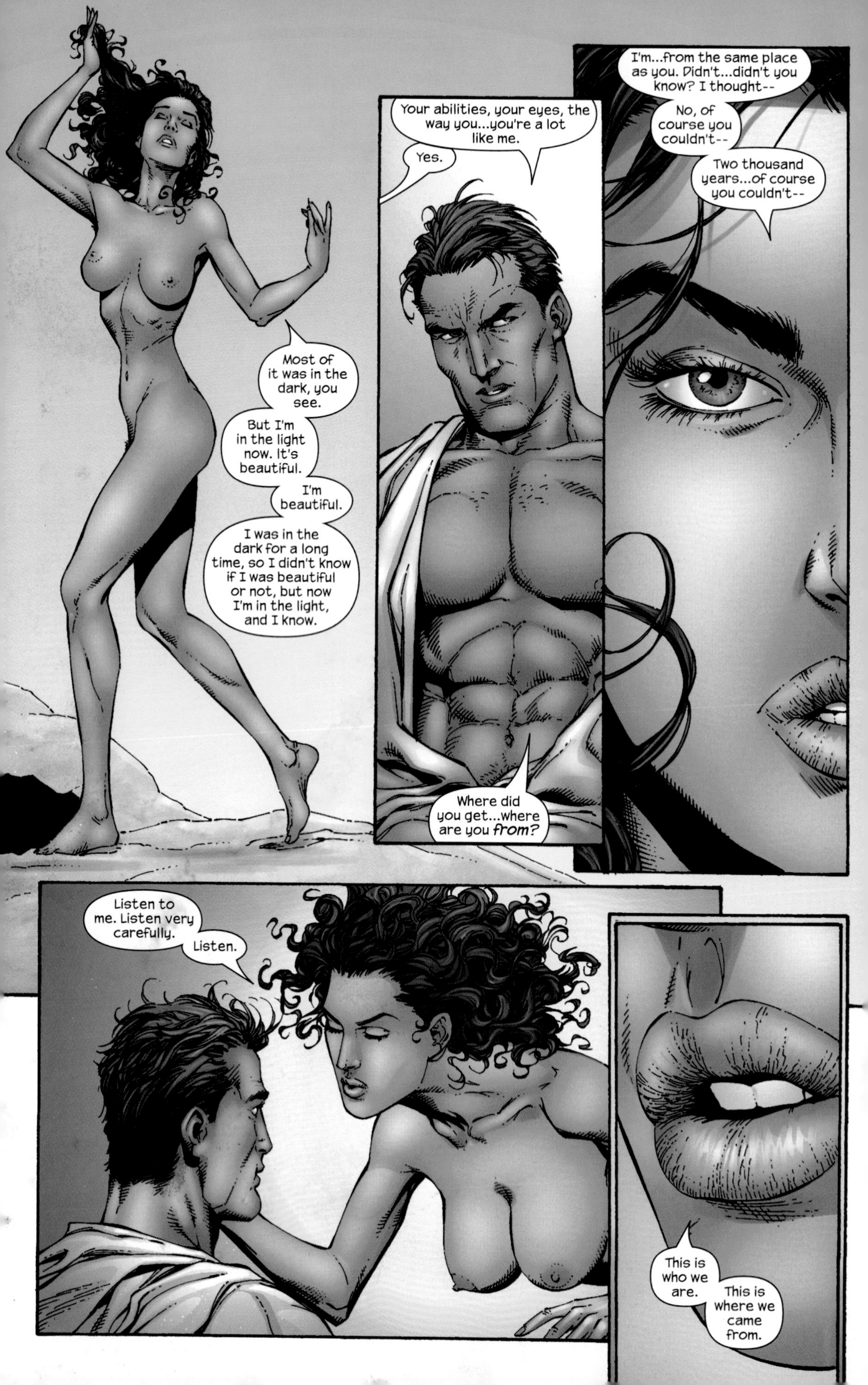
Most of it was in the dark, you see.
But I'm in the light now. It's beautiful.
I'm beautiful.
I was in the dark for a long time, so I didn't know if I was beautiful or not, but now I'm in the light, and I know.
Your abilities, your eyes, the way you...you're a lot like me.
Yes.
Where did you get...where are you *from?*
I'm...from the same place as you. Didn't...didn't you know? I thought--
No, of course you couldn't--
Two thousand years...of course you couldn't--
Listen to me. Listen very carefully.
Listen.
This is who we are.
This is where we came from.

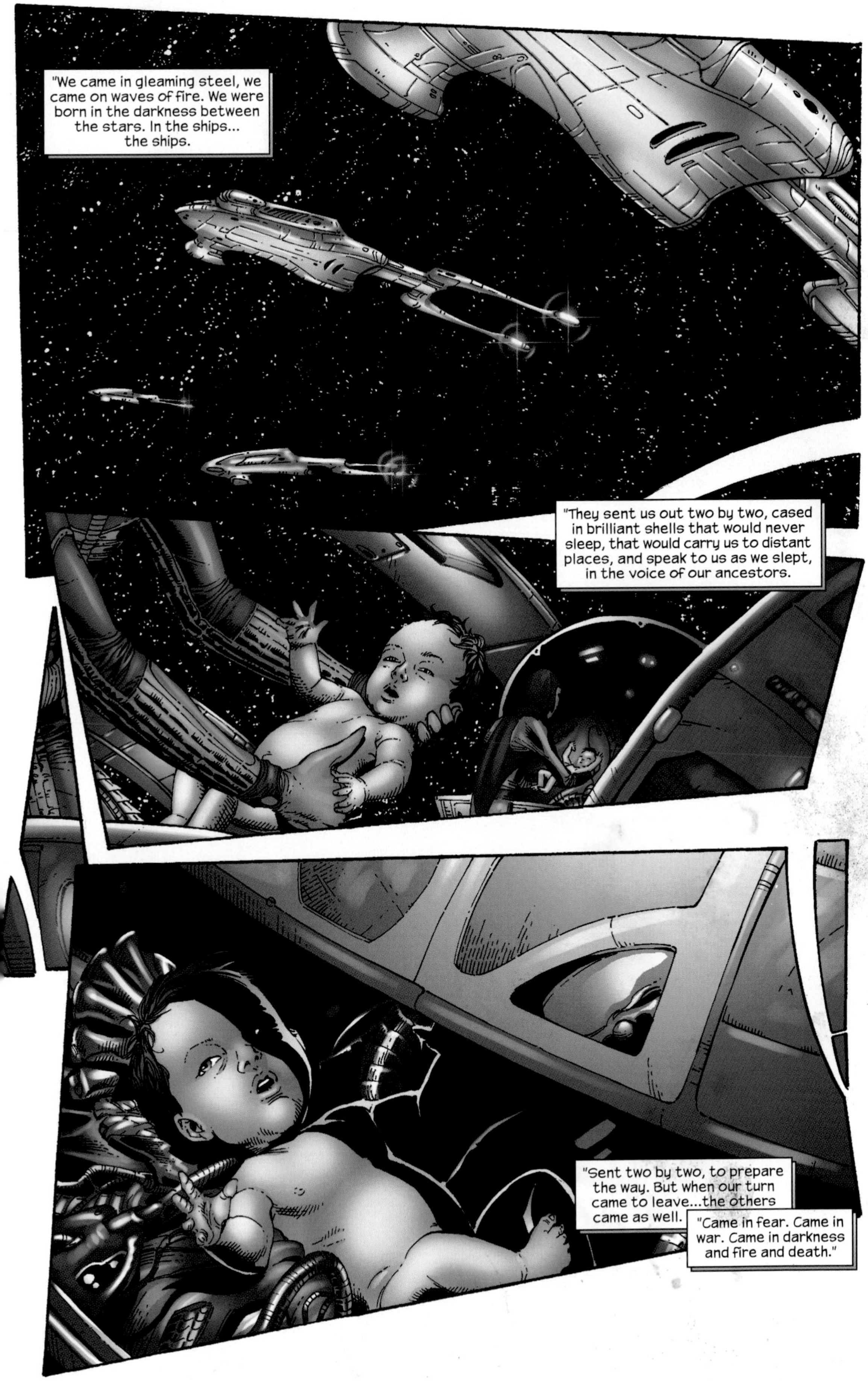
"We came in gleaming steel, we came on waves of fire. We were born in the darkness between the stars. In the ships... the ships.
"They sent us out two by two, cased in brilliant shells that would never sleep, that would carry us to distant places, and speak to us as we slept, in the voice of our ancestors.
"Sent two by two, to prepare the way. But when our turn came to leave...the others came as well.
"Came in fear. Came in war. Came in darkness and fire and death."

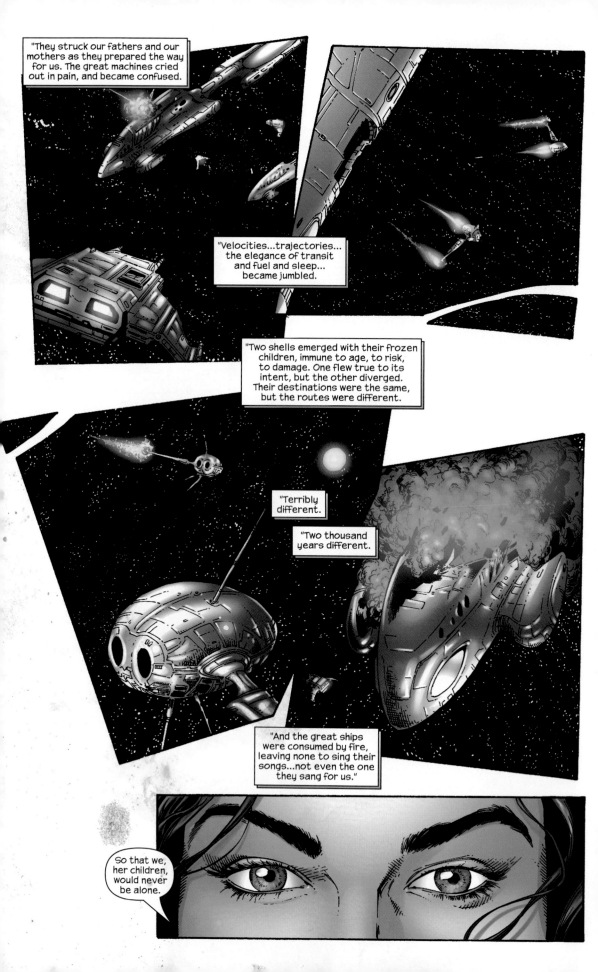

"They struck our fathers and our mothers as they prepared the way for us. The great machines cried out in pain, and became confused.

"Velocities...trajectories...the elegance of transit and fuel and sleep...became jumbled.

"Two shells emerged with their frozen children, immune to age, to risk, to damage. One flew true to its intent, but the other diverged. Their destinations were the same, but the routes were different.

"Terribly different.

"Two thousand years different.

"And the great ships were consumed by fire, leaving none to sing their songs...not even the one they sang for us."

So that we, her children, would never be alone.

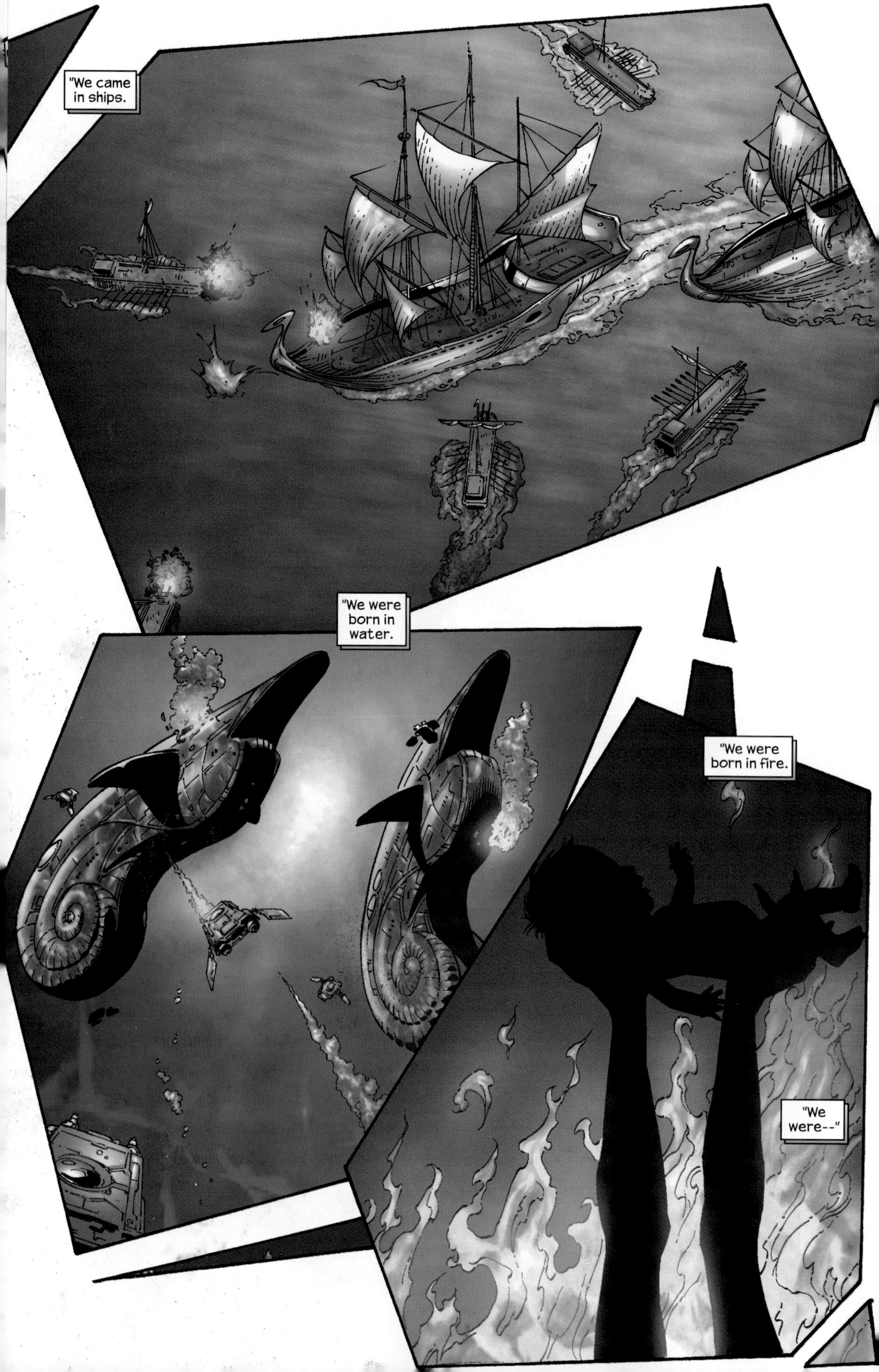
"We came in ships.
"We were born in water.
"We were born in fire.
"We were--"

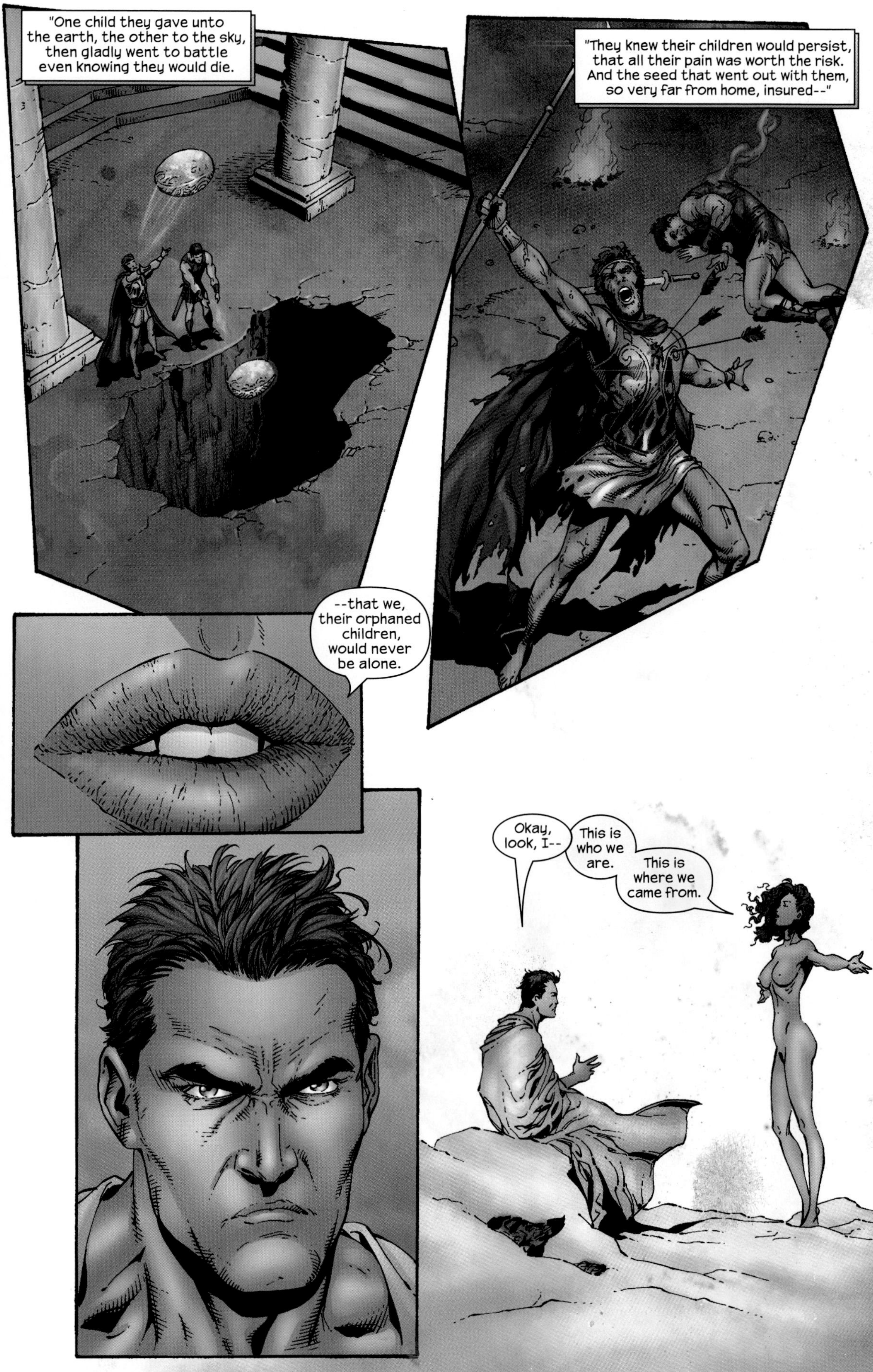
"One child they gave unto the earth, the other to the sky, then gladly went to battle even knowing they would die.
"They knew their children would persist, that all their pain was worth the risk. And the seed that went out with them, so very far from home, insured--"
--that we, their orphaned children, would never be alone.
Okay, look, I--
This is who we are.
This is where we came from.

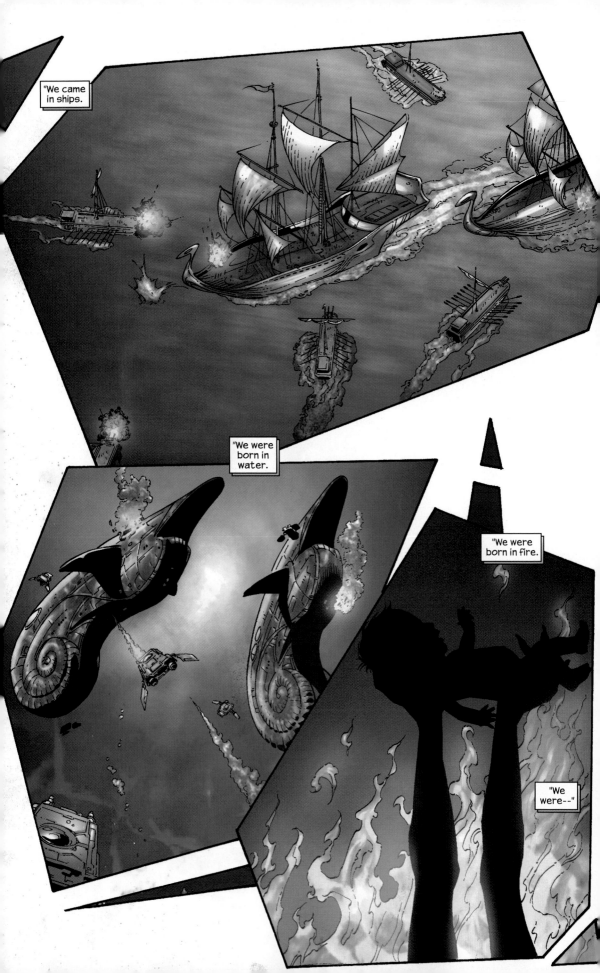

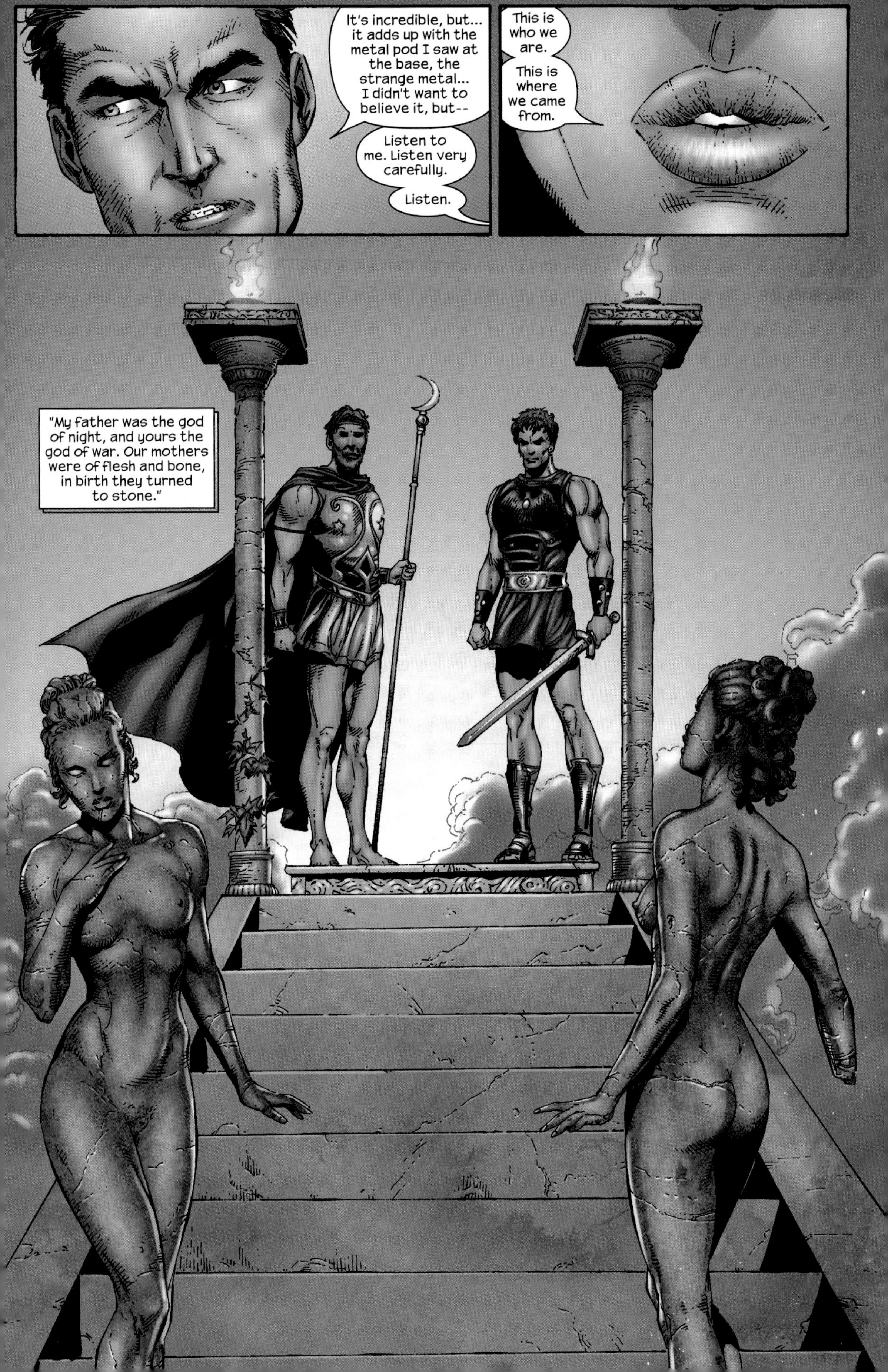
It's incredible, but... it adds up with the metal pod I saw at the base, the strange metal... I didn't want to believe it, but--
Listen to me. Listen very carefully.
Listen.
This is who we are.
This is where we came from.
"My father was the god of night, and yours the god of war. Our mothers were of flesh and bone, in birth they turned to stone."

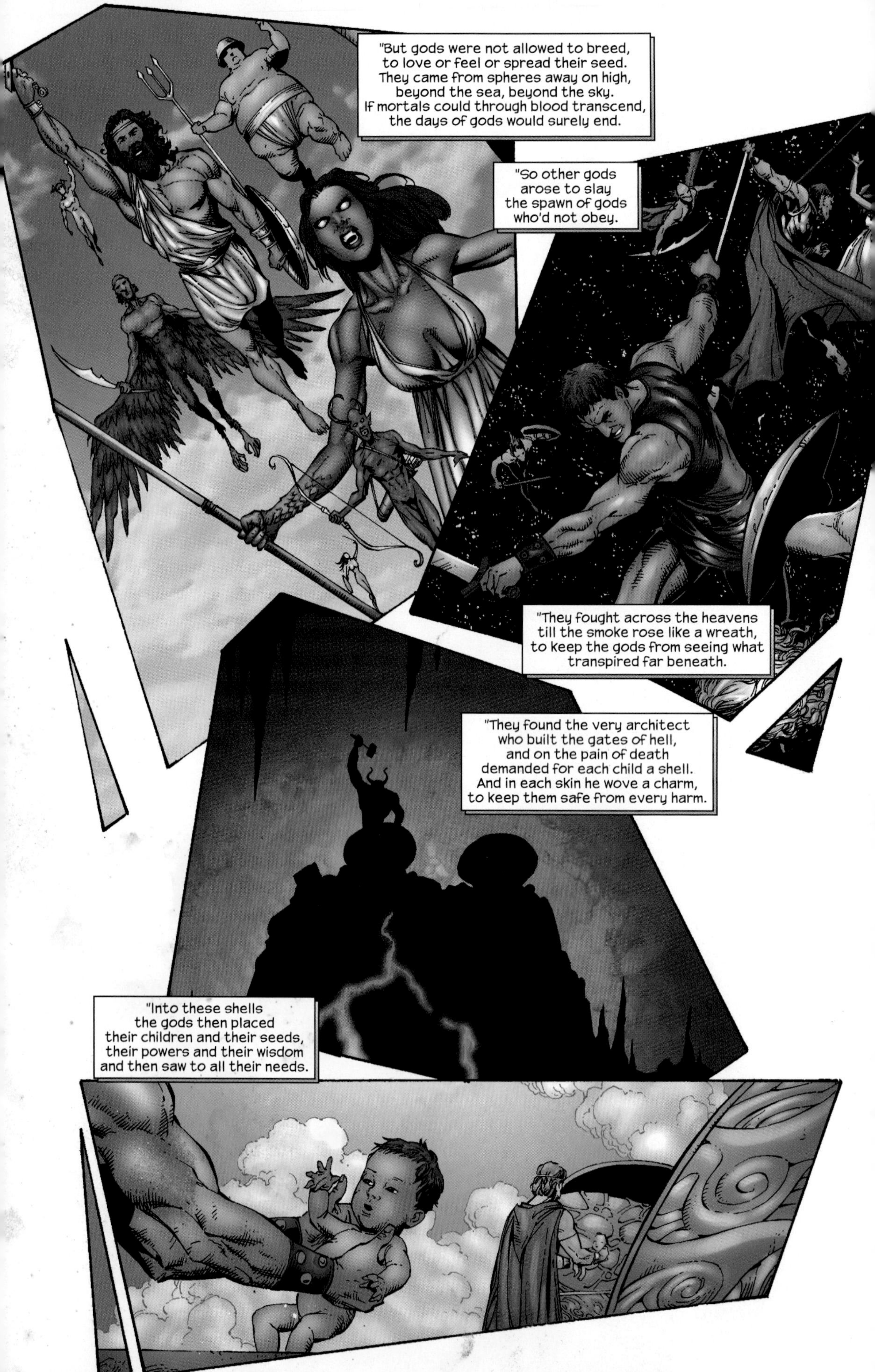
"But gods were not allowed to breed, to love or feel or spread their seed. They came from spheres away on high, beyond the sea, beyond the sky. If mortals could through blood transcend, the days of gods would surely end.
"So other gods arose to slay the spawn of gods who'd not obey.
"They fought across the heavens till the smoke rose like a wreath, to keep the gods from seeing what transpired far beneath.
"They found the very architect who built the gates of hell, and on the pain of death demanded for each child a shell. And in each skin he wove a charm, to keep them safe from every harm.
"Into these shells the gods then placed their children and their seeds, their powers and their wisdom and then saw to all their needs.

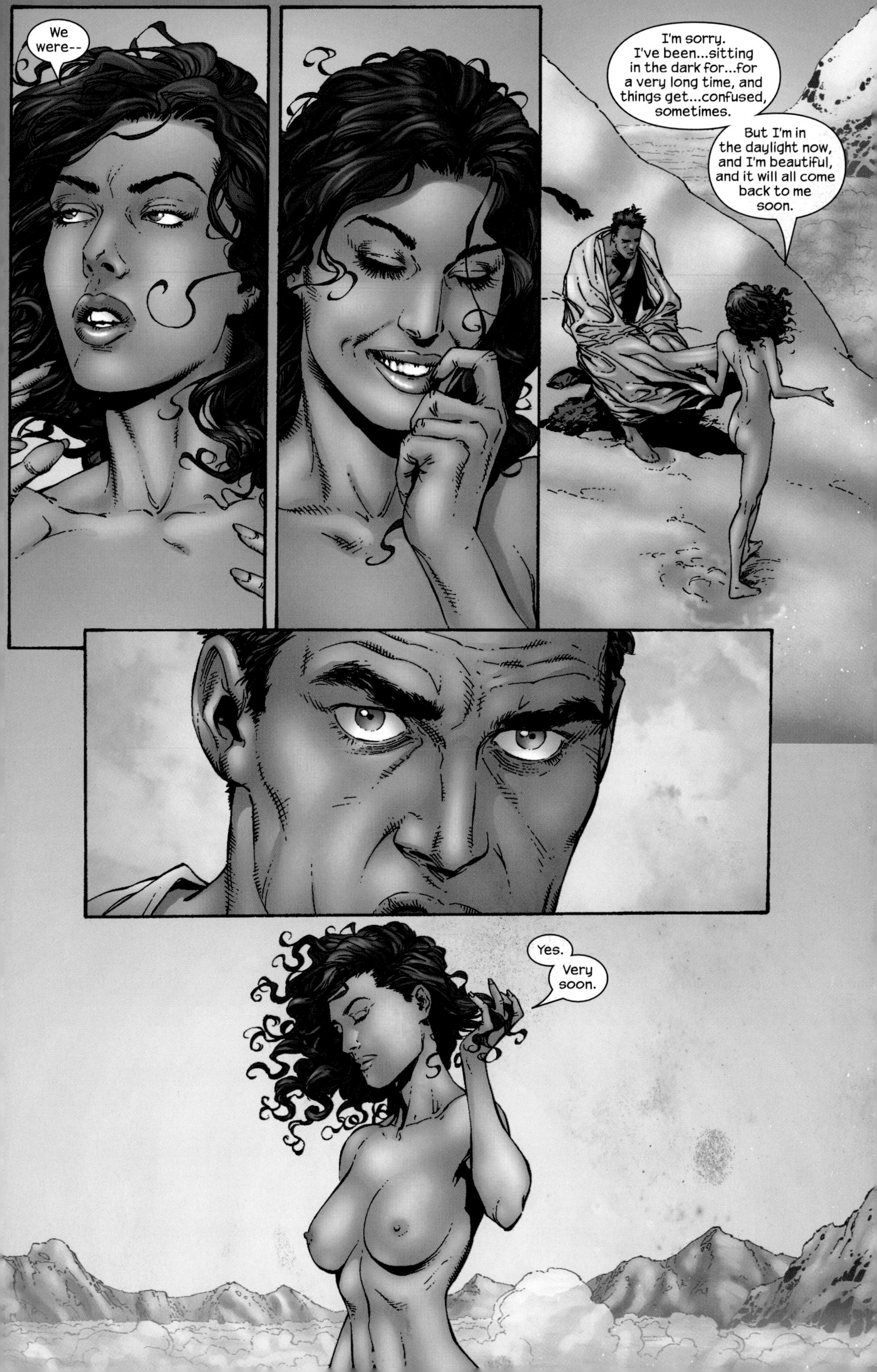
We were--
I'm sorry. I've been...sitting in the dark for...for a very long time, and things get...confused, sometimes.
But I'm in the daylight now, and I'm beautiful, and it will all come back to me soon.
Yes.
Very soon.

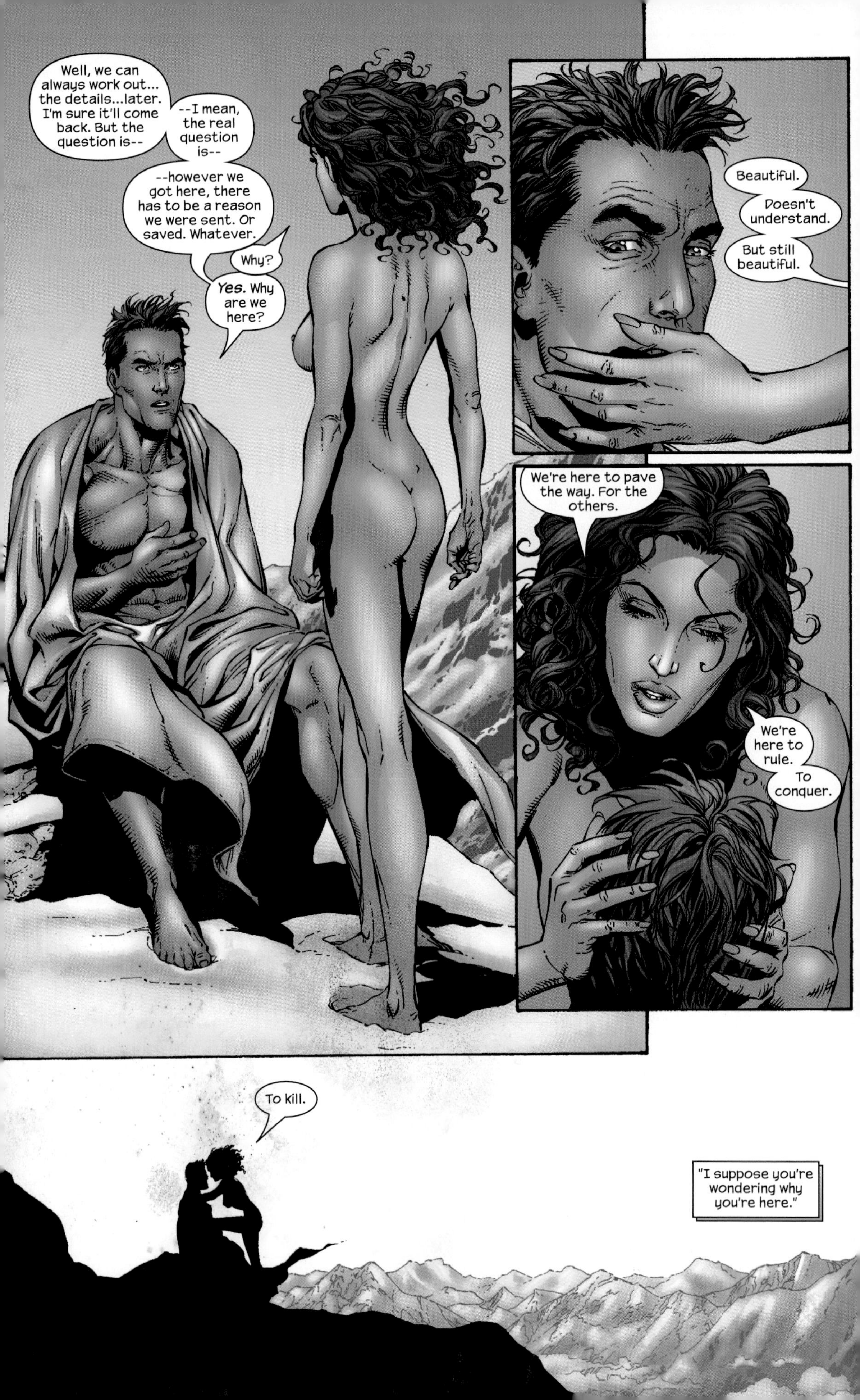

Well, we can always work out... the details...later. I'm sure it'll come back. But the question is--
--I mean, the real question is--
--however we got here, there has to be a reason we were sent. Or saved. Whatever.
Why?
Yes. Why are we here?
Beautiful.
Doesn't understand.
But still beautiful.
We're here to pave the way. For the others.
We're here to rule.
To conquer.
To kill.
"I suppose you're wondering why you're here."

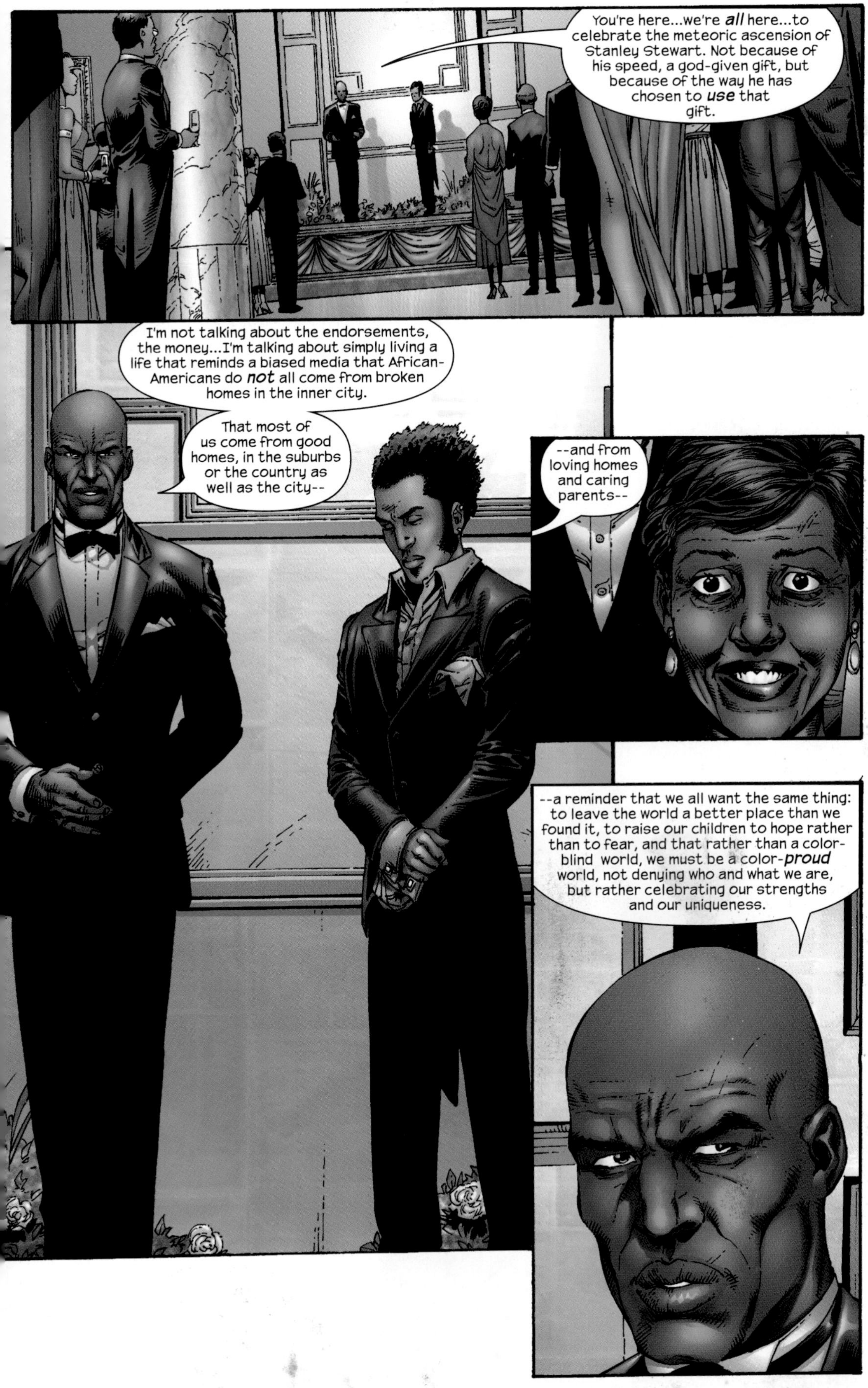
You're here...we're all here...to celebrate the meteoric ascension of Stanley Stewart. Not because of his speed, a god-given gift, but because of the way he has chosen to use that gift.
I'm not talking about the endorsements, the money...I'm talking about simply living a life that reminds a biased media that African-Americans do not all come from broken homes in the inner city.
That most of us come from good homes, in the suburbs or the country as well as the city--
--and from loving homes and caring parents--
--a reminder that we all want the same thing: to leave the world a better place than we found it, to raise our children to hope rather than to fear, and that rather than a color-blind world, we must be a color-proud world, not denying who and what we are, but rather celebrating our strengths and our uniqueness.

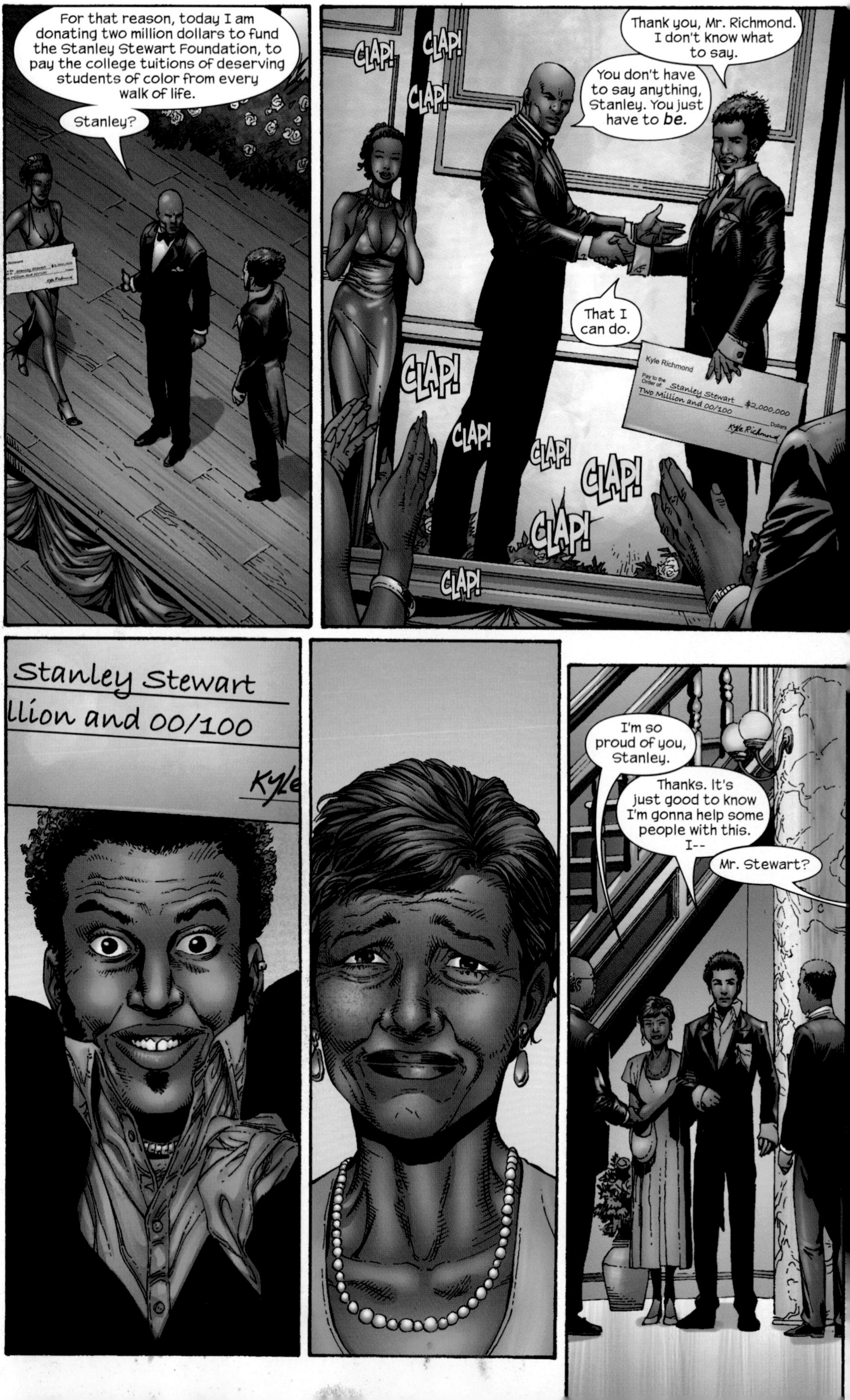
For that reason, today I am donating two million dollars to fund the Stanley Stewart Foundation, to pay the college tuitions of deserving students of color from every walk of life.
Stanley?
CLAP!
CLAP!
CLAP!
Thank you, Mr. Richmond. I don't know what to say.
You don't have to say anything, Stanley. You just have to *be.*
That I can do.
Kyle Richmond
Pay to the Order of: Stanley Stewart $2,000,000
Two Million and 00/100 Dollars
Kyle Richmond
CLAP!
CLAP!
CLAP!
CLAP!
CLAP!
CLAP!
Stanley Stewart
llion and 00/100
Kyle
I'm so proud of you, Stanley.
Thanks. It's just good to know I'm gonna help some people with this. I--
Mr. Stewart?

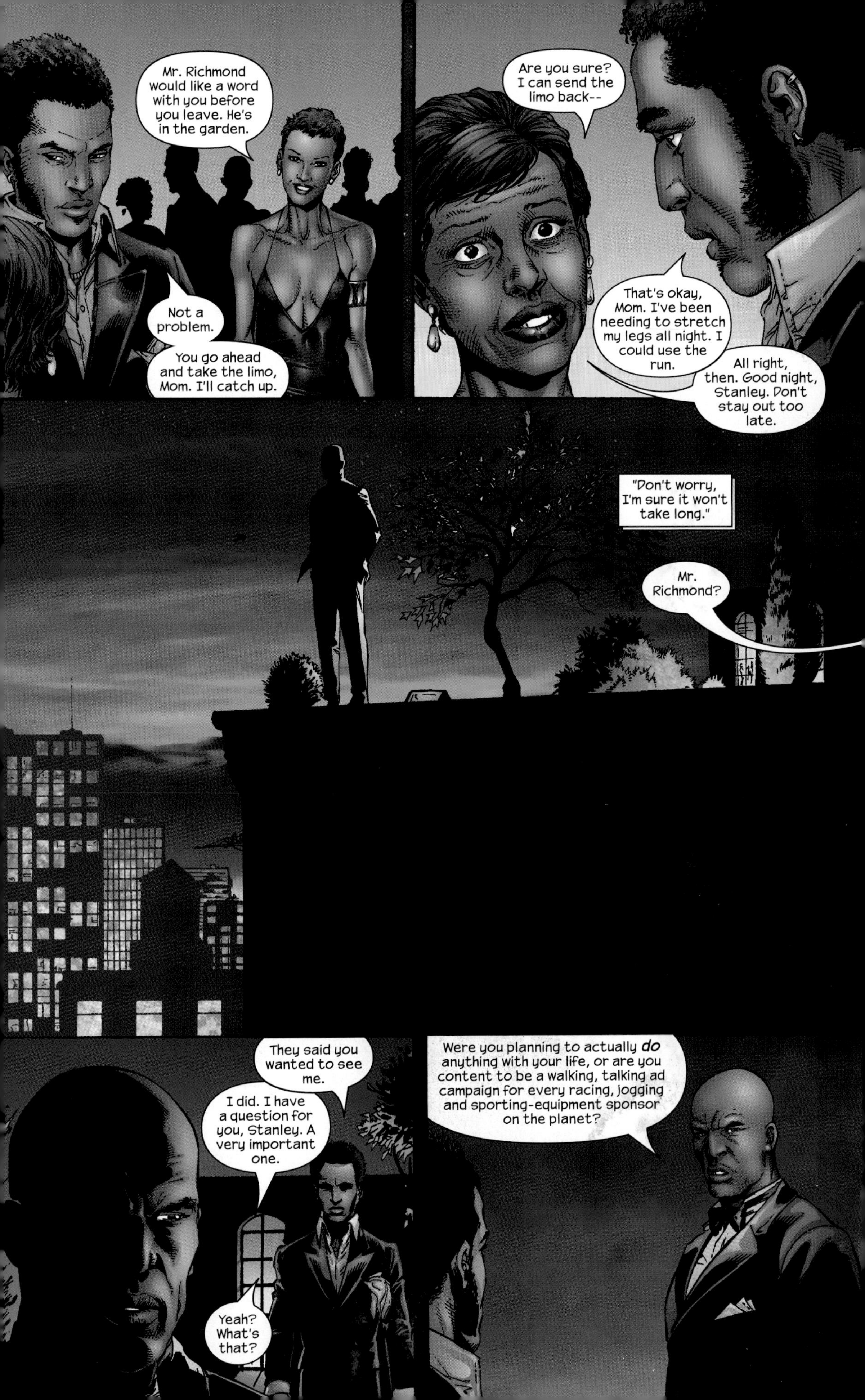

Mr. Richmond would like a word with you before you leave. He's in the garden.
Not a problem.
You go ahead and take the limo, Mom. I'll catch up.
Are you sure? I can send the limo back--
That's okay, Mom. I've been needing to stretch my legs all night. I could use the run.
All right, then. Good night, Stanley. Don't stay out too late.
"Don't worry, I'm sure it won't take long."
Mr. Richmond?
They said you wanted to see me.
I did. I have a question for you, Stanley. A very important one.
Yeah? What's that?
Were you planning to actually do anything with your life, or are you content to be a walking, talking ad campaign for every racing, jogging and sporting-equipment sponsor on the planet?

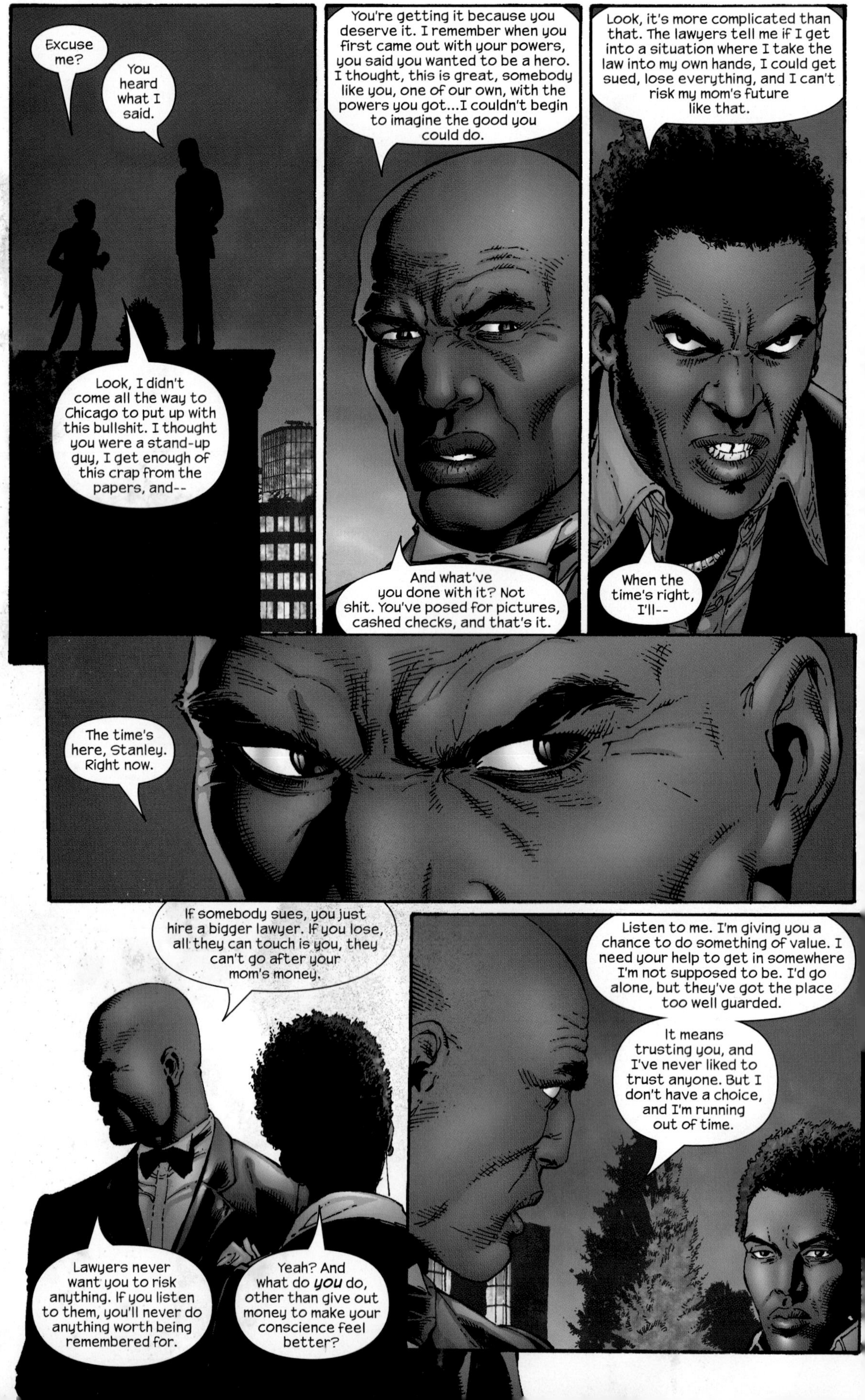
Excuse me?
You heard what I said.
Look, I didn't come all the way to Chicago to put up with this bullshit. I thought you were a stand-up guy, I get enough of this crap from the papers, and--
You're getting it because you deserve it. I remember when you first came out with your powers, you said you wanted to be a hero. I thought, this is great, somebody like you, one of our own, with the powers you got...I couldn't begin to imagine the good you could do.
And what've you done with it? Not shit. You've posed for pictures, cashed checks, and that's it.
Look, it's more complicated than that. The lawyers tell me if I get into a situation where I take the law into my own hands, I could get sued, lose everything, and I can't risk my mom's future like that.
When the time's right, I'll--
The time's here, Stanley. Right now.
If somebody sues, you just hire a bigger lawyer. If you lose, all they can touch is you, they can't go after your mom's money.
Lawyers never want you to risk anything. If you listen to them, you'll never do anything worth being remembered for.
Yeah? And what do *you* do, other than give out money to make your conscience feel better?
Listen to me. I'm giving you a chance to do something of value. I need your help to get in somewhere I'm not supposed to be. I'd go alone, but they've got the place too well guarded.
It means trusting you, and I've never liked to trust anyone. But I don't have a choice, and I'm running out of time.

Take this. There's an address on the back. It cost me a lot to get that address, so don't let it get away.

Watch the news tonight. If you understand where I'm coming from, meet me there at midnight. If not...

Then not, that's all.

Good night, Stanley.

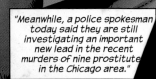

"Meanwhile, a police spokesman today said they are still investigating an important new lead in the recent murders of nine prostitutes in the Chicago area."

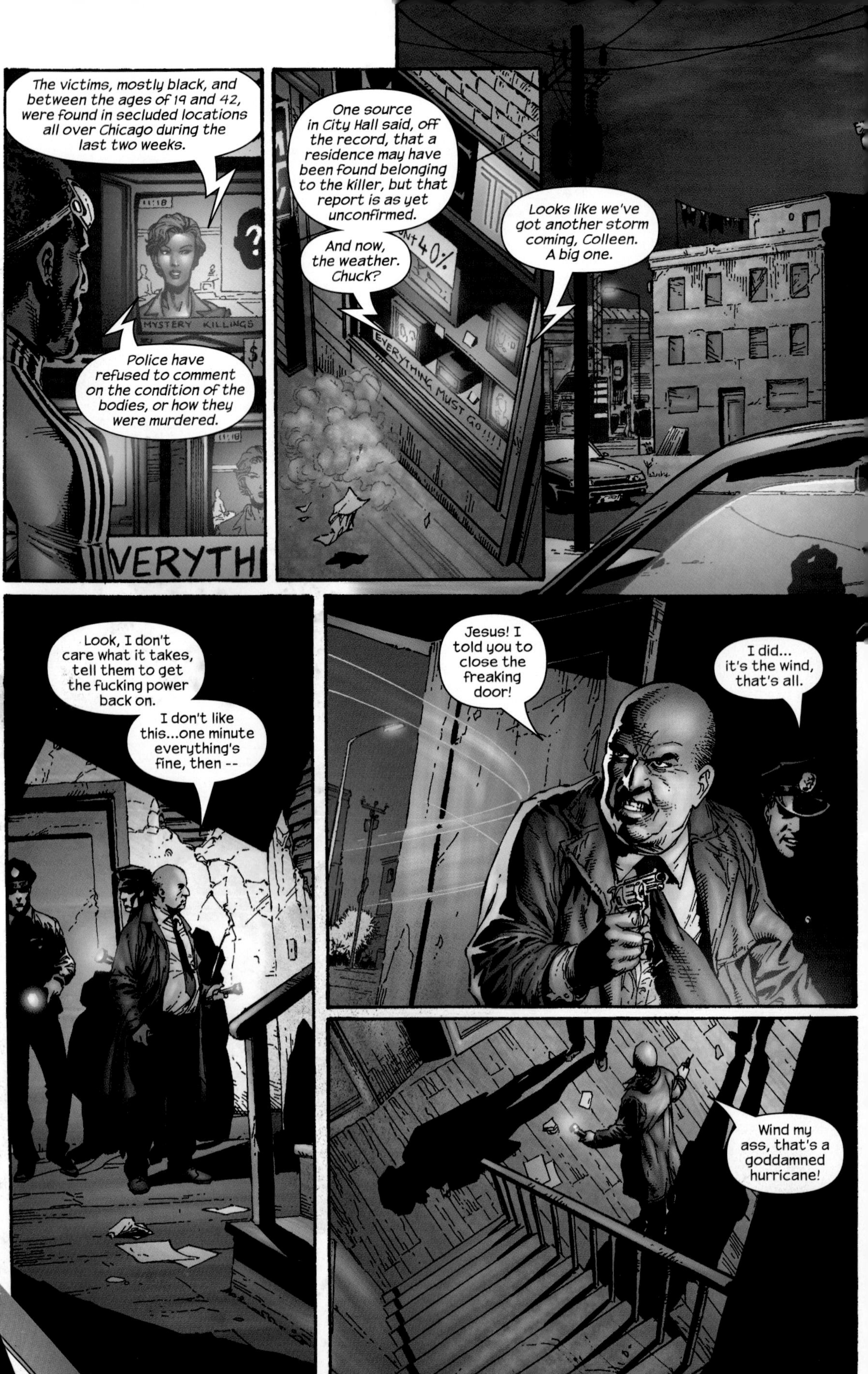
The victims, mostly black, and between the ages of 19 and 42, were found in secluded locations all over Chicago during the last two weeks.
MYSTERY KILLINGS
Police have refused to comment on the condition of the bodies, or how they were murdered.
VERYTH
One source in City Hall said, off the record, that a residence may have been found belonging to the killer, but that report is as yet unconfirmed.
And now, the weather. Chuck?
Looks like we've got another storm coming, Colleen. A big one.
EVERYTHING MUST GO!!!!
Look, I don't care what it takes, tell them to get the fucking power back on.
I don't like this...one minute everything's fine, then --
Jesus! I told you to close the freaking door!
I did... it's the wind, that's all.
Wind my ass, that's a goddamned hurricane!

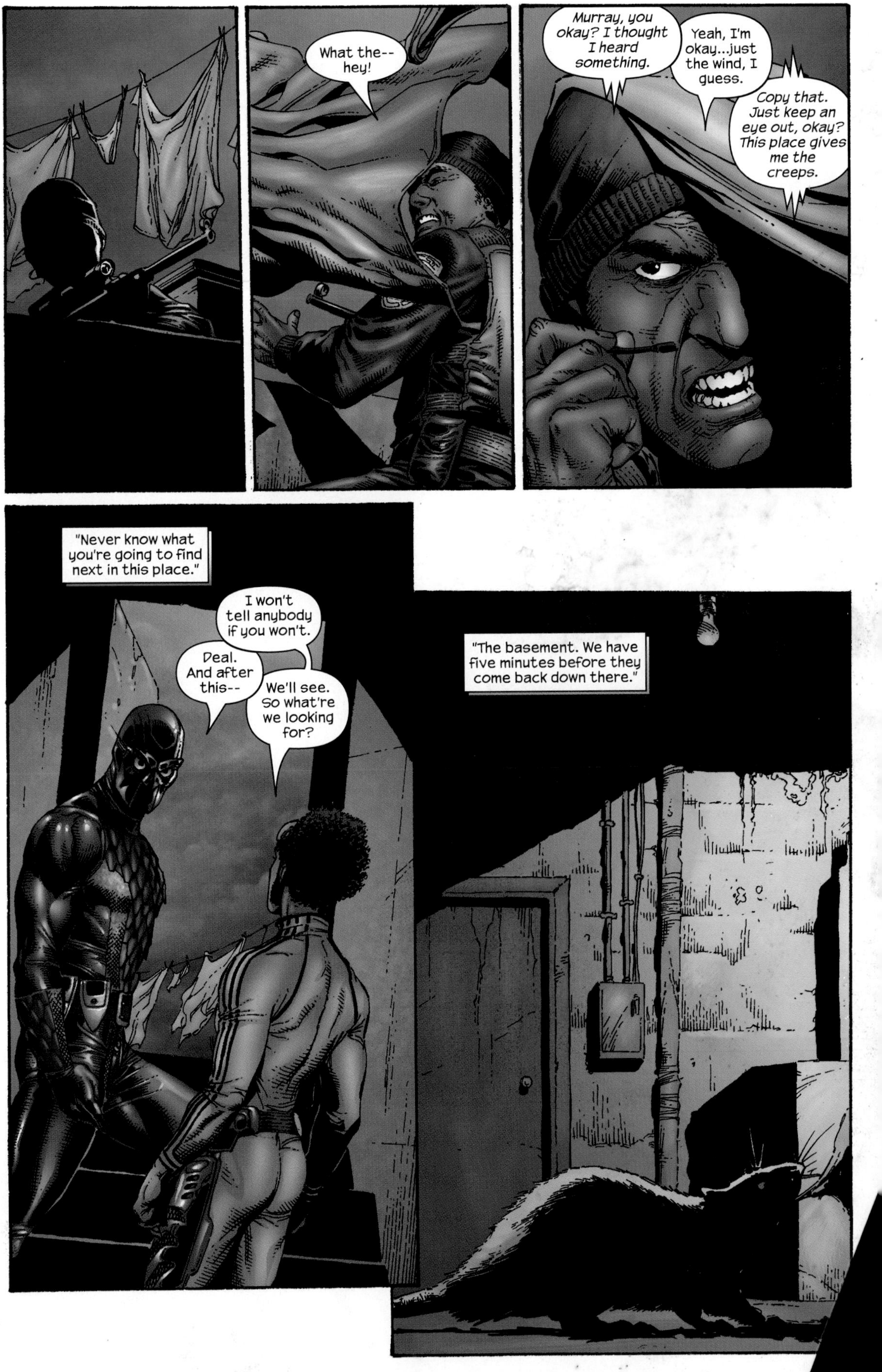
What the--
hey!
Murray, you okay? I thought I heard something.
Yeah, I'm okay...just the wind, I guess.
Copy that. Just keep an eye out, okay? This place gives me the creeps.
"Never know what you're going to find next in this place."
I won't tell anybody if you won't.
Deal. And after this--
We'll see. So what're we looking for?
"The basement. We have five minutes before they come back down there."

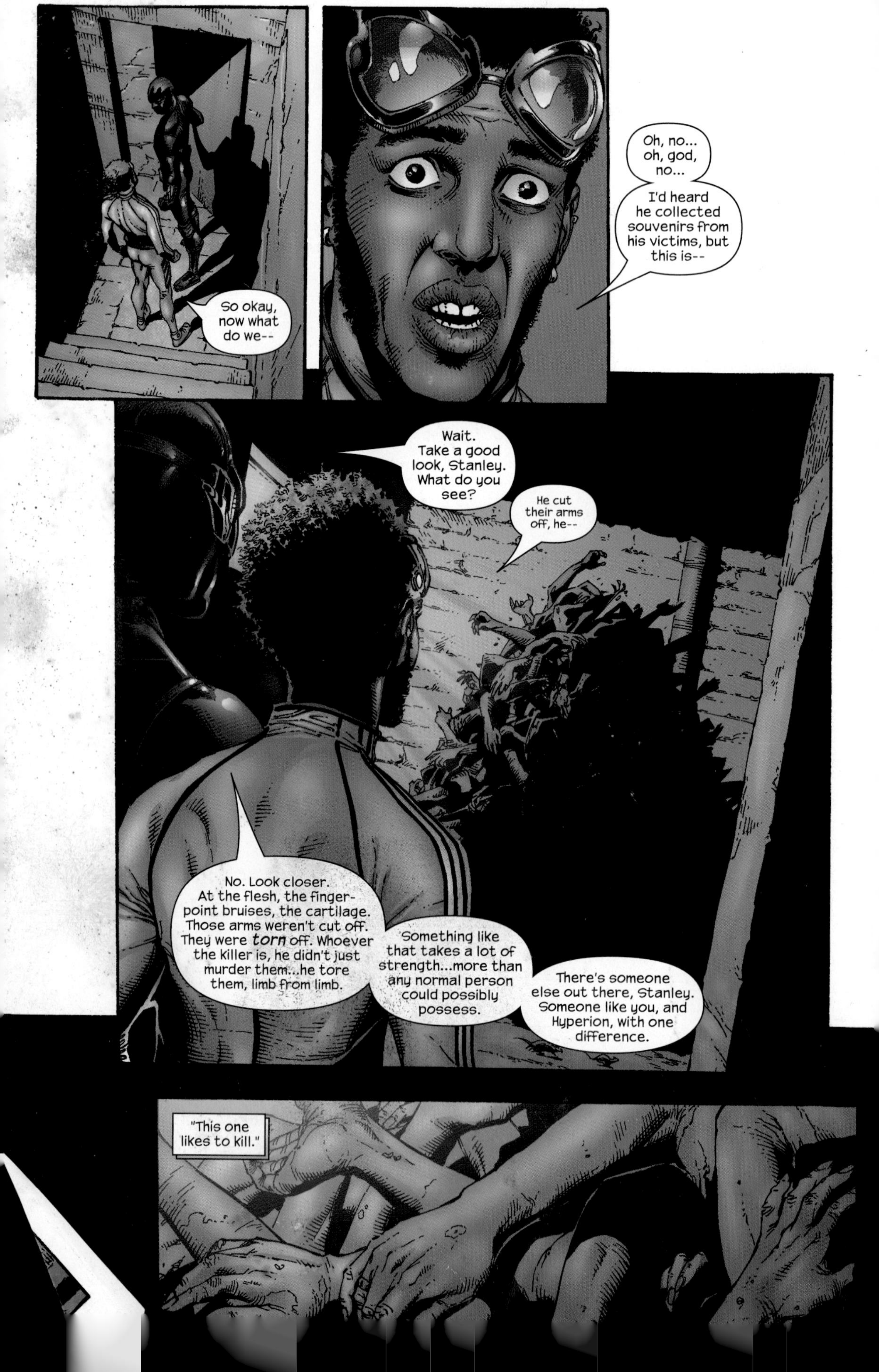
So okay, now what do we--
Oh, no... oh, god, no...
I'd heard he collected souvenirs from his victims, but this is--
Wait. Take a good look, Stanley. What do you see?
He cut their arms off, he--
No. Look closer. At the flesh, the finger-point bruises, the cartilage. Those arms weren't cut off. They were *torn* off. Whoever the killer is, he didn't just murder them...he tore them, limb from limb.
Something like that takes a lot of strength...more than any normal person could possibly possess.
There's someone else out there, Stanley. Someone like you, and Hyperion, with one difference.
"This one likes to kill."

#12

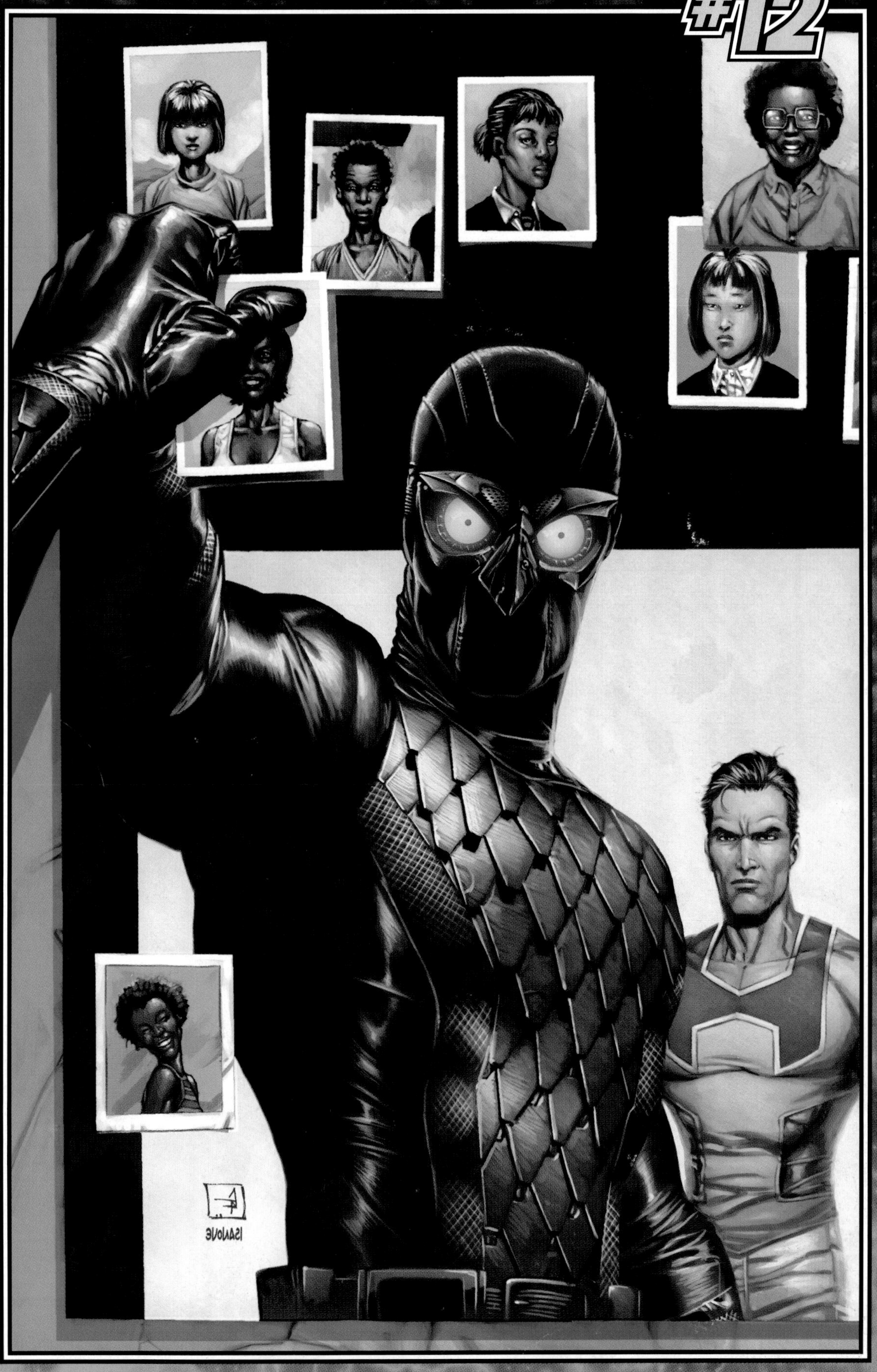

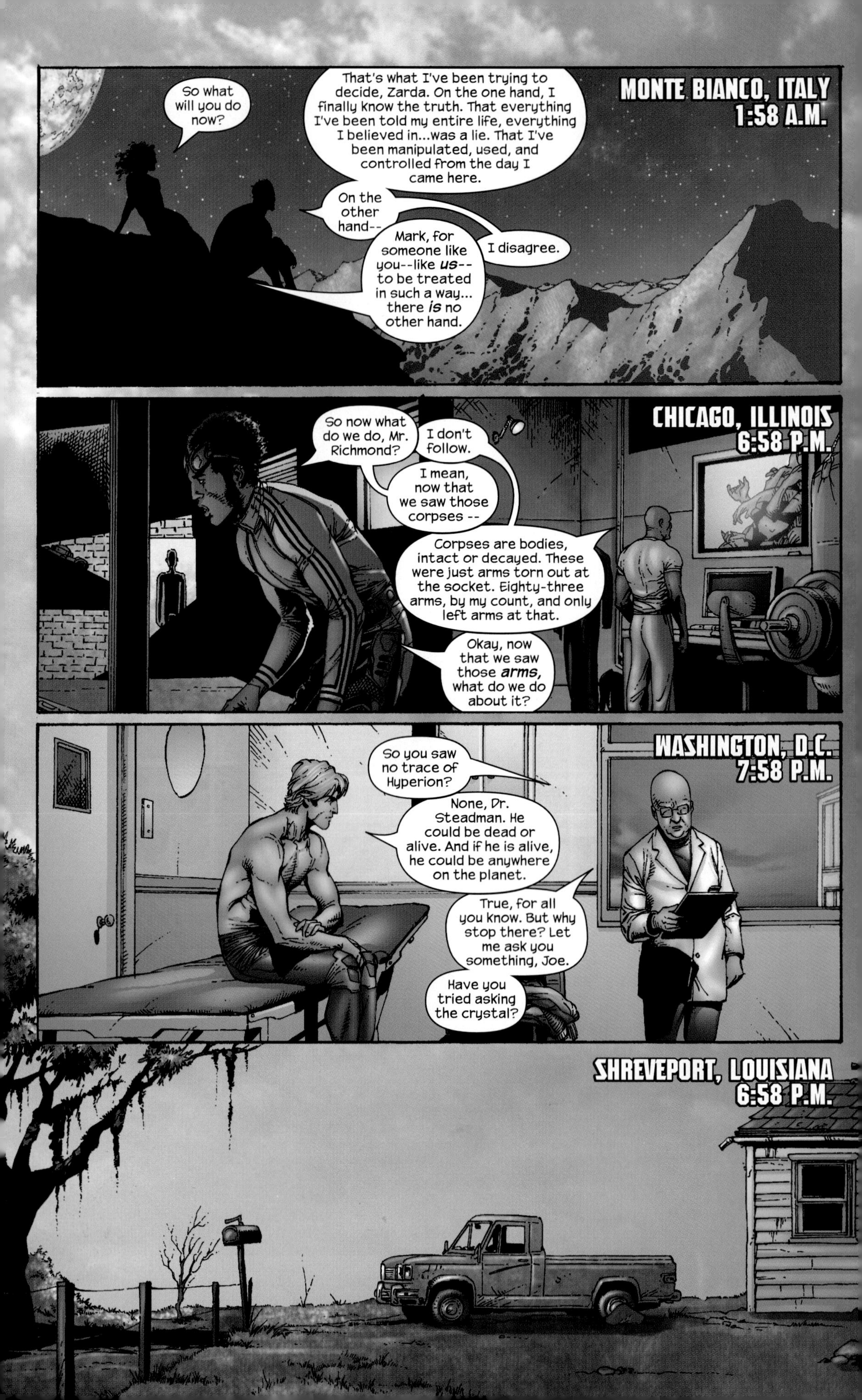
MONTE BIANCO, ITALY 1:58 A.M.
So what will you do now?
That's what I've been trying to decide, Zarda. On the one hand, I finally know the truth. That everything I've been told my entire life, everything I believed in...was a lie. That I've been manipulated, used, and controlled from the day I came here.
On the other hand--
I disagree.
Mark, for someone like you--like us--to be treated in such a way... there is no other hand.
CHICAGO, ILLINOIS 6:58 P.M.
So now what do we do, Mr. Richmond?
I don't follow.
I mean, now that we saw those corpses --
Corpses are bodies, intact or decayed. These were just arms torn out at the socket. Eighty-three arms, by my count, and only left arms at that.
Okay, now that we saw those arms, what do we do about it?
WASHINGTON, D.C. 7:58 P.M.
So you saw no trace of Hyperion?
None, Dr. Steadman. He could be dead or alive. And if he is alive, he could be anywhere on the planet.
True, for all you know. But why stop there? Let me ask you something, Joe.
Have you tried asking the crystal?
SHREVEPORT, LOUISIANA 6:58 P.M.

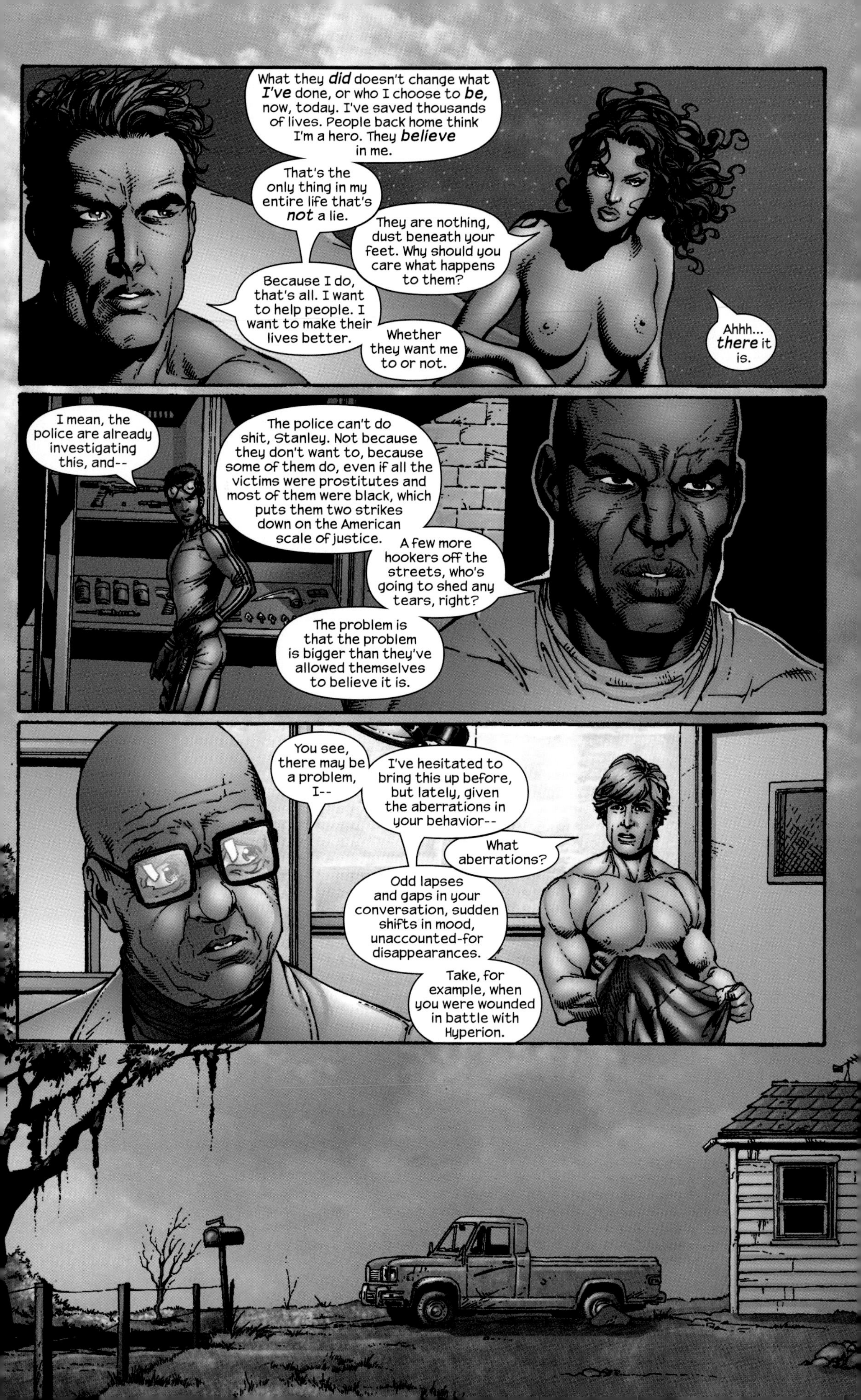
What they *did* doesn't change what *I've* done, or who I choose to *be,* now, today. I've saved thousands of lives. People back home think I'm a hero. They *believe* in me.
That's the only thing in my entire life that's *not* a lie.
They are nothing, dust beneath your feet. Why should you care what happens to them?
Because I do, that's all. I want to help people. I want to make their lives better.
Whether they want me to or not.
Ahhh... *there* it is.
I mean, the police are already investigating this, and--
The police can't do shit, Stanley. Not because they don't want to, because some of them do, even if all the victims were prostitutes and most of them were black, which puts them two strikes down on the American scale of justice.
A few more hookers off the streets, who's going to shed any tears, right?
The problem is that the problem is bigger than they've allowed themselves to believe it is.
You see, there may be a problem, I--
I've hesitated to bring this up before, but lately, given the aberrations in your behavior--
What aberrations?
Odd lapses and gaps in your conversation, sudden shifts in mood, unaccounted-for disappearances.
Take, for example, when you were wounded in battle with Hyperion.

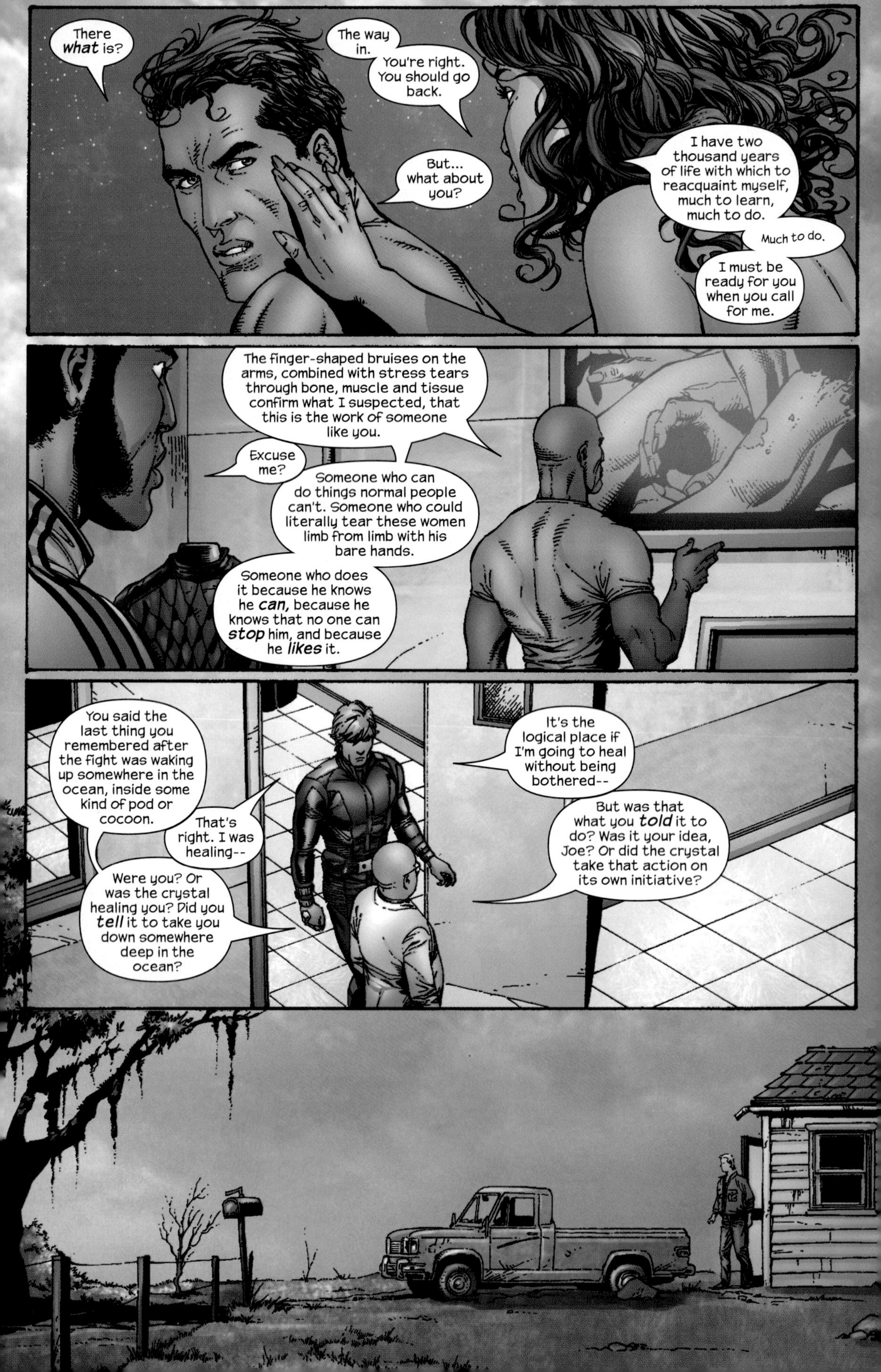
There what is?
The way in.
You're right. You should go back.
But... what about you?
I have two thousand years of life with which to reacquaint myself, much to learn, much to do.
Much to do.
I must be ready for you when you call for me.
The finger-shaped bruises on the arms, combined with stress tears through bone, muscle and tissue confirm what I suspected, that this is the work of someone like you.
Excuse me?
Someone who can do things normal people can't. Someone who could literally tear these women limb from limb with his bare hands.
Someone who does it because he knows he can, because he knows that no one can stop him, and because he likes it.
You said the last thing you remembered after the fight was waking up somewhere in the ocean, inside some kind of pod or cocoon.
That's right. I was healing--
Were you? Or was the crystal healing you? Did you tell it to take you down somewhere deep in the ocean?
It's the logical place if I'm going to heal without being bothered--
But was that what you told it to do? Was it your idea, Joe? Or did the crystal take that action on its own initiative?

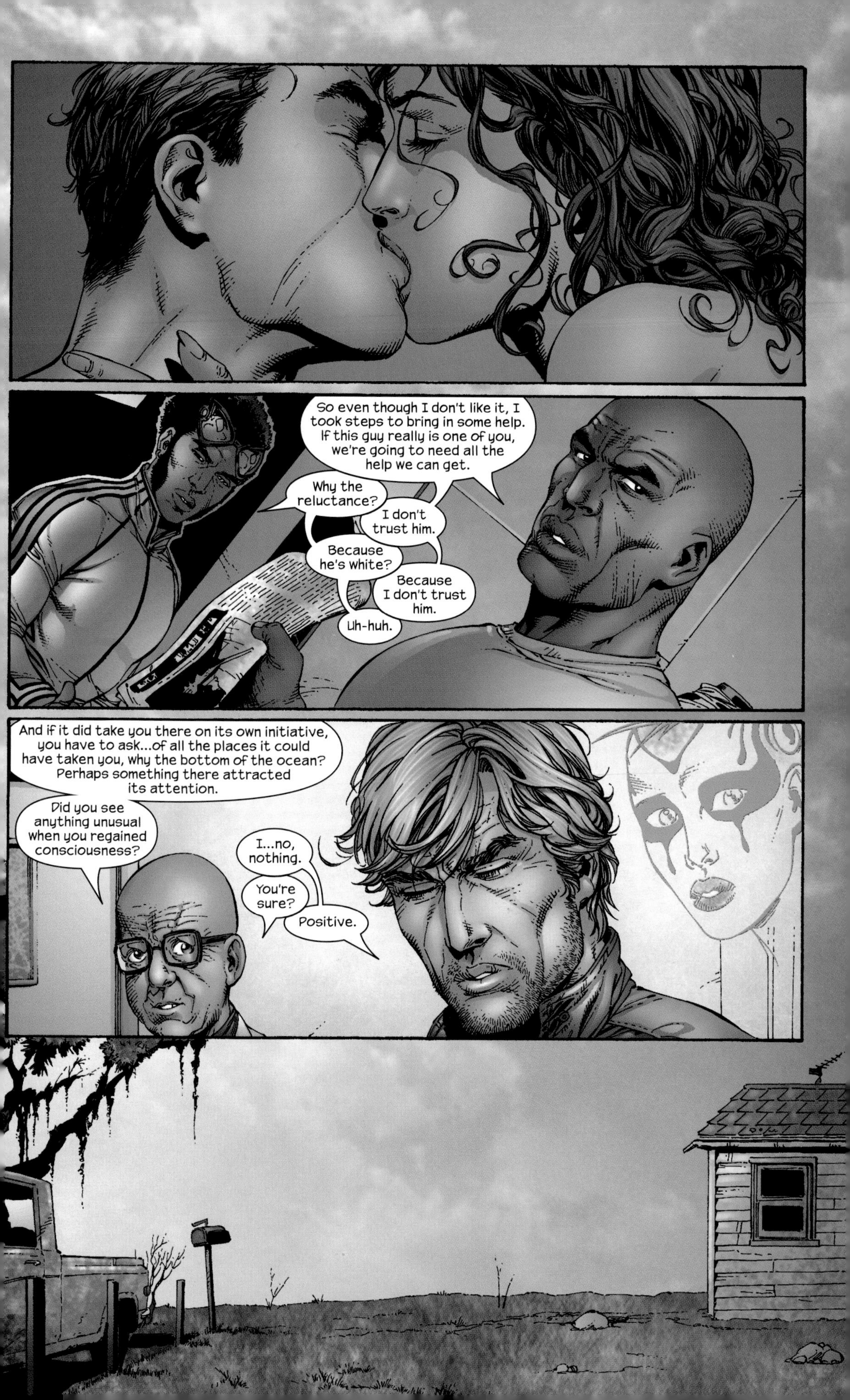
So even though I don't like it, I took steps to bring in some help. If this guy really is one of you, we're going to need all the help we can get.
Why the reluctance?
I don't trust him.
Because he's white?
Because I don't trust him.
Uh-huh.
And if it did take you there on its own initiative, you have to ask...of all the places it could have taken you, why the bottom of the ocean? Perhaps something there attracted its attention.
Did you see anything unusual when you regained consciousness?
I...no, nothing.
You're sure?
Positive.

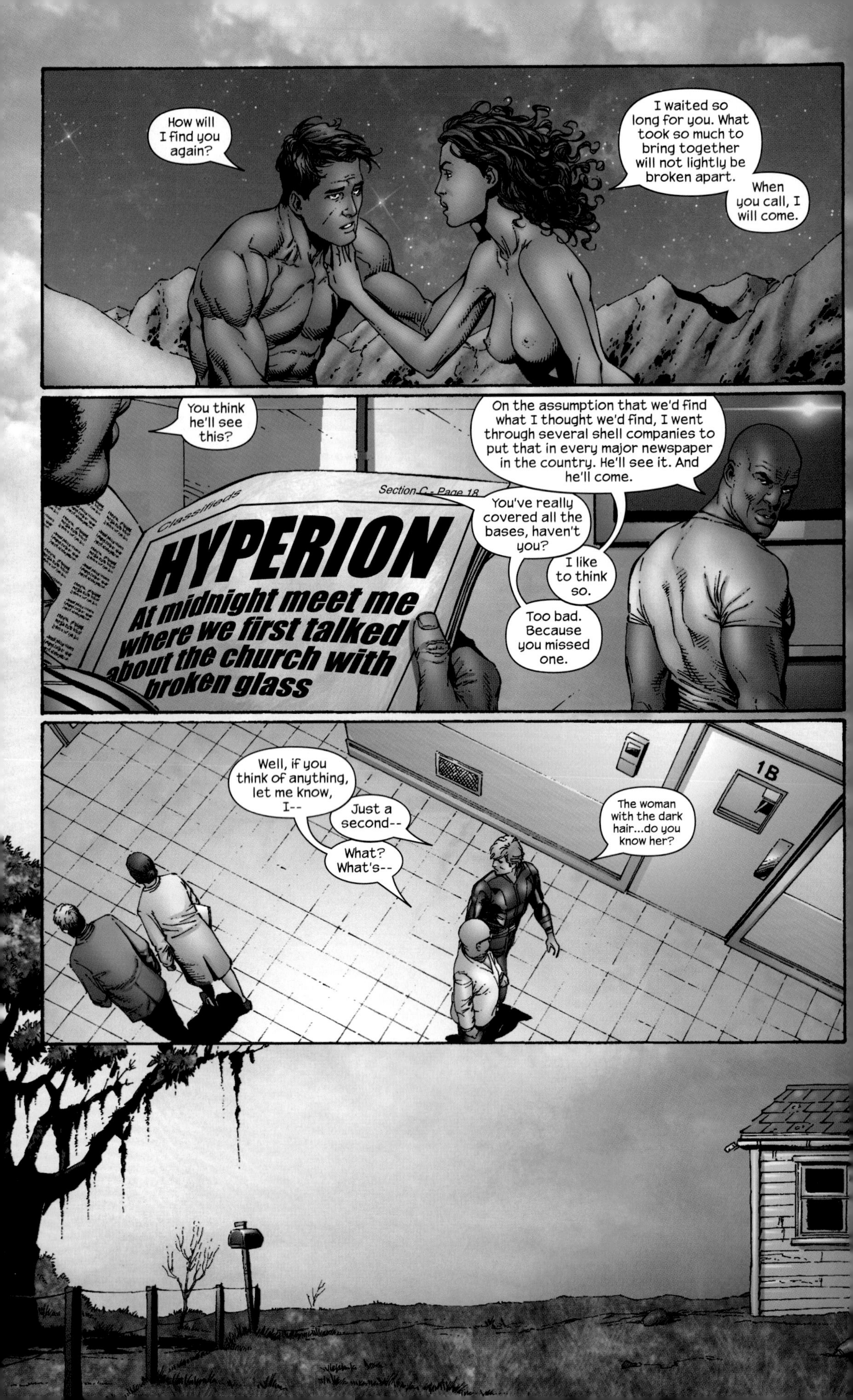
How will I find you again?
I waited so long for you. What took so much to bring together will not lightly be broken apart.
When you call, I will come.
You think he'll see this?
On the assumption that we'd find what I thought we'd find, I went through several shell companies to put that in every major newspaper in the country. He'll see it. And he'll come.
Classifieds
Section C - Page 18
HYPERION
At midnight meet me where we first talked about the church with broken glass
You've really covered all the bases, haven't you?
I like to think so.
Too bad. Because you missed one.
Well, if you think of anything, let me know, I--
Just a second--
What? What's--
1B
The woman with the dark hair...do you know her?

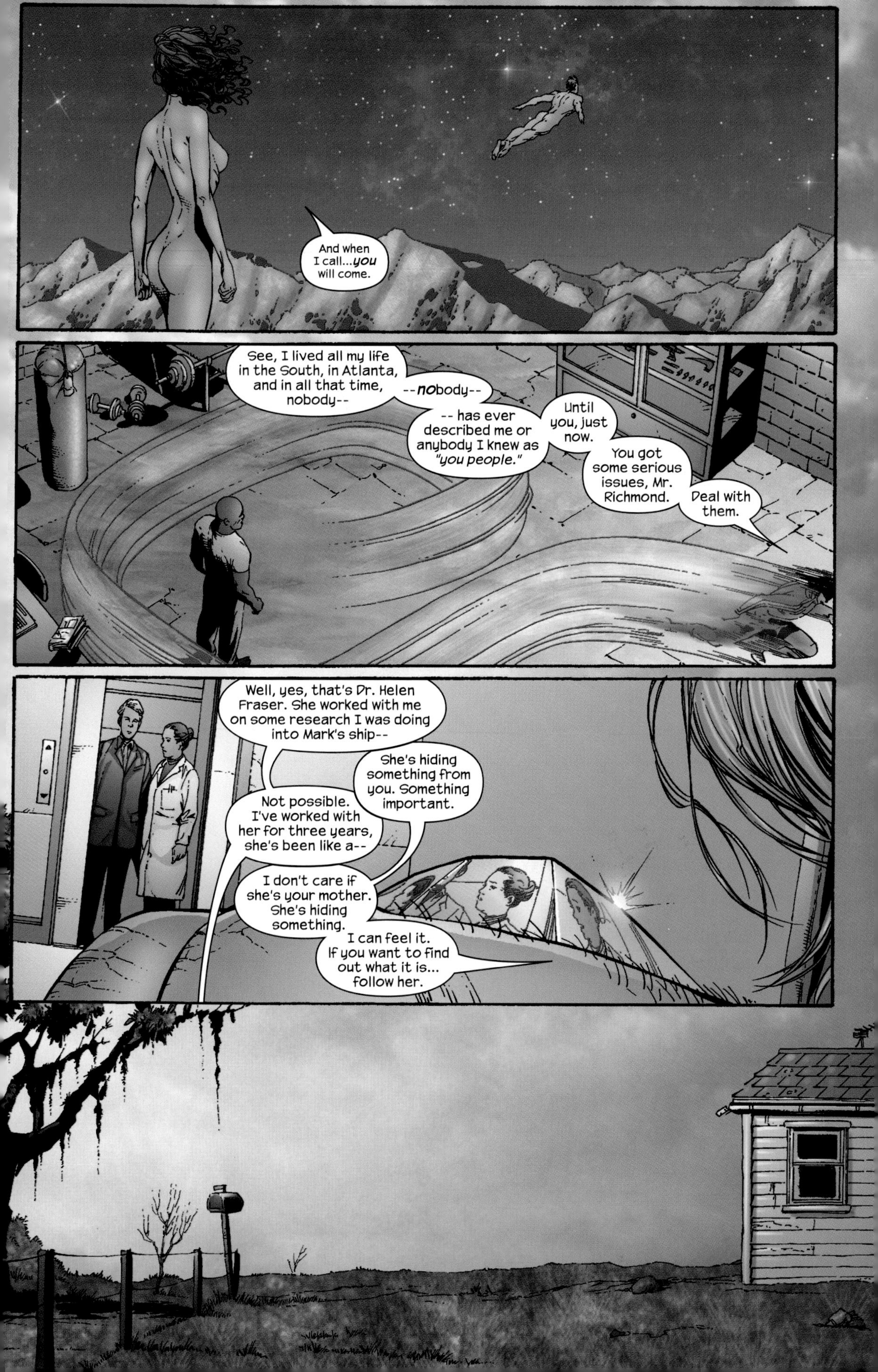
And when I call...you will come.
See, I lived all my life in the South, in Atlanta, and in all that time, nobody--
--nobody--
-- has ever described me or anybody I knew as "you people."
Until you, just now.
You got some serious issues, Mr. Richmond.
Deal with them.
Well, yes, that's Dr. Helen Fraser. She worked with me on some research I was doing into Mark's ship--
She's hiding something from you. Something important.
Not possible. I've worked with her for three years, she's been like a--
I don't care if she's your mother. She's hiding something.
I can feel it. If you want to find out what it is... follow her.

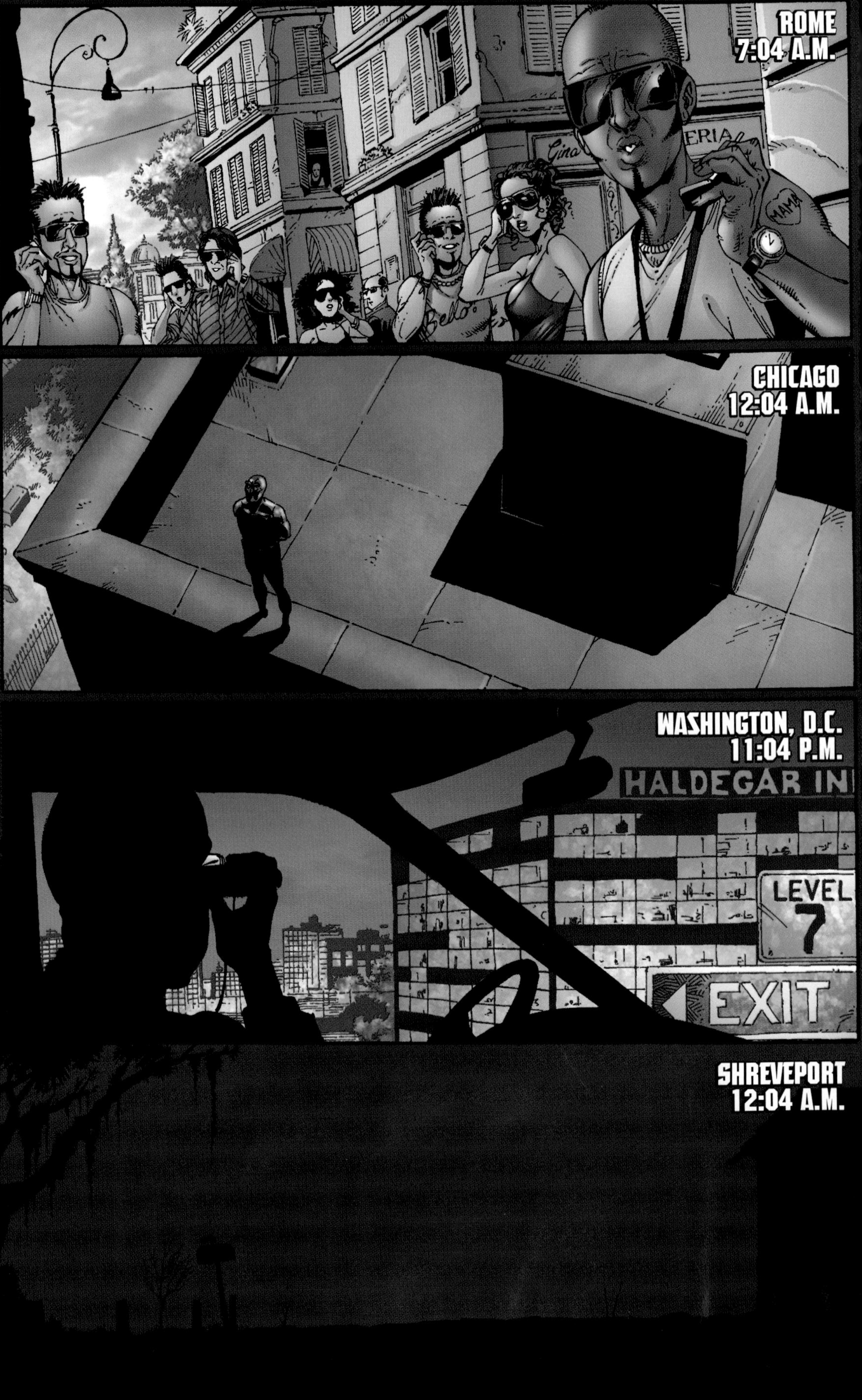
ROME
7:04 A.M.
MAMA
CHICAGO
12:04 A.M.
WASHINGTON, D.C.
11:04 P.M.
HALDEGAR IN
LEVEL
7
EXIT
SHREVEPORT
12:04 A.M.

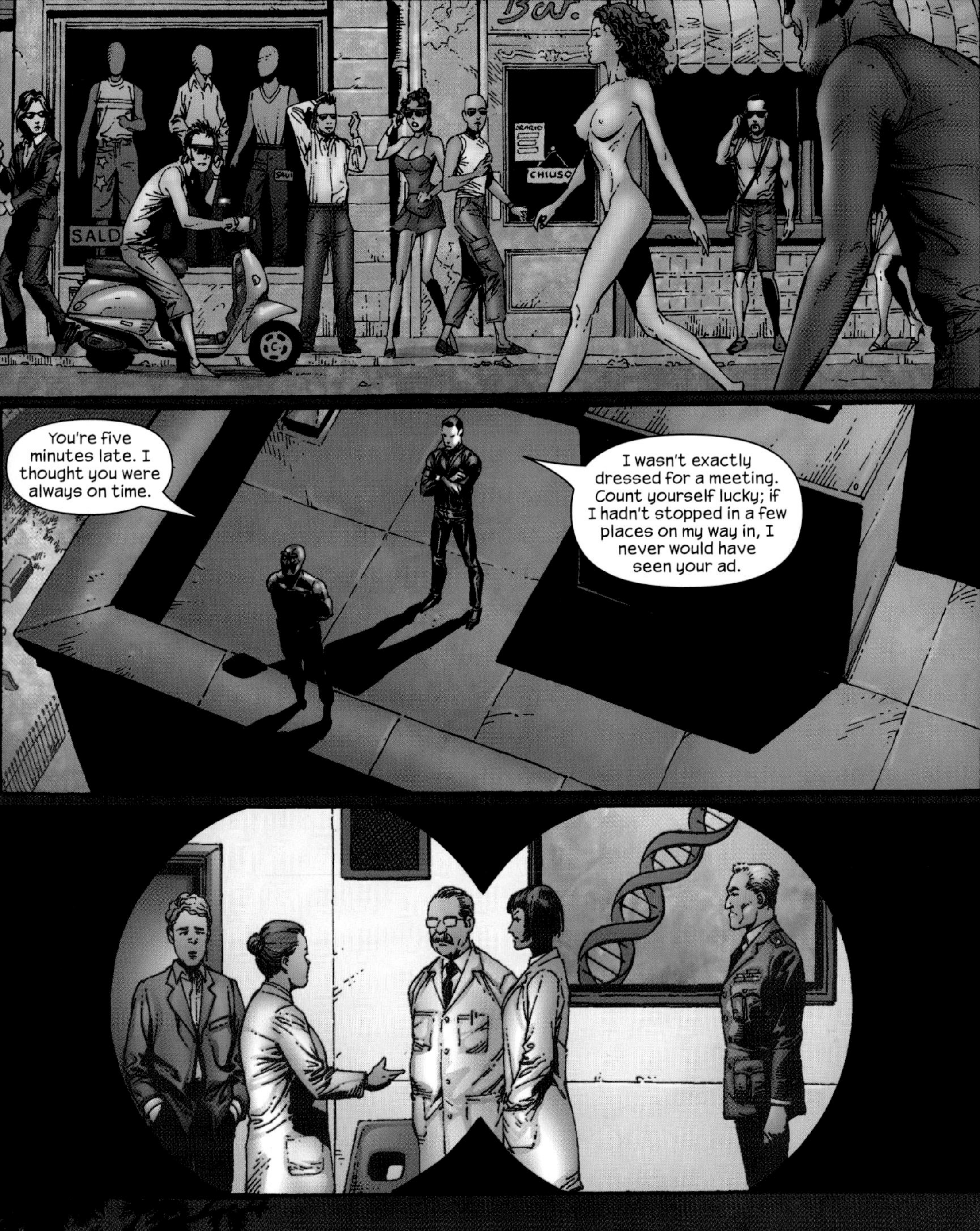

CHIUSO
You're five minutes late. I thought you were always on time.
I wasn't exactly dressed for a meeting. Count yourself lucky; if I hadn't stopped in a few places on my way in, I never would have seen your ad.

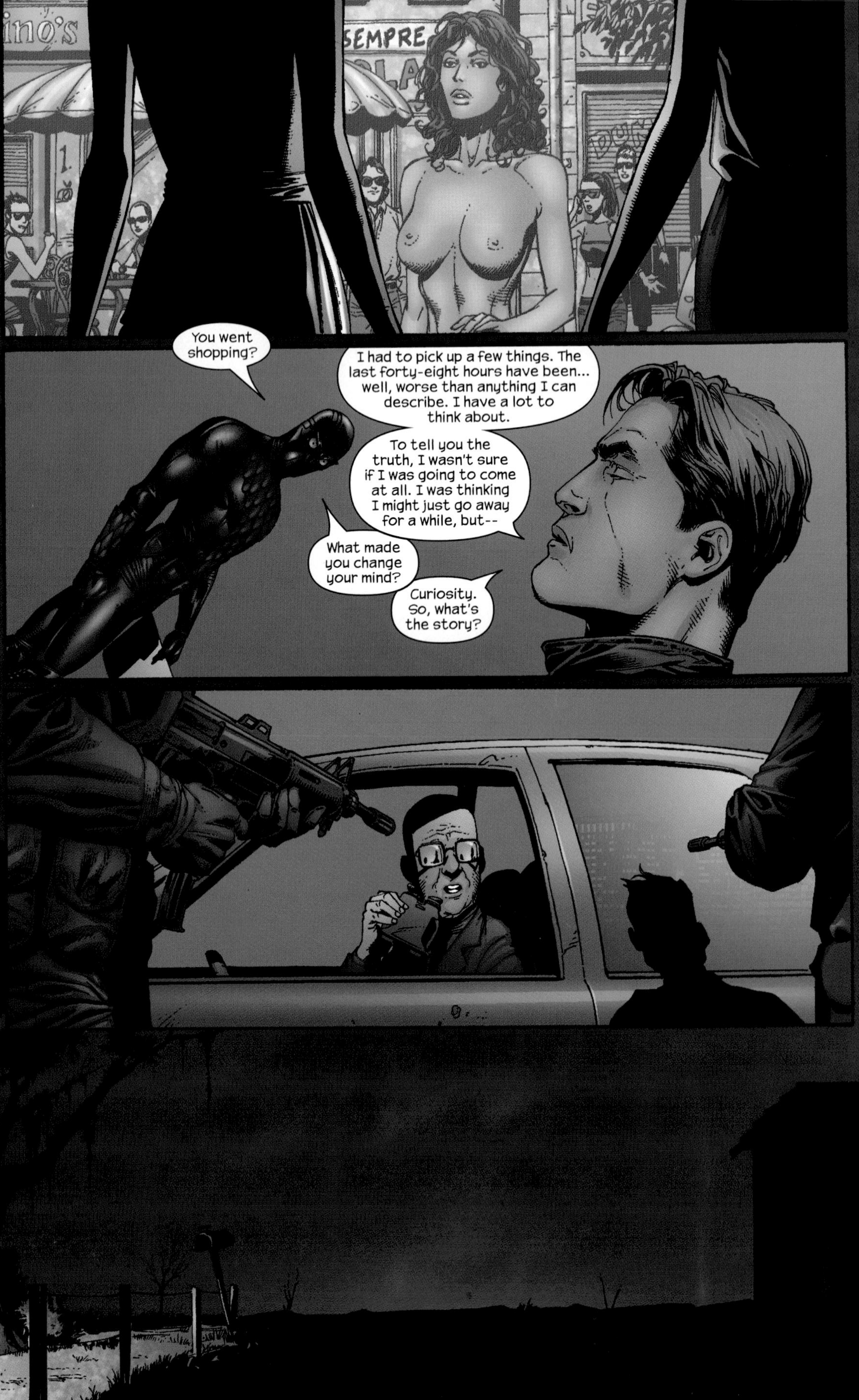
ino's
SEMPRE
You went shopping?
I had to pick up a few things. The last forty-eight hours have been... well, worse than anything I can describe. I have a lot to think about.
To tell you the truth, I wasn't sure if I was going to come at all. I was thinking I might just go away for a while, but--
What made you change your mind?
Curiosity. So, what's the story?

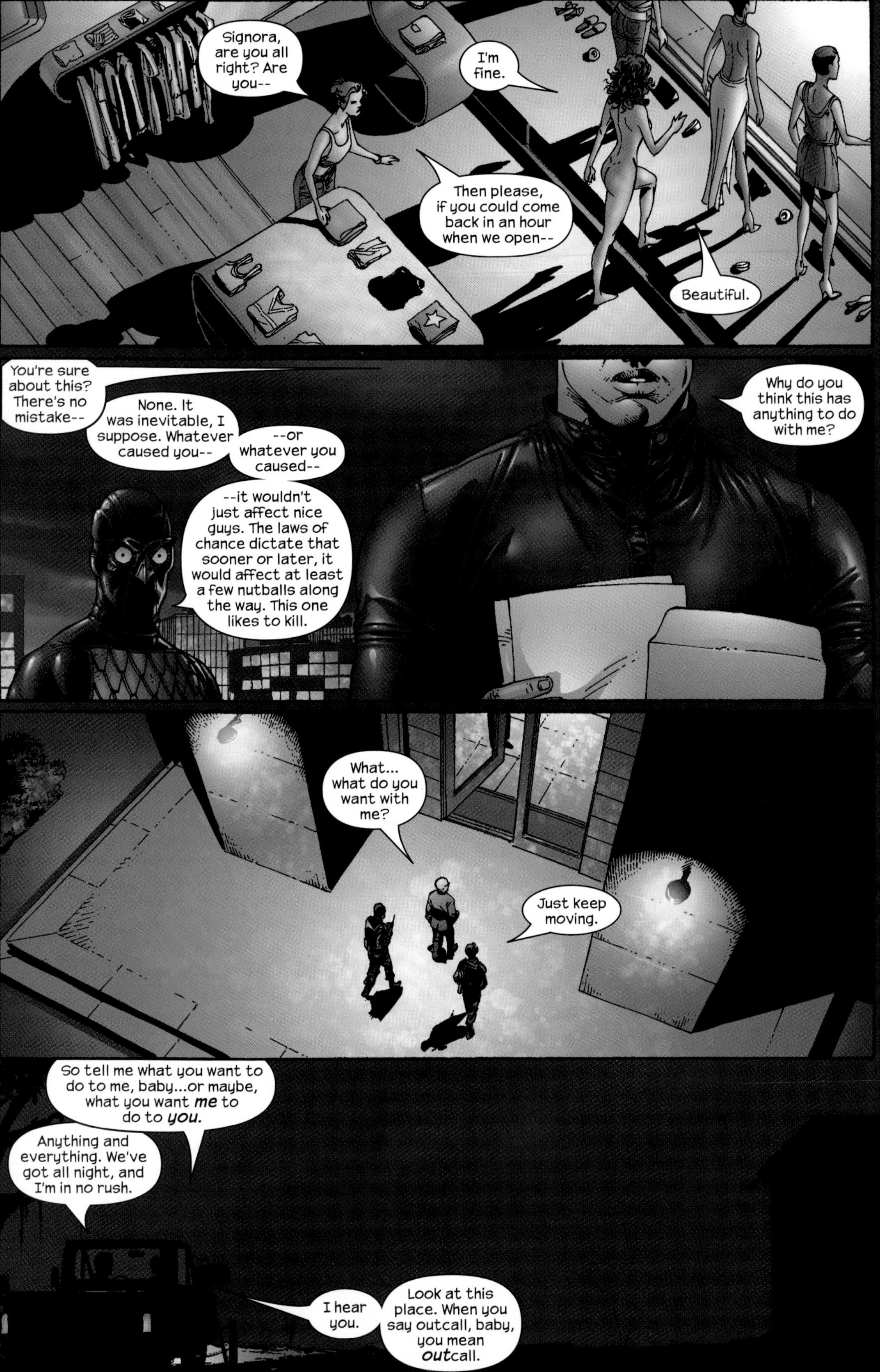
Signora, are you all right? Are you--
I'm fine.
Then please, if you could come back in an hour when we open--
Beautiful.
You're sure about this? There's no mistake--
None. It was inevitable, I suppose. Whatever caused you--
--or whatever you caused--
--it wouldn't just affect nice guys. The laws of chance dictate that sooner or later, it would affect at least a few nutballs along the way. This one likes to kill.
Why do you think this has anything to do with me?
What... what do you want with me?
Just keep moving.
So tell me what you want to do to me, baby...or maybe, what you want *me* to do to *you*.
Anything and everything. We've got all night, and I'm in no rush.
I hear you.
Look at this place. When you say outcall, baby, you mean ***out***call.

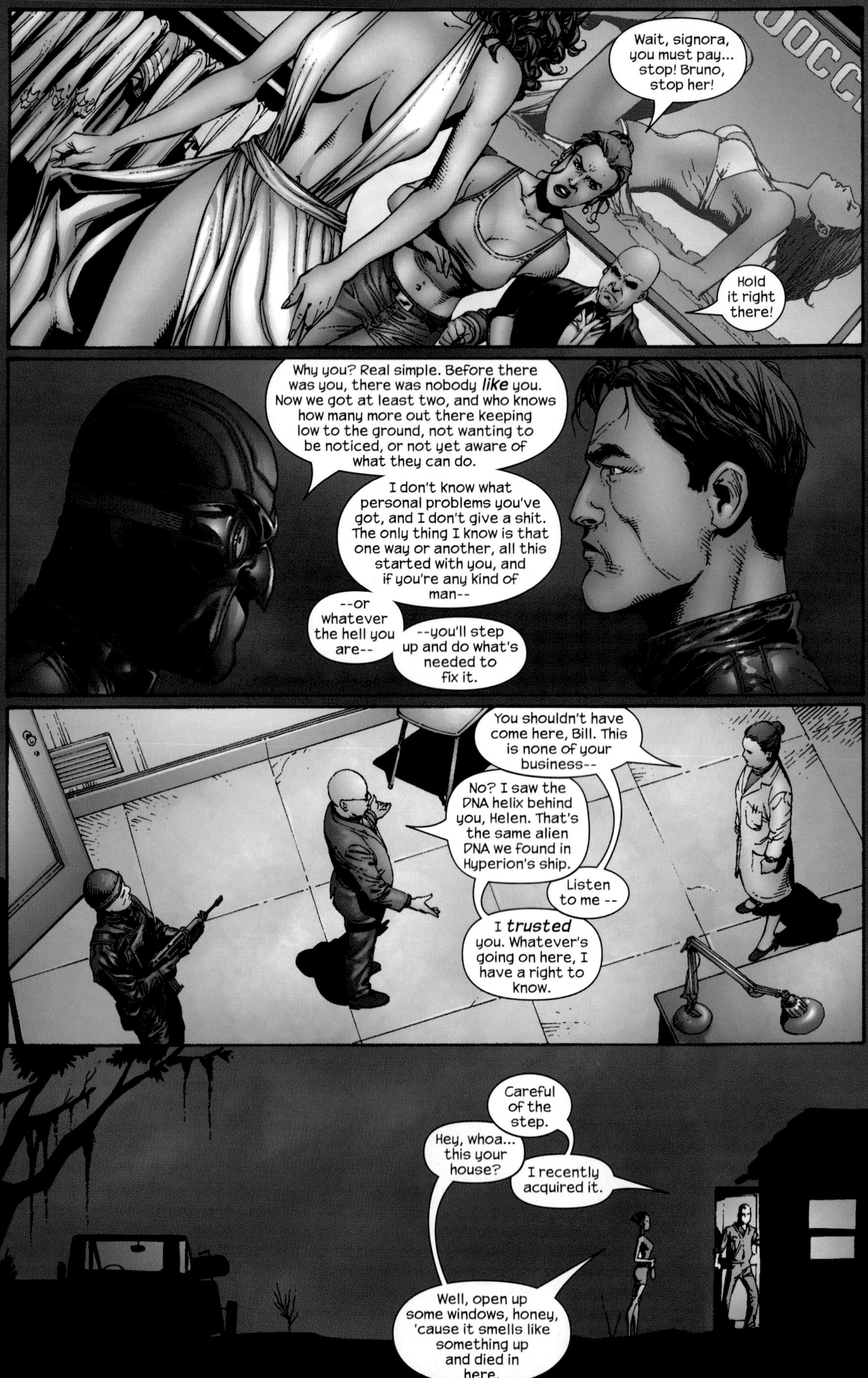
Wait, signora, you must pay... stop! Bruno, stop her!
Hold it right there!
Why you? Real simple. Before there was you, there was nobody *like* you. Now we got at least two, and who knows how many more out there keeping low to the ground, not wanting to be noticed, or not yet aware of what they can do.
I don't know what personal problems you've got, and I don't give a shit. The only thing I know is that one way or another, all this started with you, and if you're any kind of man--
--or whatever the hell you are--
--you'll step up and do what's needed to fix it.
You shouldn't have come here, Bill. This is none of your business--
No? I saw the DNA helix behind you, Helen. That's the same alien DNA we found in Hyperion's ship.
Listen to me --
I *trusted* you. Whatever's going on here, I have a right to know.
Careful of the step.
Hey, whoa... this your house?
I recently acquired it.
Well, open up some windows, honey, 'cause it smells like something up and died in here.

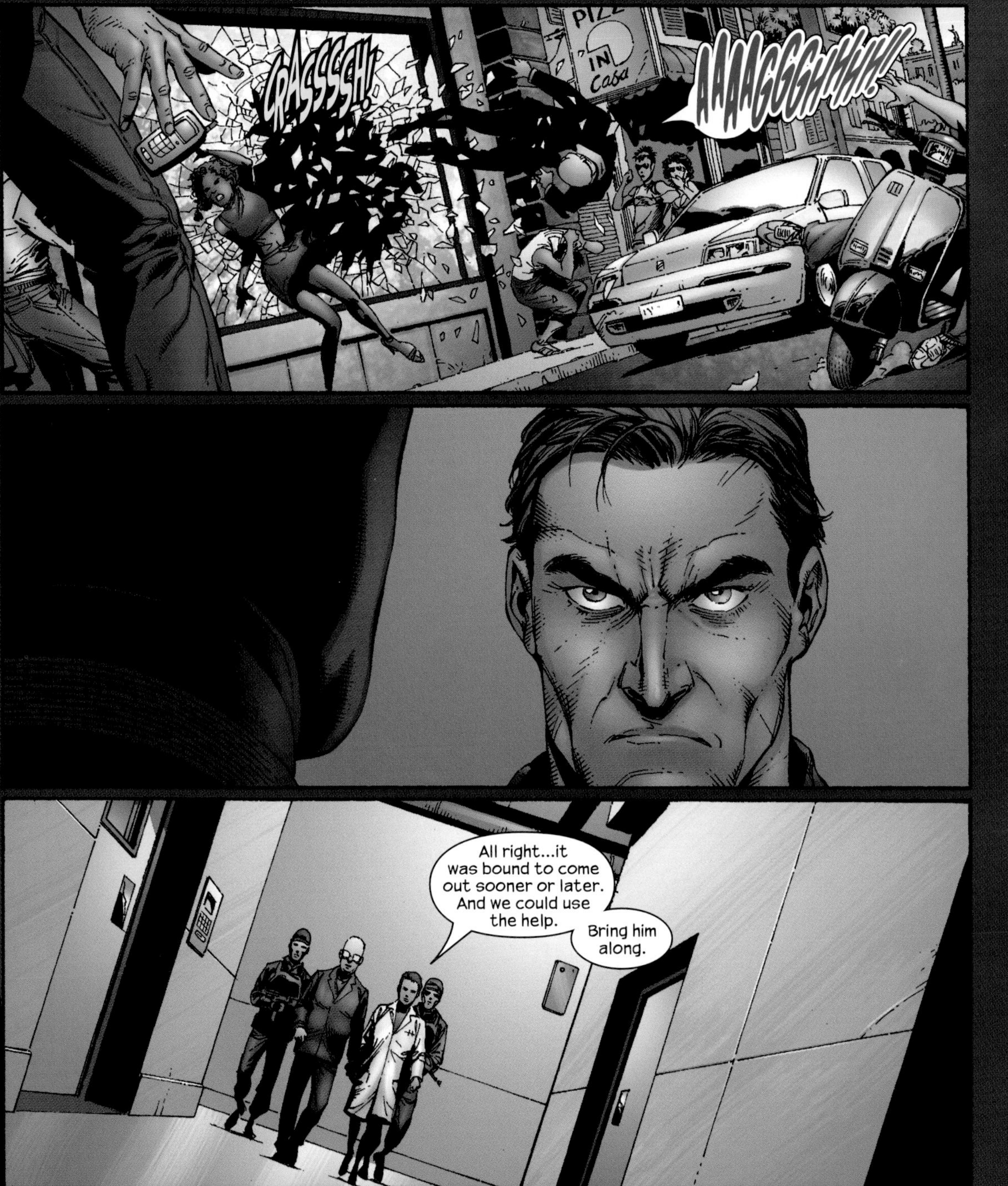
CRASSSSH!
PIZZ
IN Casa
AAAAGGGHHHH!!
All right...it was bound to come out sooner or later. And we could use the help.
Bring him along.

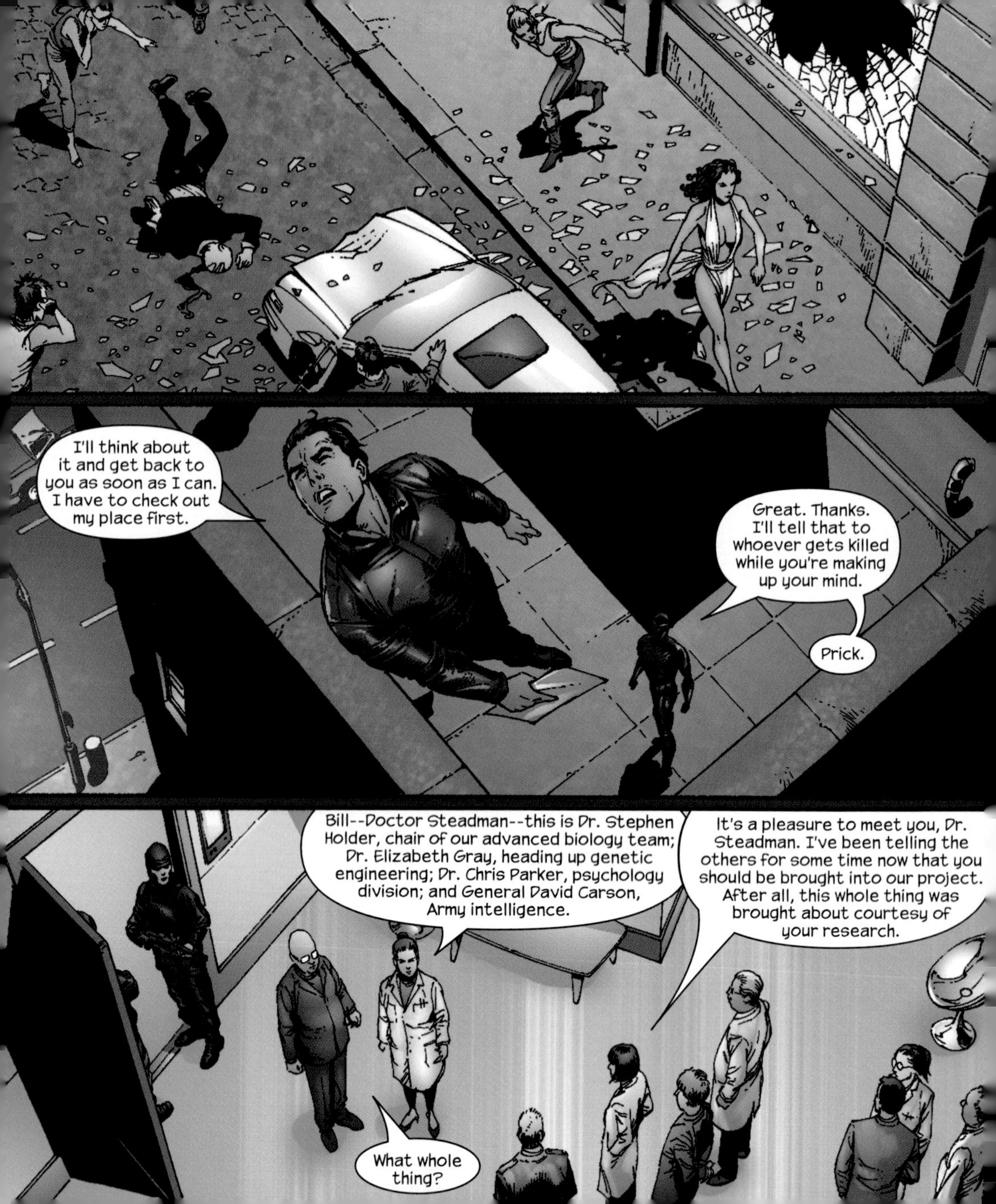

I'll think about it and get back to you as soon as I can. I have to check out my place first.
Great. Thanks. I'll tell that to whoever gets killed while you're making up your mind.
Prick.
Bill--Doctor Steadman--this is Dr. Stephen Holder, chair of our advanced biology team; Dr. Elizabeth Gray, heading up genetic engineering; Dr. Chris Parker, psychology division; and General David Carson, Army intelligence.
It's a pleasure to meet you, Dr. Steadman. I've been telling the others for some time now that you should be brought into our project. After all, this whole thing was brought about courtesy of your research.
What whole thing?

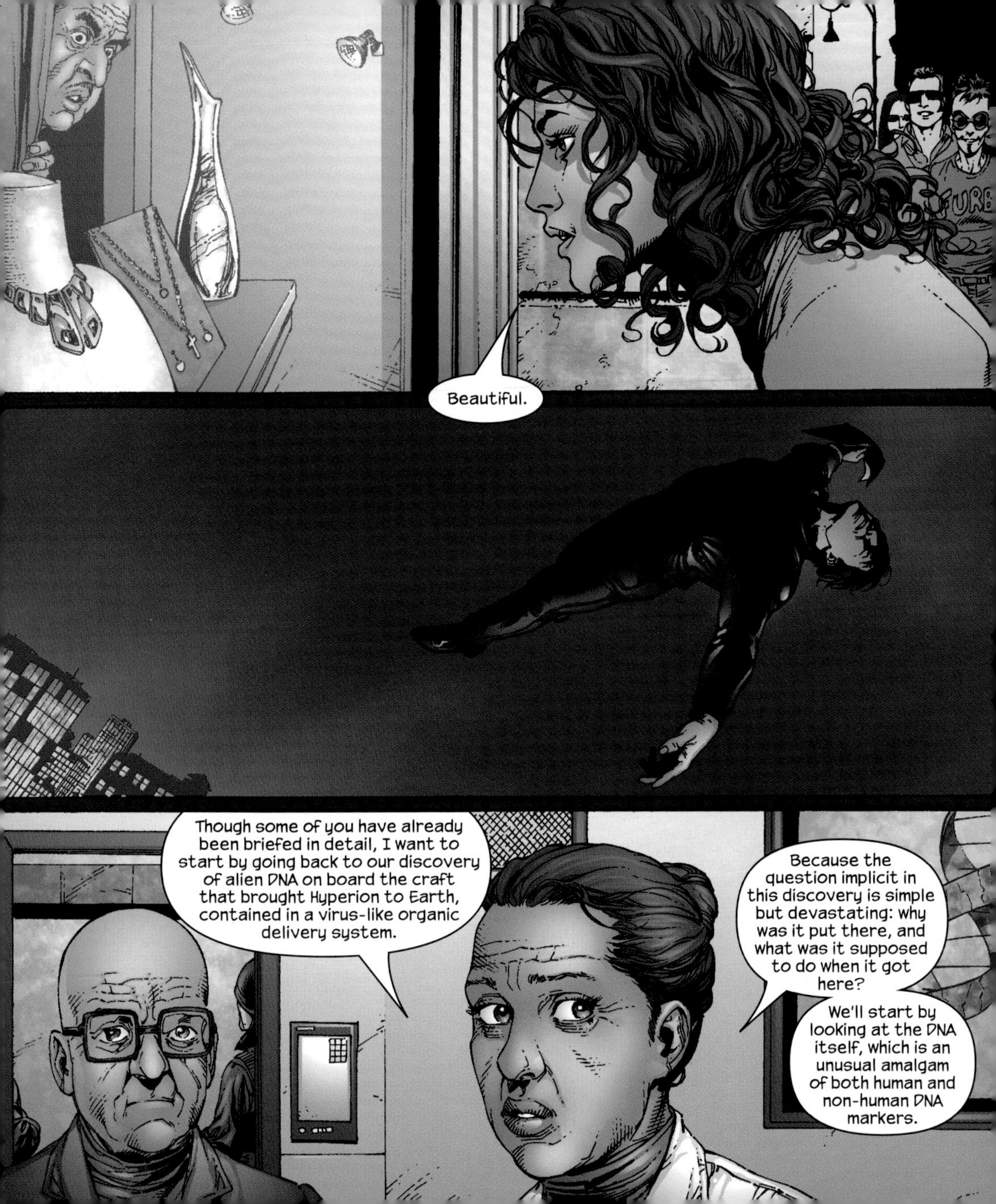
Beautiful.
Though some of you have already been briefed in detail, I want to start by going back to our discovery of alien DNA on board the craft that brought Hyperion to Earth, contained in a virus-like organic delivery system.
Because the question implicit in this discovery is simple but devastating: why was it put there, and what was it supposed to do when it got here?
We'll start by looking at the DNA itself, which is an unusual amalgam of both human and non-human DNA markers.

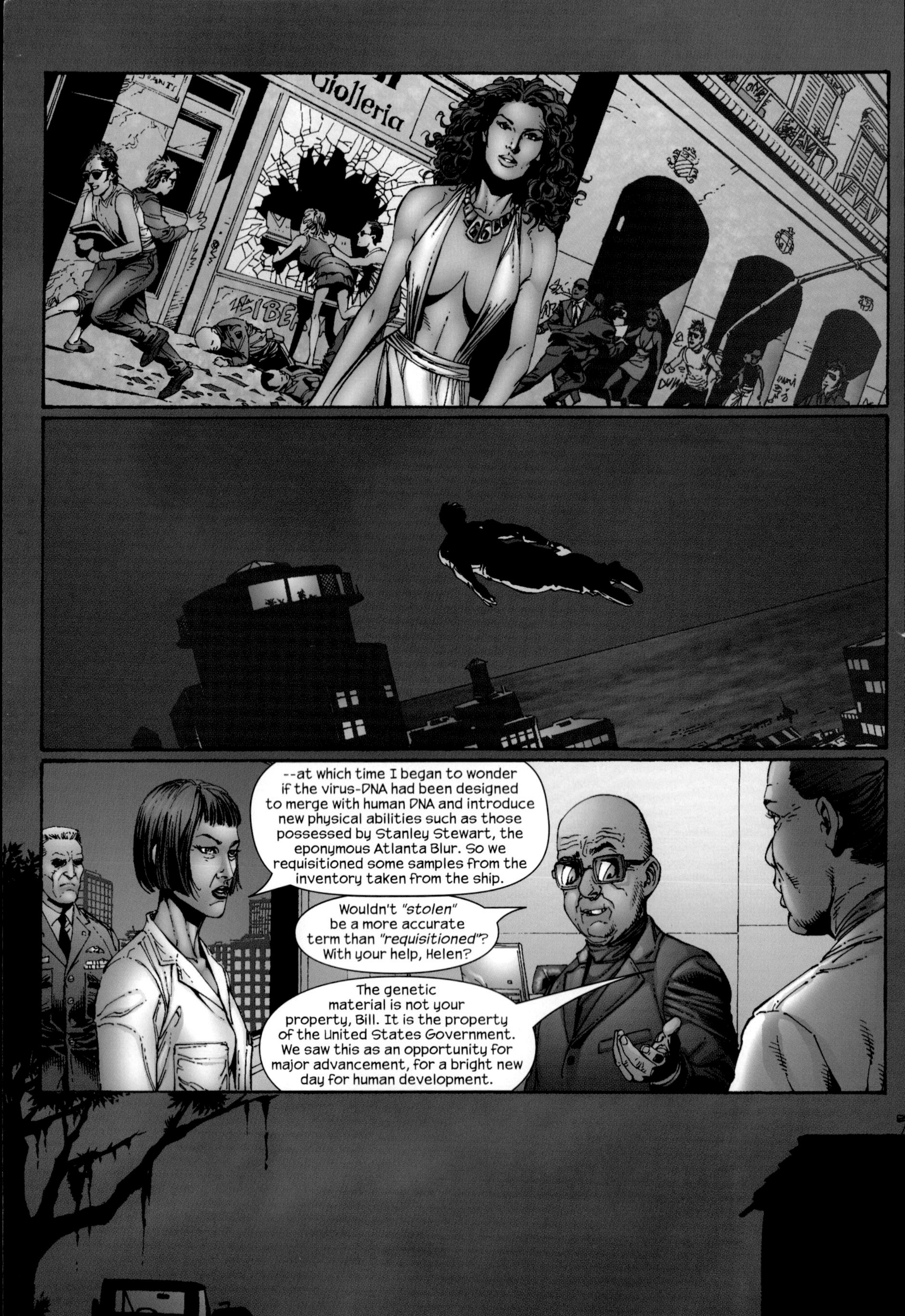
Giolleria
--at which time I began to wonder if the virus-DNA had been designed to merge with human DNA and introduce new physical abilities such as those possessed by Stanley Stewart, the eponymous Atlanta Blur. So we requisitioned some samples from the inventory taken from the ship.
Wouldn't *"stolen"* be a more accurate term than *"requisitioned"*? With your help, Helen?
The genetic material is not your property, Bill. It is the property of the United States Government. We saw this as an opportunity for major advancement, for a bright new day for human development.

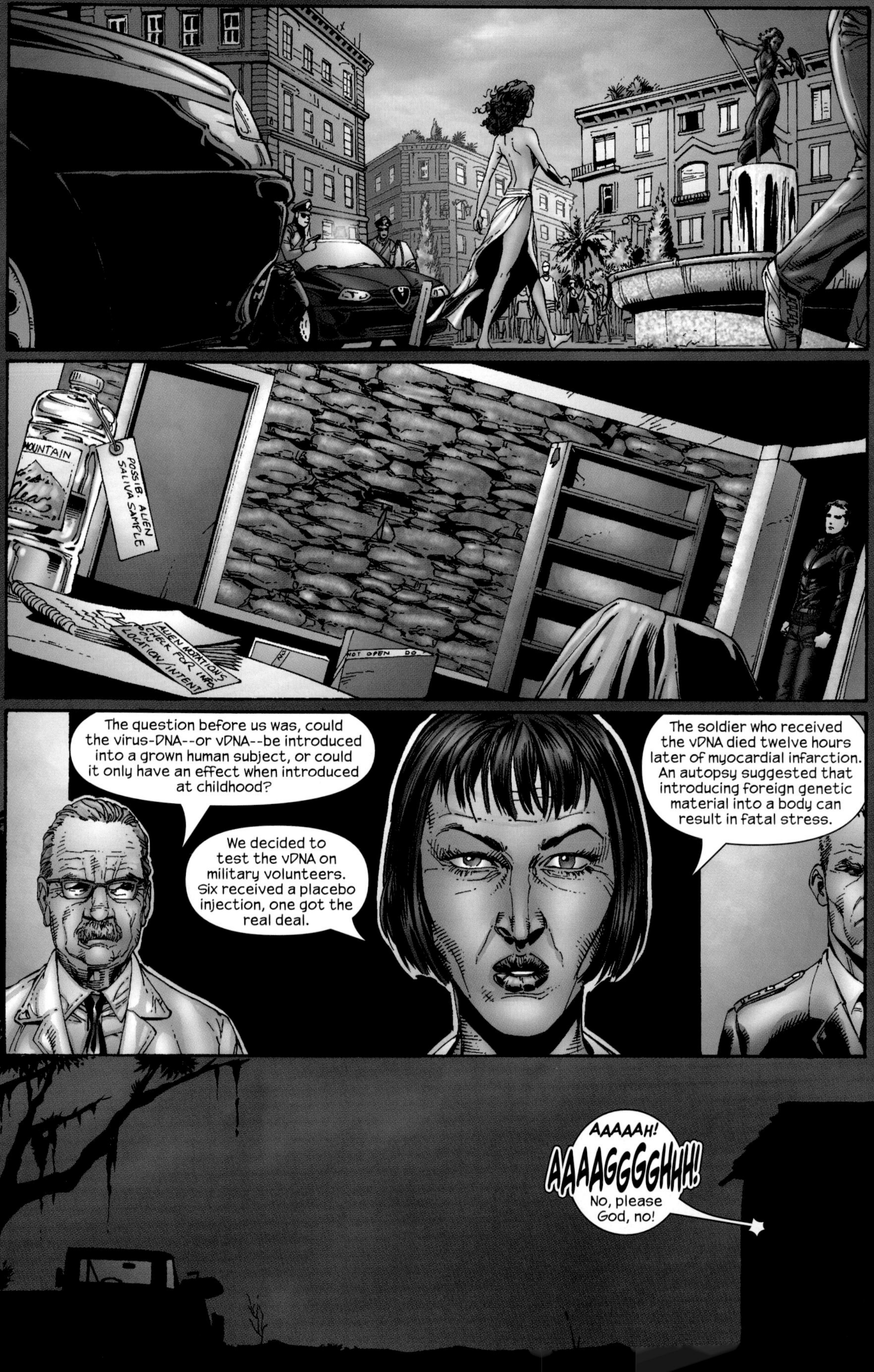
MOUNTAIN
POSSIB. ALIEN SALIVA SAMPLE
ALIEN NOTATIONS CHECK FOR INFO ON LOCATION/INTENT
NOT OPEN
The question before us was, could the virus-DNA--or vDNA--be introduced into a grown human subject, or could it only have an effect when introduced at childhood?
We decided to test the vDNA on military volunteers. Six received a placebo injection, one got the real deal.
The soldier who received the vDNA died twelve hours later of myocardial infarction. An autopsy suggested that introducing foreign genetic material into a body can result in fatal stress.
AAAAAH!
AAAAGGGGHHH!
No, please God, no!

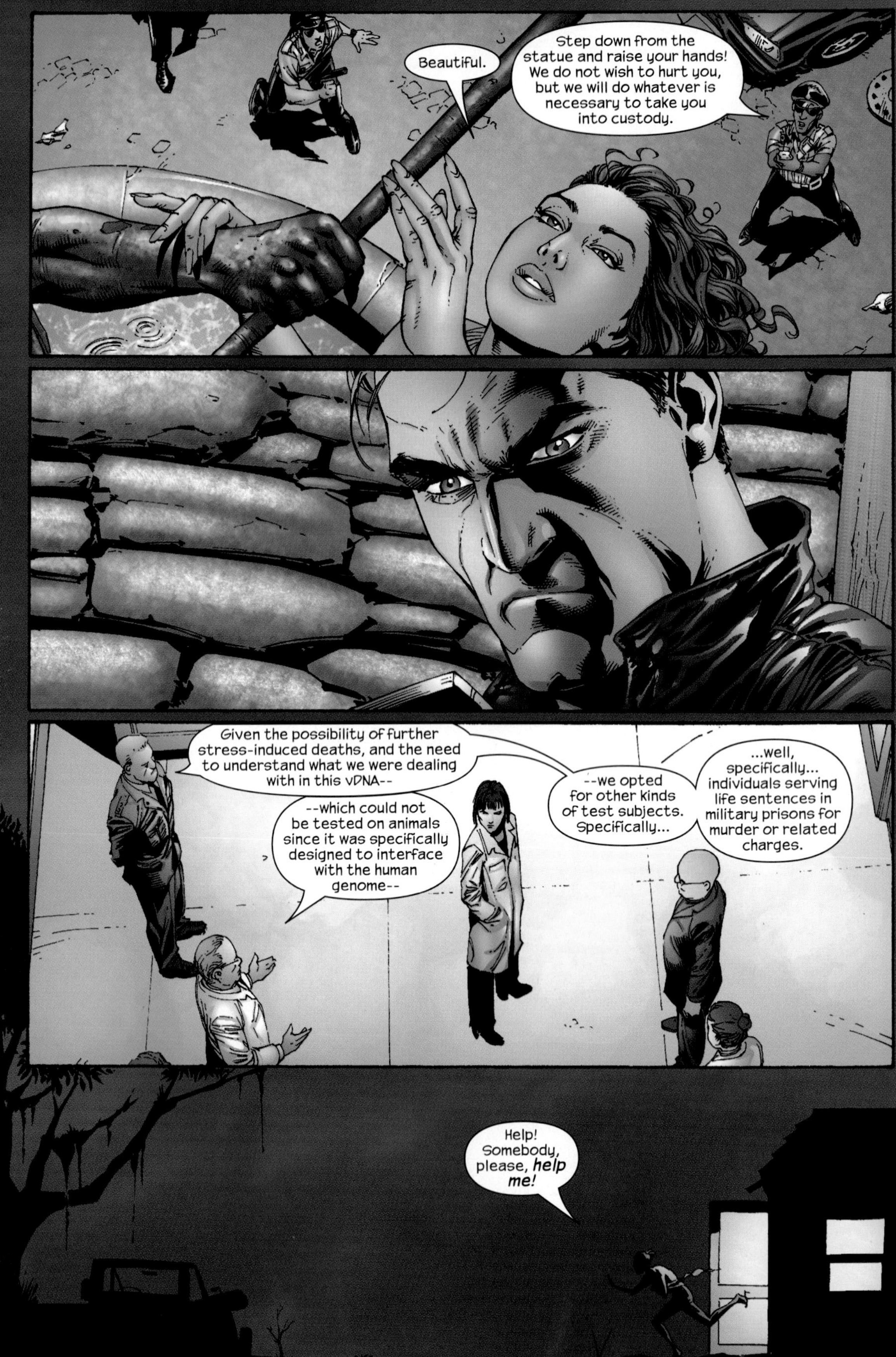
Beautiful.
Step down from the statue and raise your hands! We do not wish to hurt you, but we will do whatever is necessary to take you into custody.
Given the possibility of further stress-induced deaths, and the need to understand what we were dealing with in this vDNA--
--which could not be tested on animals since it was specifically designed to interface with the human genome--
--we opted for other kinds of test subjects. Specifically...
...well, specifically... individuals serving life sentences in military prisons for murder or related charges.
Help! Somebody, please, *help me!*

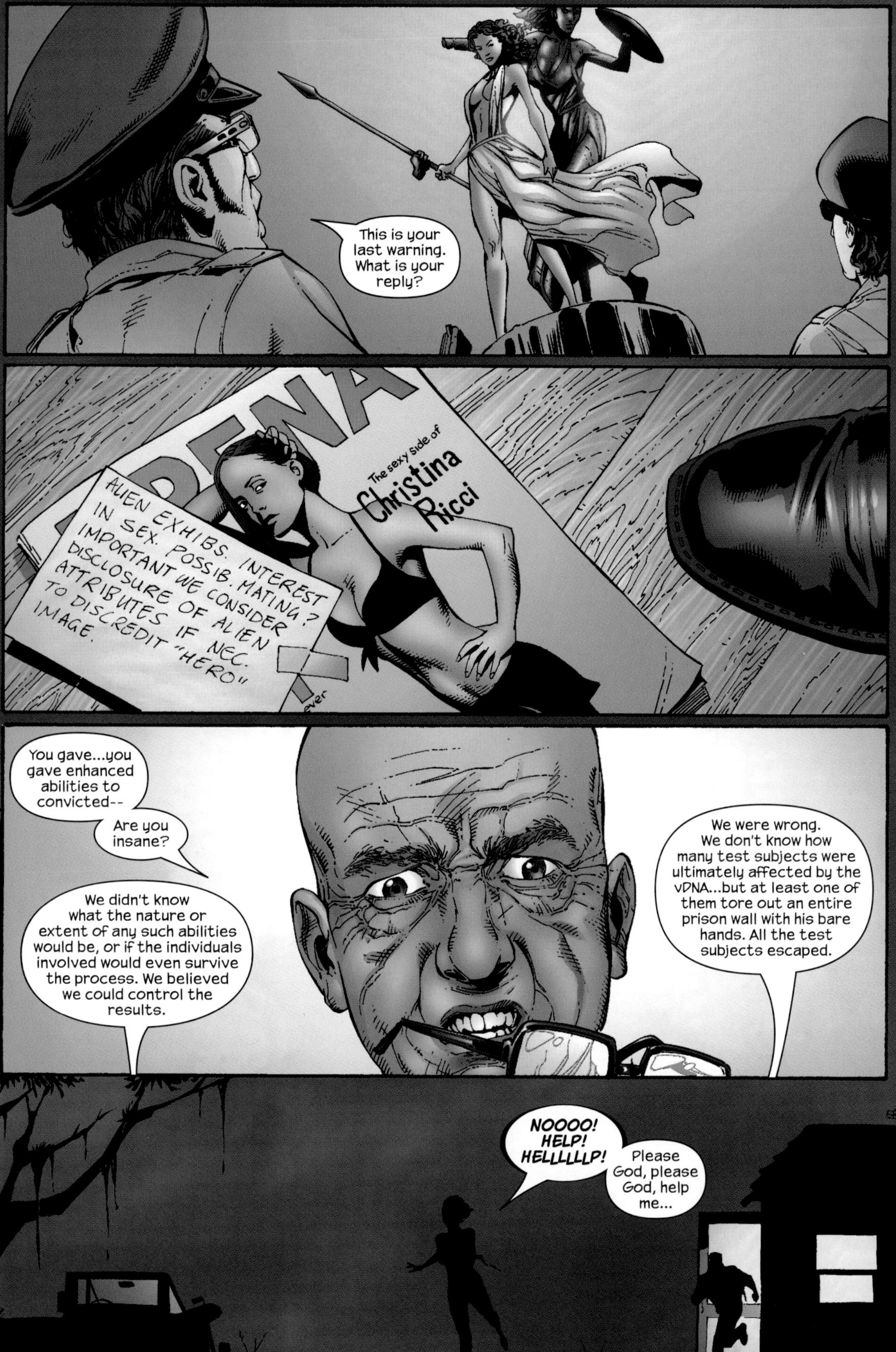
This is your last warning. What is your reply?
The sexy side of Christina Ricci
ALIEN EXHIBS. INTEREST IN SEX. POSSIB. MATING? IMPORTANT WE CONSIDER DISCLOSURE OF ALIEN ATTRIBUTES IF NEC. TO DISCREDIT "HERO" IMAGE.
You gave...you gave enhanced abilities to convicted--
Are you insane?
We didn't know what the nature or extent of any such abilities would be, or if the individuals involved would even survive the process. We believed we could control the results.
We were wrong. We don't know how many test subjects were ultimately affected by the vDNA...but at least one of them tore out an entire prison wall with his bare hands. All the test subjects escaped.
NOOOO! HELP! HELLLLLLP!
Please God, please God, help me...

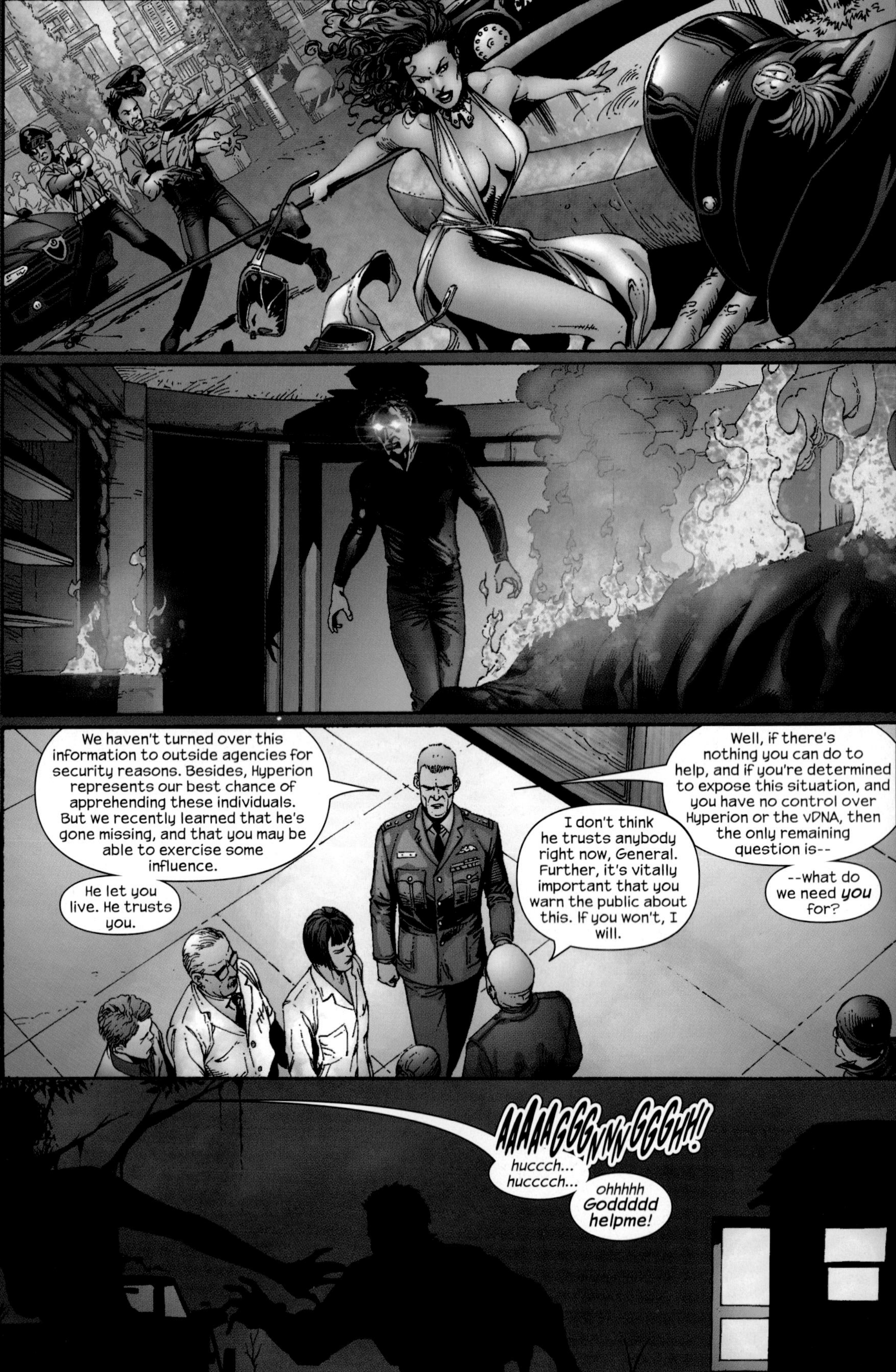
We haven't turned over this information to outside agencies for security reasons. Besides, Hyperion represents our best chance of apprehending these individuals. But we recently learned that he's gone missing, and that you may be able to exercise some influence.
He let you live. He trusts you.
I don't think he trusts anybody right now, General. Further, it's vitally important that you warn the public about this. If you won't, I will.
Well, if there's nothing you can do to help, and if you're determined to expose this situation, and you have no control over Hyperion or the vDNA, then the only remaining question is--
--what do we need *you* for?
AAAAAGGGNNNGGGHH!
hucccch... huccccch...
ohhhhh *Goddddd helpme!*

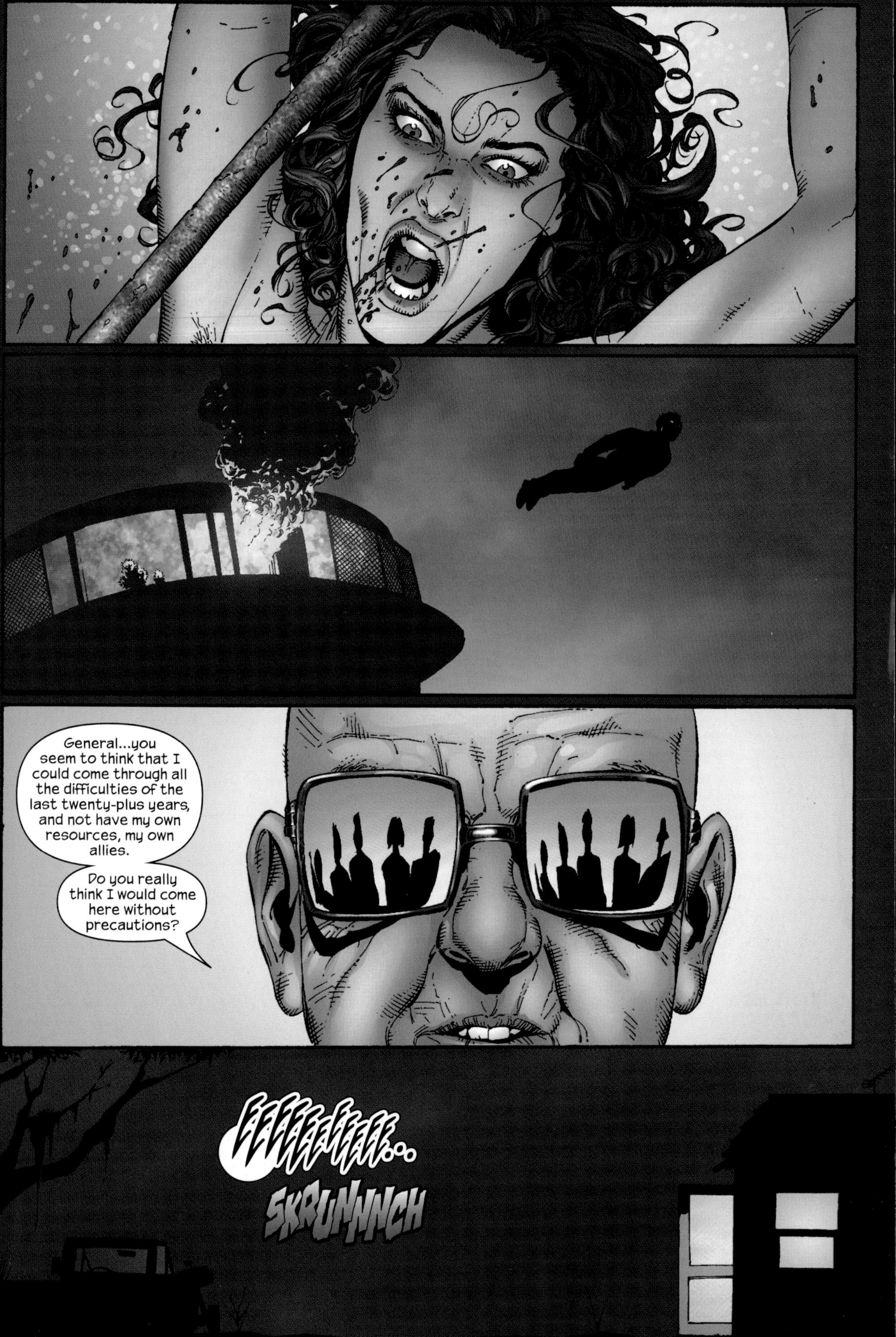

General...you seem to think that I could come through all the difficulties of the last twenty-plus years, and not have my own resources, my own allies.
Do you really think I would come here without precautions?
EEEEAAAAAAAA...
SKRUNNNCH

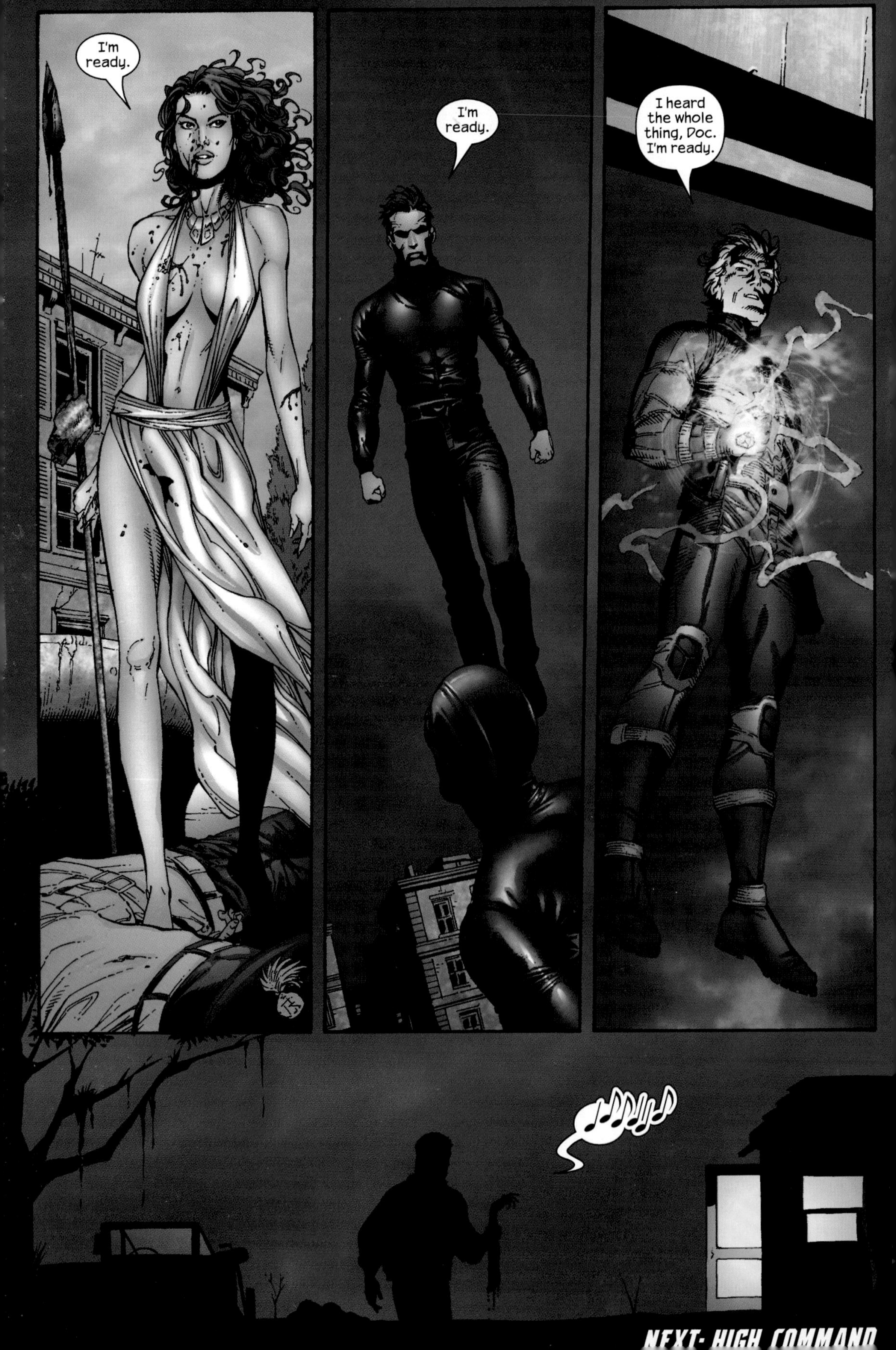
I'm ready.
I'm ready.
I heard the whole thing, Doc. I'm ready.
NEXT- HIGH COMMAND